D0500472

The Book of the **PHARAOHS**

The Book of the PHARAOHS

PASCAL VERNUS & JEAN YOYOTTE

translated from the French by DAVID LORTON

Cornell University Press *Ithaca & London*

This translation was prepared with the generous assistance of the French Ministry of Culture—Centre national du livre.

First published 2003 by Cornell University Press

Printed in the United States of America

Library of Congress Cataloging-in-Publication Data

Vernus, Pascal.
[Dictionnaire des pharaons. English]
The book of the pharaohs / Pascal Vernus and Jean Yoyotte; translated from the French by David Lorton.
p. cm.
Includes bibliographical references.
ISBN 0-8014-4050-5 (cloth : alk. paper)
1. Egypt—Civilization—To 332 B.C.—Dictionaries. 2. Pharoahs—Dictionaries. I. Yoyotte, Jean. II Lorton, David, 1945- III. Title.
DT58 .V4713 2003
932'.01'03—dc21
2002014603

Cornell University Press strives to use environmentally responsible suppliers and materials to the fullest extent possible in the publishing of its books. Such materials include vegetable-based, low-VOC inks and acid-free papers that are recycled, totally chlorine-free, or partly composed of nonwood fibers. For further information, visit our website at www.cornellpress.cornell.edu.

Cloth printing 10 9 8 7 6 5 4 3 2 1

CONTENTS

PREFACE

What if we tore off King Tut's gold mask? What lies behind the formalism, the hierarchism, and the majesty of the pharaonic monuments? To tell the truth, we see but little. The names of kings such as Cheops, Akhenaten, and Ramesses II have become part of popular culture, inspiring books and even musical compositions; yet to the historian, these monarchs remain rather pallid figures. What a difference there is between the pomp and ceremony our imagination conjures up at their very mention and the rags and tatters that scholars can ascribe to them! But this is a superficial disappointment, and we must get past it. After all, from Pharaoh on down, both individually and collectively, the Egyptians lived a full, human reality. But centuries of destruction by humans and at the hands of nature have spared only a small proportion of the products of their activities, and what is more, this remainder is ill-apportioned. What remains is essentially that which the Egyptians fashioned to last—that is, monuments of stone: temples, tombs, stelae, statues, and the like, monuments that are aesthetically eloquent but historically silent. And what survives of private tombs or dwellings for the most part informs us only indirectly of the pharaohs. Rare are papyri containing official documents and correspondence informing us of the workings of government, cabals in the palace and political factions, and *a fortiori,* the private life of the royal family. All told, one autobiographical inscription of an official, two passages from literature, and an incomplete record of a judicial investigation permit us a glimpse of three conspiracies . . . in the course of two whole millennia (see the entry Conspiracy).

There are thus too few archives for us to observe any given pharaoh in person from day to day. Temples and official monuments, however, exhibit an abundance of idealized images of the reigning sovereign, accompanied by his names. As the sole mediator between the superhuman and society, Pharaoh dedicated the temples, and on their walls, his images performed the rites. He multiplied his presence by means of his effigies, and he supplied official accounts of some of his deeds and published some of his decisions in the form of hieroglyphic texts. Everywhere, his personality was dissolved in the stereotyped image imposed by ideology. Except in rare cases, historians cannot uncover the individuality of kings, but they can at least investigate the manner in which each period, and sometimes each reign, formulated and conducted a policy. Erecting sacred monuments in Pharaoh's name to foster stability and universal prosperity was as essential a task as the management of economic activity and foreign policy; the abundance of temples and the length of their inscriptions served as global reflections of the achievements of a reign. Notwithstanding these limitations and the possibilities of analysis, we are constrained to make an objective characterization of the reigns and personalities of the "great" pharaohs, such as Tuthmosis III, Akhenaten, and Ramesses II, and to make such account as we can of the greatest possible number of less well-known sovereigns. To situate the individual monarchs in the historical context of their respective periods and thus to compose an account of those periods, this volume includes entries devoted to the periods—the "Kingdoms" and the "Intermediate Periods"—and to each of the dynasties as they succeeded one another. To broaden the cultural "landscape," brief entries deal with certain prominent nonroyal personalities. In order to assist the reader in placing the pharaohs within the perceptions and practices peculiar to ancient Egypt, other entries define essential concepts (pharaoh, coregency, etc.) and salient points having to do with monuments and institutions. Further, cities that trod the stage of history at one time or another are considered individually. A chronological table organizes the major periods of Egyptian history and notes the most illustrious royal names from each of them. The dates in this table, as well as those in the entries, are approximate: useful in terms of relative chronology, but of value only for the estimated lengths of reigns and periods; they cannot pretend to fix in time, precisely and irrevocably, the important moments and the major events. The textual and archaeological realities condemn us to this humility . . . or rather, to this humiliation.

Since the first edition of this work, excavations, text editions, and scholarly discussions have brought no truly new and certain facts, though they have offered many fresh interpretations. We feel it would be premature to include detailed accounts of all these ideas. Nevertheless, recent discoveries at predynastic sites are clarifying the problems surrounding the birth of the pharaonic state, thus justifying entries on Dynasty Zero and the problem of the Unification.

TRANSLATOR'S NOTE

English-speaking Egyptologists have no single set of conventions for the rendering of ancient Egyptian and modern Arabic personal and place names. Most of the names mentioned in this book occur in a standard reference work, John Baines and Jaromír Málek, *Atlas of Ancient Egypt* (New York, 1980), and the renderings here follow those in that volume. The major exception is the omission of the typographical sign for *ayin;* this consonant does not exist in English, and I felt that its inclusion would only distract the reader.

The Book of the **PHARAOHS**

Adoratrice

This title designates certain priestesses attached to the goddess Hathor (the Egyptian Aphrodite) or employed in the service of Atum, Min, Amun, or Sobk. The role of these priestesses was to arouse the sex drive of creator gods. When the cult of Amun was organized, the presence of the "wife of the god and hand of the god" was required to carry out various rituals.

Under Ahmose, this office, which would come to be called "divine adoratrice of Amun" in the spoken language, was conferred upon Queen Ahmose-Nofretari. She was followed by an outstanding series of princesses, some of whom became royal wives, among them the future "pharaoh" Hatshepsut.

In this period, mystical marriage to Amun did not preclude marriage to a king and motherhood, though the office had nothing to do with the legends of the divine birth of the king, one of the foundations of dynastic legitimacy, as was once long believed. Religion and politics were mingled, as suggested by unexplained changes in the office. After Tuthmosis IV, the connection between the priestess and the reigning family became less strict, and there was no adoratrice of Amun under Amenophis III. "Wives" of the god included Mut-tui, the mother of Ramesses II; Twosre, wife of Sethos II; and Tity, under Ramesses III. Yet none of the many wives and daughters of Ramesses II held the office. Princesses who were adoratrices appeared at Thebes under the Twentieth Dynasty.

In the Twenty-first Dynasty, with Maatkare, the daughter of Pinudjem, the institution experienced a transformation of great theocratic significance. From that time on, the wife of Amun, who was provided with a cartouche containing a prenomen (which was based on the name of Mut, Amun's consort), remained celibate for life. For more than half a century, queens married only to the supreme god, surrounded by virgin chantresses, and served by a rich household managed by powerful "majordomos of the adoratrice" would join with the pharaohs in embellishing the sanctuaries of Thebes. Their succession from "mother" to "daughter" was effected by adoption, and the Libyans, Kushites, and Saites each imposed a princess of their blood as spiritual "coregent." The adoratrices of the Twenty-second Dynasty (among them Karomama, famous for her bronze statue) were buried around the Ramesseum, the funerary temple of Ramesses II. Those of the Twenty-third to the Twenty-sixth Dynasties were interred at Medinet Habu—Shepenwepet I, Amenirdis, Shepenwepet II, Nitocris, Ankhnesneferibre—and their great majordomos located their tombs nearby, on the Asasif.

The Persians abolished the royal status of the adoratrice, but virgins born of local families continued to marry Amun. The name "*pallakides* (concubines) of Zeus" given to them by the Greeks creates a misimpression of sacred prostitution.

G. Robins, *Women in Ancient Egypt* (Cambridge, Mass., 1993), chapter 2.

Ahmose 1539–1514 B.C.E., Eighteenth Dynasty

In Egyptian, Ahmose (*Iahmes*) means "the moon has given birth." "Amasis," a name we assign to a pharaoh of the Twenty-sixth Dynasty, is another transcription of the same Egyptian name.

Though we begin the Eighteenth Dynasty with Ahmose, there was no rupture with the Seventeenth Dynasty, for the king was the grandson of Tetisheri, the son of Ahhotpe, and the brother of Kamose. The reason for the commencement of a new dynasty is that his reign was marked by a major event: the expulsion of the Hyksos, who had occupied Egypt for more than a century. We can see that the wars of liberation begun by Kamose required time and effort; Avaris fell only after a lengthy siege. It was then necessary to eradicate the Hyksos bastions in Palestine, to crush the Nubian chiefs who sporadically attempted to regain a foothold in Lower Nubia, which Egypt had just won back, and finally, to punish rebellions led by Egyptians who were either Hyksos collaborators or, perhaps, ambitious fellow travelers of the Theban pharaohs. Since Ahmose seems to have ascended the throne while still a minor, his mother, Ahhotpe, exercised a sort of coregency during part of his reign. When the political situation became settled, probably around year 20 of his reign, Ahmose began the great restoration efforts that Egypt so sorely needed. Mines and quarries were reopened (producing limestone from el-Maasara, alabaster from Bisra, turquoise from the Sinai), and the traditional exchanges with Byblos were reestablished. The king's construction efforts were mostly concentrated in Upper Egypt, in the areas that had belonged to the nationalist alliance forged by the Seventeenth Dynasty; his erection of a cenotaph for himself and his grandmother Tetisheri at Abydos made him a patron saint there. At the same time, the temple domains began to be reorganized, with special attention to the administration of grain revenues.

Ahmose's tomb has yet to be discovered. But we know his mummy, like many others, was deposited in the cachette of Deir el-Bahari to protect it from the depredations of tomb robbers.

See Ahmose, son of Ebana; Ahmose-Nofretari; Cachettes; Hyksos.

Ahmose, Son of Ebana

A native of el-Kab, Ahmose was the son of a soldier of Seqenenre named Beb. Ahmose's fame in antiquity resulted from his exploits, while his celebrity among Egyptologists is due to his detailed autobiography. He was scarcely married when he enlisted as a sailor in Ahmose's war of liberation against the Hyksos; he distinguished himself in the sieges of Avaris and Sharuhen, the latter a fortified Hyksos city in Palestine. Subsequently, he participated in the king's campaigns in Nubia and in the suppression of a revolt in Egypt led by Tetian.

The king's successor Amenophis I also had to campaign in Nubia. Ahmose's valor earned him the privilege of accompanying his sovereign on the royal boat, and, when the expedition returned, of being named "warrior of the ruler."

Ahmose also distinguished himself when Tuthmosis I led yet another expedition to Nubia, and he earned a promotion to "chief of the sailors." In a campaign in Syria against the empire of Mitanni, Ahmose figured prominently in the vanguard of the Egyptian army, capturing a chariot.

Ahmose reached old age prosperous and heaped with honors. On six occasions, he had been awarded the "gold of valor"; at sword point, he acquired fields and slaves, all inventoried in detail at the end of his autobiography. His affluence enabled him to make and to inscribe a tomb. He was an outstanding representative of a new social type characteristic of the New Kingdom, the soldier who rose through the ranks.

M. Lichtheim, *Ancient Egyptian Literature: A Book of Readings,* vol. 2: *The New Kingdom* (Berkeley, 1976), pp. 12–15.

See Ahmose, Amenophis I, Avaris, Hyksos, Tuthmosis I.

Ahmose-Nofretari

Ahmose-Nofretari was the wife and probably sister or half-sister of Ahmose, the first king of the Eighteenth Dynasty; she survived him, living through the reign of his successor, Amenophis I, and dying at the beginning of the reign of Tuthmosis I. She was so closely associated with some of her husband's accomplishments that it is clear she exercised a sort of coregency, as the king was long occupied with the war of liberation and its aftermath. She also exercised quasi-royal powers during the minority of Amenophis I. Aside from this political role, Ahmose-Nofretari was the first queen to hold the sacerdotal office of "wife of the god." The role was endowed with a combination of goods and landed estates by means of a complex legal fiction: the queen was given the position of second prophet of Amun, which the king soon bought back, underestimating what he paid in exchange.

In her role as "wife of the god," which included participation in a complex of ceremonies, she reorganized the cult and introduced a number of implements and objects sanctioned by her name. The prestige she earned, along with that of the funerary monuments dedicated to her and her son Amenophis I, earned her the distinction of becoming a patron saint of the Theban necropolis. She was often represented in the company of the latter king in chapels and private tombs, as well as in the temples of the gods, throughout the New Kingdom; the most popular of her images was a statue of wood covered with bitumen, which explains why the queen's body was often painted black. Her barque would go out on procession on the occasion of major festivals, the ceremonies of which included a stop at her funerary temple. After her, and thanks to her, a huge complex of landed estates and revenues remained attached to the office of "wife of the god" and "adoratrice of the god."

M. Gitton, *L'Épouse du dieu Ahmès Néfertary,* Centre de recherches d'histoire ancienne 15, Annales littéraires de l'université de Besançon 172 (Paris, 1981).

See Adoratrice, Ahmose, Amenophis I.

Alexander the Great 332–323 B.C.E.

Leading his Macedonian subjects and the Greek cities in an assault on the Persian empire, Alexander conquered Anatolia, Syria, and Phoenicia; in 332, without a blow being struck, he entered Egypt, which was discontented in the wake of its recent reconquest by the Persians. This liberating Horus from afar, who quickly became "Pharaoh Alexander," successor of "Pharaoh Darius," passed through Memphis and journeyed to Siwa Oasis, where the god Amun was said to have recognized him as his son. Upon Alexander's return, he founded Alexandria, a Greek city and Mediterranean port, on the margin of the Egyptian realm.

His internal system of government was a continuation of that of the Persians. He installed military governors and garrisons, but he left the management of civil affairs to Egyptian nomarchs who were supervised by Cleomenes of Naukratis, a Greek born in Egypt. The brilliant Macedonian then departed to conquer the East, where he died at Babylon in 323, both a hero in the Greek sense of the word and a despot in the Achaemenid style. Alexander was "beloved of Re" and "son of Amun"—and later transformed into the bodily son of this god (or of Nectanebo II), according to the myth of the divine birth of the king. Alexander's Egyptian subjects immediately endowed him with the attributes of a pharaoh. The temple of Luxor, which was restored during his reign, preserves his cartouches. The rear sanctuary at Karnak was similarly "signed" by his half brother Philip Arrhidaeus (323–317 B.C.E.), and the hypostyle hall of the great temple of Thoth at Hermopolis is decorated in the name of Alexander Aigos, his son, the third and last Macedonian pharaoh (317–311 B.C.E.).

Alexander's body would later be transferred from Babylon to Memphis and then entombed at Alexandria by order of Ptolemy I, a former commander in the armies of the conqueror and the founder of an Alexandrian dynasty.

See Macedonian (Dynasty), Nectanebo, Ptolemy.

Alexandria

Now the second city of Egypt and more illustrious than ever, this urban center was founded in 332/331 B.C.E. as the westernmost of the eleven *Alexandreia* of which the great conqueror was the eponymous hero. As a result of the remarkable developments that this Mediterranean port and its cultural institutions experienced during the Greco-Roman era, its name symbolizes the birth and the flowering of Hellenistic civilization. In fact, we might wonder to what extent this city, on which Hellenists have focused so much attention, even concerns the pharaohs or falls within the purview of Egyptologists.

Prior to Alexander's conquest, the small, rocky offshore strip of land at the northwest corner of the Nile delta separating the sea from the vast Lake Mariut was occupied only by a post for coast guard ships, while the marshes of the lake were inhabited by uncouth cowherds. The Egyptian, Demotic, and Coptic designation of the city of Alexandria continued to be Raqote (Rakotis), literally, "the construction," either in the sense of "lasting construction" in contrast to the huts of the cowherds, or, according to a recent hypothesis, the ongoing "construction site" begun by the Greeks. The isle of Pharos, about 875 yards wide, on which Ptolemy II had a lighthouse erected, served as a port of call for sailors coming from the Aegean before they proceeded east along the coast to present themselves at the royal customhouse at the entrance to the westernmost branch of the Nile. The cowherds were responsible for discouraging pirates from infiltrating Egyptian soil.

An up-to-date city, laid out geometrically in the Greek style, was built on this quasi no-man's-land. It was the residence of the dynasty, as well as the seat of government and of a central administration whose principal language was Greek. For the first time, the Egyptian state provided a seaport for its naval and commercial strategies. Themselves the pupils of Greek philosophers and amateurs at Greek literature, the Ptolemies made their capital into a conservatory and a center for the development of the Hellenic patrimony. The Museum, a sort of permanent seminar, was founded, along with the famous Library, whose scholars gathered and collated manuscripts containing Greek literary and scholarly works, enhancing them with learned commentaries. Contrary to a notion that is still current, though, nothing indicates that the Museum collected hieroglyphic, hieratic, or Demotic papyri containing the knowledge accumulated by the native tradition, nor is there is any basis to the idea that the works of the Alexandrian thinkers and scholars, Eratosthenes and others, were based on the sacred lore of the priestly scribes of Memphis, Thebes, and Heliopolis.

That is not to say, however, that we can simply imagine a purely Greek "home base" at the edge of Egypt (*ad Aegyptum*), a colony almost totally closed to natives and to their beliefs and practices. Various facts lead us to reconsider the Egyptian aspect of this Hellenic city and to assess in what ways the pharaonic heritage was present, visible, and alive there:

1. Undeniably, from the beginning, the early Ptolemies chose Osiris-Apis as the patron of Alexandria. The inhabitants of Memphis, including colonists of Greek stock, had already been worshiping him as the this-worldly and other-worldly form of the supreme deity, who was at the same time Re, Ptah, and Osiris. In the Serapeum that was constructed on the highest hill, Bryaxis created a statue of this Serapis that made him resemble Zeus, Hades, and Asclepius, but certain chapels were conceived and consecrated according to native ritual, as shown by typically pharaonic foundation deposits with hieroglyphic inscriptions that imply the participation of Egyptian priests.
2. European travelers were exploring Alexandria as long ago as the eighteenth century. Since then, the city has been investigated by local and national archaeological authorities and by the citizens of Alexandria. Its now submerged parts have been the object of recent exploration by the Center for Alexandrian Studies and the European Institute of Underwater Archaeology. Throughout the city, these investigators have found a remarkable quantity of objects and fragments in pharaonic style, often bearing hieroglyphic inscriptions, mingled with the remains of Greek style and language. These Alexandrian *aegyptiaca* are mostly monuments capable of being moved—statues, sphinxes, obelisks (including "Cleopatra's Needles," a pair of New Kingdom obelisks now in London and New York), and so forth—but there are also fragments of architecture: columns, parts of walls, door frames, and notably, seven unusual, small walls constructed under kings of Dynasty Twenty-six and under

> Nectanebo I of Dynasty Thirty, which are now scattered among the museums of Bologna, Alexandria, Vienna, and London (where they are incorrectly said to have stemmed from Rosetta!). Many of these royal monuments date to earlier dynasties, but they cannot be cited to affirm that the pharaohs had founded a port city adorned with vast sanctuaries. Inscriptions attest that they were taken from temples in the interior of the land, mostly from Heliopolis, as has been known for more than a century. Moreover, a number of stray stones bear traces showing they were recut and reused as building material, sometimes several times, during the Greek and Roman eras.

We must distinguish between works in the pharaonic style that date to the Ptolemaic Period and those that date to kings earlier than Alexander and were imported from other sites. The former—notably the colossi of Lagide kings and Isiac queens found at the foot of the Qayt-Bey fortress and in the suburb of Eleusis, or the group of Philadelphoi found on Pharos—show that the Macedonian sovereigns were pleased to exhibit their divine omnipotence in the guise of pharaohs in the bosom of their Hellenic city. As elsewhere, the beautiful Egyptian-style statues of native dignitaries are votive images that these officials set up in the temples of Alexandria. From the third century on, men from the nomes holding priestly office frequented the royal court, and in the second and first centuries, some of them, who were both traditional and Hellenized, held high government offices in the capital, including the all-powerful office of minister of finance.

The question arises of determining under what circumstances, for what purpose, and at what dates antiquities going back to the Sesostrids, the Ramessides, the Saites, and the Sebennytic kings were removed to Alexandria. It would seem that the sphinxes, along with the images of kings presenting offerings, were simply incorporated into the ritual furnishings of the Serapeum and other temples, where they materialized the pharaoh's presence and actions while affirming the prestigious and immemorial continuity of the divine kingship. Architectural elements such as window and door frames, screen walls, and monolithic columns were perhaps integrated into new buildings for the same reasons, before being abruptly reused during the reorganizations of the Roman era.

Heliopolis, the principal source of large stone monuments, had apparently declined in importance by the beginning of the Ptolemaic Period. After the year 30 B.C.E., when its decrepitude was patent, the Roman emperor decided to transport obelisks from that city to Rome, in homage to the Sun and as testimony to the domination he had established over all the world. Should we or should we not impute the final destruction of the temples of Heliopolis to the Romans? On many points, the complicated history of these *pharaonica* of Alexandria will need to be methodically investigated in order to determine the place of pharaohs, hieroglyphs, and Egyptologists in the archaeology of Alexandria.

P. Fraser, *Ptolemaic Alexandria,* 3 vols. (Oxford, 1972); F. Goddio et al., *Alexandria: The Submerged Royal Quarters* (London, 1998).

See Alexander the Great, Ptolemy.

Amarna

The name Amarna is commonly used in reference to the capital city created *ex nihilo* around 1349 B.C.E. by Amenophis IV when he changed his name to Akhenaten. The city is referred to more exactly as el-Armana (in Arabic, "the people of the Amran tribe," which inhabited the site in more recent times); the designation Tell el-Amarna, widespread though it might be, is toponymically incorrect. Egyptologists often use the term "Amarna" to qualify the religion that Akhenaten founded, as well as the unusual style of statuary and relief that he favored; the term "Atenist" would be preferable. In fact, the revolution in question did not originate at Amarna; the city was its (relatively late) manifestation.

It was not until four years after the proclamation of his doctrine and its new style that the king, inspired by his god Aten, decided to set aside a vast domain that extended from the eastern to the western mountains a little south of Hermopolis. Its boundaries were demarcated by a dozen rock-cut stelae recounting the first visit to the site (year 4), its occupation (year 6), and the confirmation (year 8) of this permanent foundation, whose name was Akhetaten, "the Horizon of the Disk." Its inhabitants, its soil, and all its resources were to be at the service of the Sun alone.

The new city, whose layout was specified by the king himself, was quickly built on a vast plain on the east bank of the river. It would be home to the holy royal family and the spiritual and political center of the empire. The principal government ministers and departments were settled there. But we must reject the oft-repeated notion that Akhenaten wished to dwell exclusively in his utopia: he in fact commanded that if he, Nefertiti, or their eldest daughter happened to die outside Amarna, they were to be brought back and buried in the rock-cut tomb that he ordered prepared in the eastern mountain.

Abandoned under Tutankhamun, the capital lasted scarcely longer than the heresy; after the departure of the court, it quickly declined. During the reign of Ramesses II, its temples were dismantled, and their materials were reused at Hermopolis and Asyut. The abandoned homes collapsed, and their remains were not damaged by later occupation. Amarna is practically our only evidence of the urban environment in a new city. The royal city properly speaking, which was rather compact and a bit anarchic, was located in the center of the plain. Its core was the immense "house of Aten," which was linked by a bridge to the huge "house of the king." Other Aten sanctuaries and the buildings housing the government ministries (including the famous office containing the diplomatic archives) were spread out around them. Two quarters, at the northern and southern ends of the plain, contained other official buildings, notably the Maru-Aten in the south, which was both a cult place of the sun god and the royal family and a pleasantly landscaped residence.

Thanks to the exceptional preservation of the buildings, archaeologists have been able to reconstruct the plans of the spacious homes of the nobles, as well as the houses of the so-called workmen of the Tomb and of the government bureaucrats. The home of the sculptor Thutmose yielded a celebrated collection of finished and unfinished works. The scenes and inscriptions carved in the rock-cut tombs of the courtiers on the eastern mountain are our principal source for reconstructing the Atenist doctrine, and they furnish many lively representations of temples, palaces, and religious and secular activities from the time when the Horizon of the Disk was the pharaoh's splendid residence.

E. Hornung, *Akhenaten and the Religion of Light* (Ithaca, 1999), chapter 5.

Amasis 570–526 B.C.E., Twenty-sixth Dynasty

What we know of this king from his numerous monuments and from Herodotus illustrates the successes and the tensions of Saite Egypt. Greek and Carian settlers had been the instruments of the victories effected by the dynasty that succeeded Psammetichus I. Claiming that it had been sacrificed by Apries during his disastrous campaign in Libya, the native military caste brought Amasis to power and crushed the foreign auxiliaries by the sheer force of numbers. "Amasis the king," as Gaston Maspero well put it, "forgot the injuries done to Amasis the pretender." This general from a small town in the Saite nome understood that the technological future lay with the cities of Greece, and once he became "son of Neith," he pursued a resolutely philhellenic policy: alliance with Cyrene, gifts to Delphi and Samos, expansion of the trading center of Naukratis, and the transfer of the Ionian and Carian military colonists to Memphis. His only military venture was the conquest of Cyprus, whose art was influenced by that of Egypt. Around 570 B.C.E., Egypt had barely escaped a Babylonian invasion, but the prudent Amasis refrained from intervening in Asia while Cyrus of Persia annexed Anatolia and then the Babylonian realm.

Amasis supposedly invented the obligatory declaration of income. The evidence seems to confirm his role as legislator in the area of tax and customs regulations, and it attests to the scale of his monumental programs (the sacred lake of Sais and the naoi of Sais and Mendes). The introduction of a gown in the latest style on the statues of high officials perhaps denotes the modernism of their master. Amasis' personality became the subject of legend (in a Demotic story and Greek anecdotes). He was supposedly a scandalous drinker and an indelicate practical joker, but his inscriptions reveal him establishing a permanent cult for his statues and extending his divine protection to his ministers. Herodotus wrote, "It is said that the reign of Amasis was a time of unexampled material prosperity for Egypt; the river gave its riches to the earth and the earth to the people."

The Persian conqueror had the cartouches of this usurper mutilated in vain. The people retained an image of the xenophilic *parvenu* that conformed exactly to the theological model of a pharaoh.

A. de Sélincourt, *Herodotus: The Histories* (Harmondsworth, Middlesex, 1972), p. 199.
See Apries, Sais, Saite (Dynasties).

Amenemhet (Ammenemes)

This name, which means "Amun is in front," was borne by several pharaohs of the Twelfth and Thirteenth Dynasties. The reigns of those of the Thirteenth Dynasty—Amenemhet V, VI, and VII—were brief and obscure.

Amenemhet I 1991–1962 B.C.E., Twelfth Dynasty

Amenemhet I was the founder and first king of the Twelfth Dynasty. Prior to that, he was undoubtedly the vizier of Mentuhotpe IV, the last king of the Eleventh Dynasty, whose reign was so troubled that ancient Egyptian historiography did not recognize him at all. Were these troubles the cause or the result of the attempt at a dynastic change? In any event, once in power, Amenemhet I clearly marked the advent of a new era by locating his capital at Lisht (in Egyptian, *Itj-tawy,* "the one who seizes the Two Lands") in the south of the plain of Memphis. He endeavored to reestablish an order that had been seriously compromised by civil war, reestablishing the traditional landholding patterns and favoring the recruitment of administrators. To the latter end, he inspired the writing of the Summa (in Egyptian, *Kemyt*), a compilation of standard written formulas, and of the *Satire of the Trades,* which paints a highly disparaging picture of callings other than that of a scribe. Amenemhet I consolidated the boundaries of Egypt by means of operations in Nubia, Libya, and Palestine, and especially by constructing the "Wall of the Ruler," a system of fortresses protecting the eastern delta from Asiatic infiltration.

It is clear that he was unable to complete this major effort to annul the effects of the First Intermediate Period. Thus, in Middle Egypt, the nomarchs maintained the aristocratic and regionalist traditions that had ruined the Old Kingdom. The problem was that the legitimacy of the new dynasty was fragile. Still, the king endeavored to reinforce it by commissioning a work of propaganda, the Prophecies of Neferti, in which, during the beneficent reign of good King Snofru, a seer predicted that Egypt would be rescued from a period of chaos by a savior from the south named Ameny, an obvious short form of the name Amenemhet. He also attempted to secure the succession by making his son, Senwosret I, coregent in year 20 of his reign, but this effort was in vain. As a result of a conspiracy concocted in the harem, Amenemhet I was assassinated in his year 30 and was buried in the pyramid he had erected at Lisht. Senwosret I then commissioned an apocryphal work, the Instruction of Amenemhet I, a political testament defending the latter's accomplishments and advocating their continuation by his successor.

Amenemhet II 1929–1895 B.C.E., Twelfth Dynasty

Amenemhet II was the third king of the Twelfth Dynasty. He ruled thirty-eight years, partly as coregent with Sesostris I, his father and predecessor, and partly with Sesostris II, his son and successor. He increased commercial relations with the exotic trade centers of Punt, Syria-Palestine, and even Cyprus; a treasure of gold and silver objects, some of Aegean type, was deposited in the foundations of the temple of Tod. Amenemhet II undertook important construction work in the temple of Hermopolis, and he built his pyramid at Dahshur, south of Saqqara.

Amenemhet III 1843–1796 B.C.E., Twelfth Dynasty

Amenemhet III was the sixth pharaoh of the Twelfth Dynasty. During his long reign, this dynasty, and the Middle Kingdom more generally, reached its culmination, to the extent that the pharaonic state was able to tighten its control over the resources and the productive forces of Egypt and neighboring lands.

The system that Senwosret III had established in Nubia had regularized commerce with the south. In the north, on the Lebanese coast around Byblos, principalities developed with a highly Egyptianized ruling elite who served as intermediaries between Egypt and the Near East (Syria-Palestine, the Aegean).

Willingly or otherwise, a large Asiatic workforce began to settle in Egypt. Mines and quarries were intensively exploited: diorite from Nubia, granite from Aswan, hard stone from the Wadi Hammamat, limestone from Tura, and especially, turquoise and copper from Sinai.

The administrative reform begun by Senwosret III was completed. It led to a multiplication of new titles and the emergence of a middle layer of minor bureaucrats who achieved sufficient affluence to set up inscribed funerary monuments for themselves.

As a result of his control over goods and over the forces of production, Amenemhet III conducted an intense building program in which technology served to express an austere classicism. He built two pyramids, one at Saqqara and the other at Hawara in the Faiyum. The latter's funerary temple and associated town constituted an ensemble so complex that the Greeks called it a Labyrinth; other traces of his construction activities are still visible at Biahmu. The king's funerary cult lasted into the Greco-Roman era, when he was worshiped under the name Lamares, which was based on his throne name, Nimaatre.

See Senwosret III.

Amenemhet IV 1799–1787 B.C.E., Twelfth Dynasty

Amenemhet IV was the seventh king of the Twelfth Dynasty. He reigned for twelve years, some of them as coregent with his predecessor, Amenemhet III, who might have been his uncle. Amenemhet IV continued the work of his predecessor, maintaining extensive relations with Asia and constructing temples, especially in the Faiyum.

Amenhotpe, Son of Hapu

This provincial son of a lowly scribe from Athribis, a town in the middle of the delta, was born in the reign of Tuthmosis III and died in his eighties in year 31 of Amenophis III. Amenhotpe had one of the most brilliant careers to which an ordinary private person could aspire in pharaonic Egypt, thanks to his abilities and to the favor of the king. Amenophis III, who recognized his talent, appointed him as a royal scribe, assigning him at first to religious writings. Later, the king made him a "royal scribe of recruits"; Amenhotpe's duties were to administer the numerous personnel of the various institutions that composed the state. He also had to organize the change of status of the serfs of the royal domain, who were transferred permanently to the domain of Amun. In addition, he oversaw the maintenance and movements of the troops who patrolled the delta coast and the eastern and western desert plateaus, and he raised and organized an expeditionary force charged with putting down a revolt in Nubia.

The king was so satisfied with his services that he entrusted him with a burdensome responsibility: that of supervising, as "overseer of all works," the many construction projects he undertook at Thebes. Thus, Amenhotpe directed quarrying at Heliopolis, and then the transport of the Colossi of Memnon and the colossus of the Tenth Pylon of the temple of Karnak. These services received their due reward: the king presented him with statues that were placed in the temple to serve as intermediaries between Amenhotpe and visitors. The king also entrusted him with the administration of the domain of one of his daughters, Satamun, and he put him in charge of organizing his first jubilee, even permitting him to play an officiating role in the cermony. Finally, Amenhotpe was granted the right to erect a funerary temple near that of the king; its personnel benefited from a tax-immune status that would be reconfirmed even after the New Kingdom. By way of a prebend, he was also awarded the office of "overseer of prophets of Khentekhtai," the god of Athribis, his hometown.

Amenhotpe's tomb must surely have equaled that of contemporaries such as Ramose and Khaemhet. It has yet to be discovered, though its approximate location is known; in any case, Egytologists are certain that it was pillaged and severely damaged, to judge from the remains of it scattered throughout museums and private collections.

His brilliant career made it possible for Amenhotpe to survive to posterity, not only as an intercessor or patron saint, but also as a deity. He was believed to be the son of the god Apis (because of his father's name, Hapu), and he was associated with Imhotep, another deified man. Sanctuaries and oratories were built for his worship, and as late as the Ptolemaic Period, crowds of suppliants came to find the solution to their troubles or a cure for their ailments, either from his oracle or in the silence of incubation (visions seen in dreams). He was even identified with Asclepius by the Greeks.

A. Varille, *Inscriptions concernant l'architecte Amenhotep, fils de Hapou,* Bibliothèque d'Étude 44 (Cairo, 1968); D. Wildung, *Egyptian Saints: Deification in Pharaonic Egypt* (New York, 1977).

See Amenophis III, Imhotep.

Amenophis

When speaking of kings, Egyptologists often use the Greek form Amenophis as the equivalent of the Egyptian name Amenhotpe, which means "Amun is satisfied." This convention is followed here for the pharaohs named Amenhotpe in Egyptian. Nevertheless, it should be mentioned that the name form rests on a confusion: the Greek name Amenophis actually transcribes the Egyptian name Amenemope, "Amun is in Opet"; the actual Greek transcription of Amenhotpe is Amenothes.

Amenophis I 1514–1493 B.C.E., Eighteenth Dynasty

Amenophis I was the second king of the Eighteenth Dynasty, son and successor of Ahmose and Ahmose-Nofretari. He reigned twenty years and seven months. He was faced with the task of continuing the policy of restoration and fresh undertakings that Ahmose had barely begun. Like his predecessor, he subdued rebellions in Nubia, where permanent Egyptian occupation would extend as far as the Second Cataract, and which was placed under the jurisdiction of a special administrator, the viceroy of Kush; the mining of local gold could thus be systematically organized. Within Egypt, Amenophis I's efforts were turned especially to the cities that had participated in the alliance put together by the Theban kings, in particular el-Kab, where he built a temple. In the temple of Karnak, he constructed an alabaster way station for the divine barque. More generally, Amenophis I breathed new life into Egyptian culture: during his reign, in both the art and the inscriptions, we can follow the progressive elimination of the legacy of the Second Intermediate Period and the return to a classicism inspired by the Middle Kingdom.

Amenophis I stimulated a policy of inventorying and copying old works that was continued by his successors, in particular Tuthmosis III. Amenophis I did not hesitate to introduce innovations. He was the first to separate the royal tomb from the funerary temple, and he founded the organization charged with excavating and decorating the tomb; he thus became the patron saint of the workmen of Deir el-Medina, who created cult places where oracular consultations were carried out near certain of his monuments and images. Moreover, from the New Kingdom on, the seventh month of the calendar was called "that of Amenophis," referring to the festival of the deified king. In most of his posthumous cults, he was associated with his mother, Ahmose-Nofretari, who was herself considered to have been the founder of new practices.

See Ahmose; Ahmose, son of Ebana; Ahmose-Nofretari.

Amenophis II 1428–1401 B.C.E., Eighteenth Dynasty

Amenophis II was the seventh king of the Eighteenth Dynasty (counting Hatshepsut), son of Tuthmosis III and Queen Merytre-Hatshepsut. He reigned twenty-eight years (1428–1401), three of them as coregent with his father. From the beginning of his sole reign, he was obliged to defend the Egyptian hegemony so brilliantly consolidated in the Levant by Tuthmosis III. In his year 7, he led an expedition against a coalition of princes in the region of Takhsy, between the Orontes and the Euphrates; seven of them were put to death by Amenophis II himself, and their corpses were hung from the walls of Thebes and Napata. Nonetheless, it is not certain that his victory was total; it has even been suspected that Egypt abandoned certain territories to the allies of Mitanni. In year 9, a second expedition conducted north of Carmel obtained better results: Mitanni, Babylon, and the Hittite empire sent offers of peace.

Amenophis II completed the work undertaken by his father in the temple of Amada, and he continued the embellishment of the sanctuaries of Thebes and its region without neglecting the rest of the land. He built his funerary temple south of that of Tuthmosis III. His mummy was discovered in his sparsely decorated tomb in the Valley of the Kings.

With the reign of Amenophis II, a profound change came into play. Although Hatshepsut and Tuthmosis III had felt constrained to institute an artistic and cultural neoclassicism inspired largely by the Middle Kingdom, ideology now began to open up to the times, taking innovations into account. Egypt's imperialism in the Levant had opened its civilization to Asia, and royal terminology came to include metaphors based on Asiatic deities. A new theme described the king's physical abilities: Amenophis II had a passion for horses, which he broke in and maneuvered with great panache; he steered a boat with the greatest of skill, thanks to his expert handling of the oar; and his arrows pierced thick sheets of copper. Behind the obvious rhetoric of such proclamations, we see a genuine state of mind: most of the high officials of his reign were not chosen from the descendants of powerful lineages, but from the companions of the king's youth and military years.

G. Steindorff and K. C. Seele, *When Egypt Ruled the East,* 2d ed. (Chicago, 1957), chapter 8; C. Lalouette, *Thèbes ou la naissance d'un Empire* (Paris, 1986), chapter 6.
See Sport, Tuthmosis III, Tuthmosis IV.

Amenophis III 1391–1353 B.C.E., Eighteenth Dynasty

The ninth king of the Eighteenth Dynasty, Amenophis III was the son of Tuthmosis IV and Queen Mutemwia. He reigned thirty-eight years and seven months. His chief wife was Queen Teye, whom he associated closely with the official events of his reign; she influenced the affairs of state, especially when illness diminished the king's capacities at the end of his life.

She bore him at least two sons, one of them the future Amenophis IV/Akhenaten, and four daughters. One of the latter, Satamun, exercised the ritual functions of a queen, though this does not mean that Amenophis III actually married her, as is often maintained with a somewhat superficial taste for the spectacular.

The great accomplishments of his reign arouse astonishment and admiration, with no need for embellishment. In fact, if there ever was a pharaoh who resembled the stereotype of an oriental despot, it was certainly Amenophis III, with his obvious propensities for refinement, ostentation, and perhaps indolence. From his time on, great military campaigns were over; despite a police action in year 5 in Nubia, in the area of the Fourth Cataract, Amenophis III preferred to assure Egyptian hegemony in Asia through diplomacy, repeatedly affirming and consolidating friendly relations with Mitanni, the great power of the day. In year 10, he married Gilukhepa, the daughter of Shuttarna, the king of Mitanni; subsequently, he married the sister of Tushratta, another king of that land, along with the sister of the king of Babylon, and then their daughters and that of the king of Arzawa. When Amenophis III was ill, Tushratta sent him the image of the goddess Ishtar of Nineveh, whose healing powers were renowned. But diplomacy had its limits, and it did not prevent the king of Amurru from forming a coalition of small states intent on freeing themselves from the Egyptian sphere of influence.

This reversal occurred only at the end of a reign that otherwise marked the apogee of Egypt's power and wealth, thanks to the influx of Nubian gold and enormous quantities of raw materials and finished products delivered by countries that were to one degree or another subject to the pharaoh. Along with goods came ideas, customs, beliefs, and also people. Egyptian society became highly cosmopolitan, and there was a change of style that had already become perceptible under Amenophis II. Art furnishes an excellent example. Without renouncing the traditional conventions, a new delicacy and sensitivity modified Egypt's strict hierarchism; who has not admired the reliefs from the tombs of Ramose or Khaemhet? The style of clothing and jewelry changed, and the hieroglyphic writing system became progressively more open to the vernacular, which until then had been written with the cursive script. Religion was also transformed, not only by the introduction of foreign deities, but also by its turn toward a more concrete concept of the solar cult. Under the name Aten, the sun disk itself became the object of devotion, and we know to what extremes Akhenaten would take this tendency.

Amenophis III's style of rule was in tune with the changes in Egyptian culture. To be sure, ostentation and pomp had always characterized a pharaoh's acts and deeds, but this king took the splendor of his office to new heights. Deeming each of his acts to be worthy of more publicity than would be assured by traditional methods, he issued series of scarabs that were sent to the four corners of his empire to aggrandize them: they commemorated his marriages to Teye and Gilukhepa, his bull hunt in the desert in year 2, the total number of lions he slaughtered during the first years of his reign, and sailing on the gigantic *hod* (irrigation basin) that was dug near where Teye was born.

Amenophis III's monumental activity was itself a form of publicity. He erected a series of temples in Nubia, and the reliefs of that at Soleb illustrate the royal jubilee. He transformed the small chapel of Luxor into a temple, the elegantly slender colonnades of which still bear testimony to the splendor of his epoch. He also effected repairs or additions to many of the temples of Egypt. Amenophis constructed a palace at el-Malqata, south of Medinet Habu; in front of it was an artificial lake (Birket Habu) about 1100 yards wide by 2700 yards long. Of his funerary temple, only its huge statues, the Colossi of Memnon, remain for tourists to admire today; at the beginning of the Roman era, one of them was said to emit a moaning sound at dawn, but an earthquake put an end to the phenomenon. Amenophis III's tomb was located in a branch of the Valley of the Kings; its decoration, which was painted on stucco, is now in highly damaged condition. The identification of his mummy is uncertain.

G. Steindorff and K. C. Seele, *When Egypt Ruled the East,* 2d ed. (Chicago, 1957), chapter 8; C. Lalouette, *Thèbes ou la naissance d'un Empire* (Paris, 1986), chapter 7; A. P. Kozloff and B. M. Bryan, *Egypt's Dazzling Sun: Amenhotep III and His World* (Cleveland, 1992); D. O'Connor and E. Cline (eds.), *Amenhotep III: Perspectives on His Reign* (Ann Arbor, 1998).

See Amenhotpe, son of Hapu; Amenophis IV, alias Akhenaten; Teye.

Amenophis IV, alias Akhenaten

1353–1336 B.C.E., Eighteenth Dynasty

A long-standing hypothesis held that the government of the sumptuous but classical Amenophis III coexisted for more than eleven years with that of his son, the no less sumptuous but scarcely classical Amenophis IV. Most specialists today believe that this hypothesis was based on illusory facts that required us to imagine, contrary to the great mass of evidence, an unbelievable situation in which the two kings supposedly coexisted in peace but lived in parallel universes: two courts, two administrations, two incompatible religions, with both kings ruling the same kingdom while ignoring each other. In reality, at the change of reigns, there was an enormous rupture. When he came to power, Amenophis IV behaved like a prophet, revealing his sole god: "Re-Harakhty who rejoices in the horizon in his name of Shu (Light) which is in the Disk (Aten)"; this new formulation was written in two cartouches to express the sovereignty of the sun. Huge buildings were hastily built of small blocks (*talatat*) at Karnak, the home of the cult of Amun, King of the Gods, the foremost patron of Egypt's empire. The provincial cults continued to exist, served nominally by the king but under orders to furnish offerings to the new deity.

In his year 4, the king took the name Akhenaten ("useful to the Disk") and had a huge territory called the "Horizon of Aten" (*Akhet-Aten*) prepared in Middle Egypt, in an area devoid of any earlier temple. A new city was built in this territory, and in year 6, he moved there with his mother, Teye, his wife Nefertiti, his daughters, his court, and his government. Aten temples would be constructed in other cities as well: Sedeinga in the Sudan, Gurob, Memphis, and Heliopolis.

The hymns copied in the rock-cut tombs of the government officials at Amarna are addressed to Aten, the unfettered driving force of the physical cosmos, dispenser of light and air, and salvation of every living being. They are beautiful outpourings of sentiment, composed in a learned style that nevertheless borrows a great deal from the spoken language, and they sing of existence optimistically; in every way, the cosmos of Amarna was secure and beautiful. Along with Aten, the devotion of the faithful embraced only the persons of the earthly king and his wife, "in whom the perfections of the Disk are perfect": they were corporeal manifestations of the celestial father-mother, and their tender, mystical union was the manifest model of the sole god on earth. Temples and tombs represented them in public appearances and in the bosom of the palace, accompanied by their little daughters, breathing, eating, traveling about, rejoicing, offering, and praying under the huge sun whose arms radiated life (see figure 1). These epiphanies of the trinity are the common subject of huge compositions depicting various rites and other activities: fundamental ceremonies, offerings in the open-air sanctuaries, visits to the temples, reception of foreign tribute, rewarding of officials, and myriad activities of the royal subjects, all depicted in a lively style and replete with picturesque details. The only idols permitted in the homes of Amarna depicted the triad: the sun, the king, and the queen. Whether as an invention of the imagination or as the symbolic exploitation of the appearance of the king (see figure 2), the sovereigns are depicted in reliefs and in sculpture in the round with long faces hovering above androgynous bodies, a strange type that was generalized to all representations of the human figure. At the outset, the new iconography displayed a shocking expressionism, as exemplified

FIGURE 1. *Akhenaten and Nefertiti under the sun disk. Cairo Museum. Photo © 1991 by David P. Silverman.*

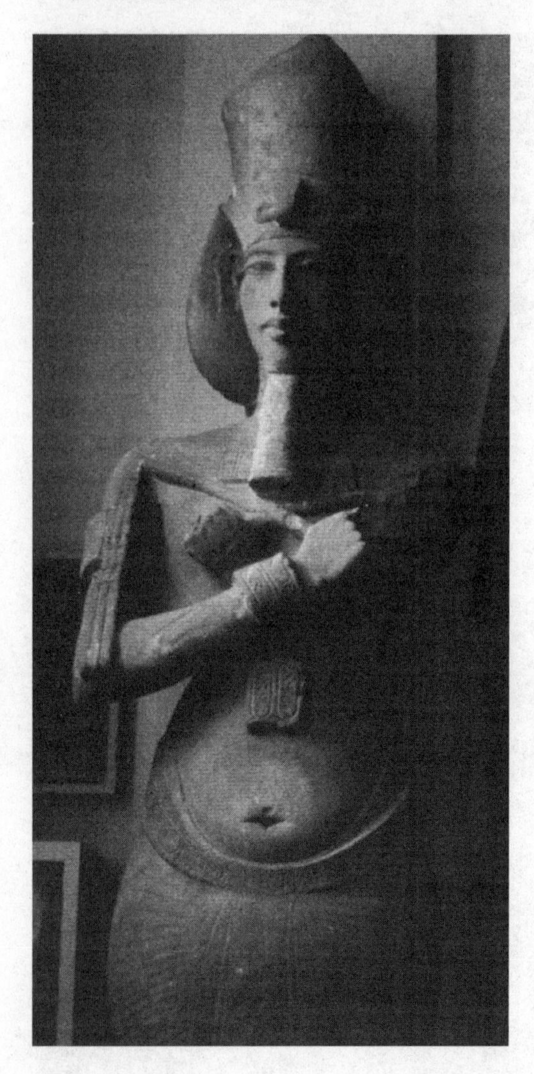

FIGURE 2. *Colossal statue of Amenophis IV/Akhenaten. Cairo Museum. Photo by Nancy J. Corbin.*

by the Karnak colossi of the king, that contrasted with the moderate aesthetic of the preceding reign, though at Amarna, it would be treated in a subtly restrained manner, as illustrated by the busts of Nefertiti.

The doctrine evolved. Signaling a theological purification, the divine titulary changed: "the Sun, celestial sovereign, rejoices in the Horizon—in his name Sun-Father (or "Luminosity") who comes as Aten." The name and images of Amun, the erstwhile supreme being who was still too present in the hearts of his subjects, were systematically effaced in the old temples. Vague attempts at censorship were also carried out on mentions of other deities and on the plural word "gods." These aberrant signs of what did not exist had to disappear.

From a handful of references, we know that besides Nefertiti, Akhenaten had a secondary wife, Kiya, who could have been the mother of Tutankhamun. But it is no longer believed that discord broke up the great theological marriage. When Nefertiti disappeared in year 14, Merytaten, the oldest of the six daughters she had borne to the king, and then the third, Akhesenpaaten, formally replaced her in representations of the epiphany of the royal couple. Akhenaten died during the eighteenth year of his reign. Archeologists found that the family tomb he had ordered to be prepared in the mountain of Amarna had been sacked. Everywhere, his cartouches and representations were destroyed during the reigns that followed. The Aten temples were dismantled and their blocks were reused as fill in new constructions. With time, the names and representations of Amun reappeared on walls. The word *aten* became what it had once been: the designation of the visible aspect of the sun and the moon.

In our own time, this "king drunk with God" has been regarded as the best of the pharaohs, a sympathetic hero, and the illustrious inventor of monotheism. The positive and simple rationality of his doctrine, the original expressions of it that he caused to be made in art and in texts, and the sudden emergence of an "ego" have a modern ring. His fleeting work marked a break with the impersonal and (to us) confusing discourse of the centuries that preceded and followed him. But in his own time, the man who was called "the enemy in Akhetaten" under Ramesses II was a misunderstood prophet and a negative monarch. Some histories have managed to make him an emancipator combating idolatrous obscurantism, a pacifist with ecumenical aims, or an anticlerical populist battling the oppression exercised by Amun and his priests; but all such portraits are refuted by the sources or are anachronistically speculative. The preserved evidence is insufficient to determine whether his revolution resolved an actual conflict between the crown and a supposed Theban lobby, as has been claimed, or to identify a military pressure group on which Akhenaten purportedly relied. From the evidence, we derive the image of an autocrat (as every pharaoh was!) who freed himself from the standard perceptions of his culture. Presumably filled with sensitivity and good intentions, he used his power to propose to this entire culture—or to impose on it—a minority theology with a doctrine of its own, leading to a radical transformation of the rites, the language of carved inscriptions, and the art. His religion had no impact on the secular administrative organs (government offices, army, police), the leadership of which was simply entrusted to declared disciples.

Until that time, kings had divine authority for the purpose of maintaining the gods and goddesses, who were resident in their hometowns and in the souls of the faithful. The king was the administrator of a religion whose representations and practices, which changed only imperceptibly in the course of the ages according to a shared logic, were experienced as manifestations that conformed to a primordial order and an immanent wisdom. It was not that individuals had been unable to appeal to their gods in trusting and affectionate terms. It was not that in the Eighteenth Dynasty, professional priests charged with invoking the divine did not wonder about the attributes or the ethical function of the gods, or the way in which this ancient world of names and forms regulating this world and the next was structured. The Theban conquerors, and all Egypt in their train, had recognized Amun-Re, patron of Thebes, as the author of imperial expansion. His oracular will had miraculously determined the course of the dynasty's history. Immense temporal holdings and a vast clergy lent expression to his recognition and corroborated his beneficent primacy. Expanding on the identity of Amun and Re by discursively clarifying the creative and legislative functions of the head of the pantheon, the Theban theologians conceived of Amun-Re as a unified and totalizing model of the notion of "god."

Relying less on mythological imagery, a new form of discourse emphasized the sun alone and described the direct effect of its distant course and its omnipresent light, its natural (so to speak) effect on all the known universe and in the existence of each individual. This New Solar Theology, however, did not exclude the other gods and goddesses; through hierarchism and homology, their existence remained compatible with that of the supreme being in the diversity of their names, idols, myths, and cult places. The favor the dynasty accorded to Amun had thus done no harm to the other gods: the pantheon honored by Amenophis III in the jubilees celebrated during the nine years preceding his death included all the gods and goddesses of Egypt. In this polytheistic culture in which all beliefs and forms were perceived as "natural," kings did not have to proclaim a dogma. It is thus wrong of us to refer to a "return to orthodoxy" in defining the liquidation of the Amarna interlude. It was with Amenophis IV that a choice (a heresy) instituted an orthodoxy, for his monotheism was the dogmatic, totalitarian, and intolerant negation of his contemporaries' religion of the One and the Many.

Given the state of the evidence, it is difficult to catch sight of the antecedents of Atenism. We see no influence of thought introduced from outside Egypt. Quite the contrary, the structures of theological elaboration, the pharaoh's monopoly on the cult, the elements of the grammar of symbolism, the ceremonial forms, the themes of divine praise (notably the idea that all races are creatures of the creator god), and the confident expression of faith all proceed from the common background of the Egyptian culture of the time. We see a sign of the recent promotion of the physical disk into a regal idol in the fact that Amenophis III proclaimed himself the "dazzling Aten," a name he had also given to his Theban palace, to his great processional barque, and to one of the regiments of his army. Priestly reflection had touched on the unity of the divine, but without translating it into an expression of contradiction. We imagine that it was thinkers in Heliopolis who took this step: setting aside the diverse formulas, myths, and rites that served to treat the mystery of the divine, these theologians retained no sign of the creator other than the disk with the luminous (Shu) breath, which was accessible without the rigamarole of the traditional imaginary realm. In fact, Amenophis IV called his god Re-Harakhty, he believed the *benben*-stone and the Mnevis bull to be the god's theophanies, and his chief priest was called "greatest of seers"; these four elements were borrowed from the tradition of Heliopolis. The "trinity" in which the royal couple shared in the status of the god, the aesthetic innovations (which generalized certain existing tendencies), and the expansive, optimistic expressions of fervor can be imputed to the genius of the ruler. Akhenaten's teaching thus consisted of creating an exclusive religion out of the concepts of certain previous thinkers, a religion he developed personally and which was implemented by artists and scribes whom he personally instructed.

We have no indication that this despotism provoked open rebellion, yet the speed with which the normal order returned, without the ravages of internecine warfare, creates the impression that the heresy had scarcely seduced either the educated class or the masses. The theophoric names of peasants had remained unchanged, and the little idols discovered in the homes at Amarna testify to the everyday survival of polytheistic habits. The queen mother Teye had passionately called her late husband the *Osiris* Amenophis. On his monument, a provincial dignitary had invoked the unique Aten, but also Osiris-Sokar and Khnum. The logic of the doctrine, though supported by the apparatus of the state and the enthusiastic will of the king, could not prevail against faith or against a nonconflictual theology from which both humble and learned derived spiritual and material benefit. The sources at Amarna inform us only of the resources of the palaces and the Atenist sanctuaries, but it is scarcely conceivable that the religious revolution did not diminish the temporal wealth of the old temples or put their priesthoods out of work. Afterwards, the religious restorers would assert that the sanctuaries had been stripped of their goods and their priests. Still, seventeen years of religious paranoia do not seem to have diminished the land's prosperity.

Though the texts expressing the theology scarcely mention the conflicts that inevitably occur in the world, certain iconographic themes that were openly retained demonstrate that the prophet-king endorsed the traditional bellicose duties according to which the pharaoh was supposed to ward off and to subject foreign peoples. Toward the middle of Akhenaten's reign, the viceroy of Kush suppressed a Nubian insurrection with the customary brutality. In Asia, triumphant Egypt had scarcely waged war during the reign of Amenophis III, despite the expansionist intentions of the Hittites and Mitanni and the intrigues of some of the vassal kinglets. Both the diplomatic archives discovered at Amarna and the Hittite sources show that the situation had deteriorated badly by the time Amenophis IV ascended the throne. During his own reign, unreliable high commissioners and the overly restricted movements of the Egyptian garrison troops proved unable to protect loyal Byblos against the ambitious dynasty of Amurru, or to prevent Hatti from eliminating the Mitannian ally and annexing Syria, or to suppress the depredations of marauding bands in Palestine. To explain this impotence by asserting that the sovereign shut himself up in his pious utopia and took no personal interest in armed defense or diplomatic maneuvers is scarcely plausible.

On the king's reign: C. Aldred, *Akhenaten and Nefertiti* (Brooklyn, 1973); idem, *Akhenaten, King of Egypt,* 2d ed. (London, 1988); D. B. Redford, *Akhenaten, the Heretic King* (Princeton, 1984); E. Hornung, *Akhenaten and the Religion of Light* (Ithaca, 1999); N. Reeves, *Akhenaten: Egypt's False Prophet* (London, 2001); G. Steindorf and K. C. Seele, *When Egypt Ruled the East,* 2d ed. (Chicago, 1957), chapter 14; C. Lalouette, *Thèbes ou la naissance d'un Empire* (Paris, 1986), pp. 505–46. *On the New Solar Theology and Amarna religion:* J. Assmann, *The Search for God in Ancient Egypt* (Ithaca, 2001), chapter 9.

See Amarna, Amenophis III, Aya, Nefertiti, Smenkhkare, Tutankhamun.

Ankhtifi

Ankhtifi was one of the strongest leaders during the Ninth Dynasty; his career lasted through the highly obscure reign of Neferkare. Ankhtifi was buried at Moalla, the cemetery of ancient Hefat, which was located between Thebes and el-Kab; the painted decoration of his tomb is in a curious provincial style, and there is a lengthy autobiography rich in information regarding the beginning of the First Intermediate Period. He succeeded a certain Hetep as nomarch of Nekhen, and he was also chosen, either by an oracle or by the king, as nomarch of the neighboring nome of Edfu to reestablish order, which had broken down during the turbulence of the epoch. He did so effectively, and he also placed the nome of Elephantine in his sphere of influence, leading to his title "overseer of foreign countries and overseer of interpreters." In times of famine, he not only succeeded in nourishing his own province, but also in sending grain as far as Dendara. Ankhtifi faced up to the initial displays of Theban ambition, leading several military expeditions (presented, of course, as victories) against the coalition formed by Thebes and Koptos. His autobiography is not without literary quality, but it demands a solid mastery of Egyptian.

J. Vandier, *Mo'alla,* Bibliothèque d'Étude 18 (Cairo, 1950).

Ankhu

Ankhu was a vizier in the first part of the Thirteenth Dynasty. He was of Theban origin, the son of a vizier and of the daughter of a prophet of Amun. His two sons Reseneb and Iymeru were also viziers, and it is likely that later viziers belonged to his family. One of Ankhu's daughters, Senebhenaes, married the "overseer of workshops" Wepwawethotpe, the descendant of a powerful family of Abydos. In this period when pharaohs succeeded one another at a rapid pace, Ankhu served several kings, including Sebekhotpe II, Khendjer, and Sebekhotpe III. We see him dealing, along with other high officials, with in-kind allocations in the festival hall of the court of Thebes; assigned by royal decree with intervening in conflicts involving jurisdiction over forced laborers; entrusting an "overseer of the phyle" with cleansing the temple of Abydos; setting up statues to his parents; and being honored on the monuments of his sons and colleagues.

See Sebekhotpe, Thirteenth Dynasty.

Apophis Fifteenth Dynasty

Apophis was the penultimate king of the Fifteenth Dynasty and the best known of the Hyksos. During his reign of more than thirty-three years, he conducted himself as an Egyptian king, commissioning construction work in the temples, such as that at Gebelein, having works of the past copied (e.g., the mathematical treatise of Papyrus Rhind), and defining his power by means of an authentically Egyptian titulary, to the point of changing his throne name three times to give ideological emphasis to the phases of his reign.

Nevertheless, according to a story entitled *The Quarrel of Apophis and Seqenenre,* he ended his *modus vivendi* with the Seventeenth Dynasty by imposing a humiliating demand, formulated allegorically, on Seqenenre. He attempted to weaken Seqenenre's successor, Kamose, by killing the latter's Egyptian collaborator at Neferusi and breaking up his alliance with the ruler of Kush. At the end of his reign, Apophis' power grew unsteady under the blows of the Theban nationalists, who would sweep away his successor Khamudi.

See Hyksos, Kamose, Seqenenre Tao, Seventeenth Dynasty.

Apries 589–570 B.C.E., Twenty-sixth Dynasty

Son of the ambitious Necho II, Apries intervened in Phoenicia. Despite his aid, Jerusalem, which had revolted against Babylon, was retaken by Nebuchadnezzar, and the Jewish people were deported. Egypt accepted some fugitives, among them the prophet Jeremiah. Apries also intervened in the west to aid the Libyan tribes against the Greeks of Cyrene. The failure of his Egyptian expeditionary force turned them against him and cost him the throne. This unfortunate Saite king is less well known from his monuments than from traditions about Amasis, who supplanted him.

Archaic (Period)

According to the historian Manetho, the period covered by the first two dynasties (beginning c. 3000–2950 B.C.E.) was governed by kings from Thinis, near Abydos in Upper Egypt. In fact, a series of very ancient tombs has been found at Abydos, many of which can be attributed to the pharaohs of the First and Second Dynasties, thanks to stelae that identify their owners. But at the Memphite cemetery of Saqqara, a British archaeologist, Walter B. Emery, discovered still larger tombs dated to the same period by a great number of sealings (but no stelae). This situation triggered a lengthy debate: were these the tombs of pharaohs? And if they were, were they real tombs, and were the tombs of Abydos cenotaphs? (The custom of building cenotaphs is well-known from a later date.) In fact, objects bearing the name of the same pharaoh were found in many tombs at Saqqara, while other tombs of similar size were built at other sites: Naqada, Giza, Abu Rawash, Tarkhan. Scholars are therefore inclined to attribute most of the tombs at Saqqara not to kings of the first two dynasties, but to their high officials, courtiers, and family members—categories that overlapped in this period.

In any case, their presence at a site where nothing earlier is known is not a matter of chance: it corresponds to a new policy formulated by the first pharaohs who were worthy of that name, that is to say, who ruled over a unified Egypt. This unification, which opened the historical period, was less the subjection of one kingdom by another than the extension of an already highly organized state in Upper Egypt into regions, more or less organized, of the delta (and perhaps Middle Egypt). Memphis was founded at the apex of the delta to facilitate better control of the newly integrated territories.

The list of First Dynasty kings includes Narmer/Menes, Aha (or, Aha/Menes), Djer, Wadj, Den, Adjib, Semerkhet, and Qaa. We know almost nothing of the political events in their reigns, except that even then, succession to the throne was not always a smooth one: a queen, Meretneith, seems to have exercised a regency that was contested, for her name and that of Adjib were systematically effaced on pottery of theirs that was found in the tomb of Semerkhet. The reign of Den manifested perceptible ideological changes that probably reflect political readjustments.

Though we do not know the details, it was probably political conflict that caused the sudden emergence of a new line of kings, the Second Dynasty (2780–2635 B.C.E.). The change occurred in a context of violence, for the First Dynasty tombs at Saqqara were pillaged and burned at that time. The kings of the new dynasty were: Hetepsekhemwy, Reneb, Ninetjer, Wadjenes, Weneg, Senedj, Nubnefer, Neferka, Neferka-Sokar, Peribsen, Sekhemib, and Khasekhemwy.

This linear enumeration can deceive; in fact, we are assured of neither its completeness nor its lack of redundancy, for the same sovereign might have been listed under two different names. Furthermore, the rifts led to the division of the land into two kingdoms, and it is probable that Wadjenes, Weneg, and Senedj ruled at Memphis, while Peribsen and Sekhemib made Abydos their capital. In fact, royal ideology codified these political conflicts, in which some have wished to recognize the ancient antagonism between an aristocracy rooted in the tradition of nomadic hunters and commoners composed of descendants of the agricultural populations of the valley. Certain changes in the writings of the Horus names of the kings of the Second Dynasty could be characterized as a process of thesis (Horus), antithesis (Seth), and synthesis (Horus and Seth). In any event, Khasekhemwy put an end to these conflicts, triumphing over a revolt by Lower Egypt and creating conditions that were propitious for a qualitative leap in the development of Egyptian civilization.

Aside from its political manifestations, Egypt of the first two dynasties was a state that was closely organized around the person of the pharaoh. The collection, preparation, and administration of consumable goods were assured by various institutions: the administration of granaries, the treasury (for manufactured goods), royal domains producing wine and oil (whose vintages were carefully dated and authenticated by the name of the responsible official); biennial inventories of gold and cultivable fields. According to a custom that probably predated the historical period, the king periodically toured the nomes to collect imposts. Lower Egypt was administered by officials who bore its seal ("sealbearer of the king of Lower Egypt"). The procurement of certain precious products that were lacking in the Nile valley (such as wood for construction) was assured by economic-military expeditions to the mines and quarries of the desert or through commercial relations, as with Byblos. The army had to be regularly used to maintain the security of the borders against incursions or raids by Libyans, Asiatic nomads, or Nubian peoples. Linked to the physical person of the pharaoh were institutions such as the palace (of which there were several for each king), the harem (which had an economic role), and officials charged with assuring his personal maintenance.

The organization of the state had its symbolic counterpart in a highly elaborate ideological system, the keystone of which was the king. He represented the supreme power in the hierarchy around which the world was organized. His entire person, as well as any objects or beings coming into contact with him, were invested with a part of that power. The institutions of the state were in some sense hypostases of the pharaoh, and their personnel acted as officiants responsible for the maintenance of one of his many manifestations. Events that affected society were interpreted and codified via a fixed repertoire of royal acts. Year by year, annals listed what was considered significant, such as the erection of statues or temples to the gods, kingship rituals (jubilee, ritual run around the walls, Uniting of the Two Lands, Reception of Upper and Lower Egypt), biennial counts, suppression of revolts, and victories over neighboring peoples. The chronological references necessary for administration were not based on the numerical position of a year in the reign, but rather by characterizing the year by the principal events that marked it. This ideological codification remained open; thus, the royal titulary (a king's names and accompanying titles) was still in the process of development.

Although the contemporary documents are laconic and formulaic, certain indications suggest that already at this time, the kings inspired the development of religious and magico-medical literature. Thus, while maintaining, at least at its beginning, certain highly archaic traits (such as funerals marked by the killing of servants to accompany an important personage in the tomb), the Archaic Period witnessed the development of most of the characteristic elements of Egyptian civilization.

W. B. Emery, *Archaic Egypt* (Baltimore, 1961); T. A. H. Wilkinson, *Early Dynastic Egypt* (London, 1999).

See Khasekhemwy, Menes, Narmer, Peribsen, Pharaoh.

Asia

In ancient Egypt, the Nile marked the frontier between Africa and Asia; Egypt was thus the link between these two continents. The "Asia" of pharaonic civilization was, of course, much smaller than what the term means to us today; it was essentially the Near East.

There was a strong Asiatic influence during the period when pharaonic civilization was taking form; in particular, Mesopotamian inspiration is perceptible in certain iconographic themes of the predynastic period and in certain predynastic objects, such as cylinder seals. Throughout its history, Egypt of the pharaohs would be induced to maintain relations with the Asiatic world.

One reason for this phenomenon was the exploitation of its eastern desert: the galena of Gebel Zeit, the gold mines of Barramiya and Samut, and the gold mines and *bekhen*-stone (graywacke) in the area of the Wadi Hammamat. The latter was also a passageway: dismantled at Koptos, boats were transported via the Wadi Hammamat to the shore of the Red Sea, where they were reassembled at the ports of Quseir and Wadi Gawasis. From those ports expeditions would depart for Africa (Punt) or for the Sinai peninsula and its indispensable mines of turquoise and copper at Serabit el-Khadim and Wadi Maghara. During such enterprises, Egyptians encountered Asiatic nomads, sometimes peaceful and ready to barter, but most often hostile and posing a threat to the expeditionary forces and their encampments.

The other reason was that the easternmost delta was a zone of permanent contact. The frontier extending from the Mediterranean shore to the Pelusiac branch of the Nile, on the one hand, and on the other hand, to the Gulf of Suez, was lined by a series of lakes: the Lake of Horus, near the eastern end of the present-day Lake Menzala, Lake Bala, Lake Timsah, and the Bitter Lakes. There were two main routes across this border. One was via the Wadi Tumilat; dried out today, it was covered with marshes and overgrowth through much of the pharaonic era. Its access was defended by the town of Pithom, and biblical tradition identifies it as one of the routes of the Exodus. The other was the depression of el-Qantara, which in the New Kingdom was controlled by the fortress of Sile and linked to the Lake of Horus and the Pelusiac branch of the Nile by a canal. Until it was silted up at the beginning of the second millennium B.C.E., it was the principal communication artery with the Mediterranean and the Near East. Its main port was located not on the shore, but in the delta, where the desert met the cultivated land; it was there that Avaris was founded, the city that became the Hyksos capital and then Pi-Riamsese. When the Pelusiac branch became unusable, the Tanite branch, a little to the north, served as the communication route with Asia.

These passageways had two functions. The Egyptians made use of them, but so did Asiatics. Archaeology has in fact revealed the presence of the latter's settlements, often ancient ones, along the axes that crossed the easternmost delta; their size varied with historical circumstances.

During the Old Kingdom, relations with Asia remained relatively sporadic: police operations on the shores of the Red Sea against nomads who threatened the port installations, expeditions to the Sinai, and especially expeditions to Byblos on the Lebanese coast, where the Egyptians went in search of pine and cedar, wood they needed for building. During the First Intermediate Period, the pressure from Asiatic infiltrators became so great on the eastern borders of Lower Egypt that the pharaohs of Herakleopolis were obliged to establish a huge defensive system there.

The effort was evidently insufficient, for Amenemhet I, the first king of the Twelfth Dynasty, boasted of having put an end to the incessant Asiatic infiltrations by means of a fortification system called "Wall of the Ruler." Additionally, the new dynasty intensified exploitation of the Sinai and commercial ties with Byblos, which from that time on would be ruled by highly Egyptianized native potentates. Egypt also opened itself to the world of Syria-Palestine; the Execration Texts display a good knowledge of the political geography of the area as far as the region of Damascus, while the Story of Sinuhe introduced the ruling classes to its exoticism. Military expeditions—one of them marked by the capture of Shekhem—were sometimes necessary to assure the regularity of imports, which included cattle and, in particular, copper, gold, lapis lazuli, other precious stones, and objects that were manufactured locally or obtained from Cyprus and the Aegean world. In the reign of Amenemhet II, four coffers filled with these raw materials and manufactured objects were buried in the foundations of the temple of Tod.

At the same time, a large number of Asiatics immigrated to Egypt, where they were employed as domestics or enrolled (willingly or by force) as workers in the major departments of the state bureaucracy. At the end of the Twelfth Dynasty, there was already a large colony of Asiatics at Avaris, the great port that gave access to Asia. Toward the middle of the following dynasty, they were an important component of a principality that made itself independent of the sovereignty of the Theban pharaohs, preparing the way, so to speak, for the Hyksos conquest of Egypt some decades later. The latter would establish an empire that straddled Egypt and the Palestinian world.

It was for this reason that the early pharaohs of the Eighteenth Dynasty had to penetrate into Palestine in their effort to eradicate the domination of the Hyksos. This action was the preliminary to a new Asiatic policy; during the New Kingdom, Egypt would establish a protectorate over Syria-Palestine, one that was guaranteed by Egyptian garrisons planted in strategic locales and reinforced by skillful diplomatic measures that included hostages and marriages. Egypt defended its protectorate with varying degrees of success against the competing imperialists of Mitanni, and then the Hittite empire. As often occurs, the culture of the conquered influenced that of the conquerors, and Egypt benefited greatly from the products and technologies of Asia. With objects and materials came vocabulary, and the Egyptian language was enriched by an ample stock of Asiatic words, some of them Hurrian or Indo-European, but most of them Semitic. Indeed, a veritable Semitic fad swept over Egypt, encouraged by the status of Akkadian, a Semitic tongue, as the language of diplomacy. Every literate person was obliged to master Canaanite idioms, and Semitic words sometimes replaced ordinary Egyptian ones; this fashion was a form of snobbism. Even Asiatic deities were introduced into the already densely populated pantheon of Egypt. Obviously, people accompanied these words, objects, and deities; numerous Asiatic colonies were installed in Egypt, in places such as Perunefer, the great port of Memphis. Many of these Asiatics were laborers assigned to the humblest and most difficult of tasks; this was the context of the story in the book of Exodus. Yet some enjoyed brilliant careers in the upper levels of the Egyptian administration and even found their way into the court, often with the title "royal butler."

After the New Kingdom, Egypt's claims of domination over Asia came screeching to a halt; the prince of Byblos was well aware of this when, during the Twenty-first Dynasty, he cruelly snubbed Wenamun, the envoy of the god Amun, letting him know clearly that the days of hegemonic arrogance were over. In fact, Shoshenq I's campaigns in Palestine were the swan song of Egyptian imperialism. They did not end in the political subjection of the Hebrew monarchy, but simply in the reinforcement of its cultural ties with Egypt, thus accounting for the borrowings from Egyptian wisdom literature in certain books of the Bible and for the use of hieratic numerals in the bookkeeping of the kingdom of Israel. After that, Egyptians looked to Asia not with the greedy gaze of a conqueror, but rather to calculate the appetite of the next invader. Egypt became subject to the Assyrians, and then, on two occasions, to the Persians. During the interludes of independence, relations were confined to commerce, and such few military ventures as those of Taharqa and Necho II came quickly to an end.

See Amenemhet I, Hittites, Hurrians, Hyksos, Necho II, Ramesses II, Sethos I, Shoshenq, Sinuhe, Taharqa, Tuthmosis III.

Autobiography

The autobiographical genre flourished in pharaonic Egypt because of beliefs in survival. To survive in the hereafter, deceased persons needed for the living to recite the necessary formulas, in particular the offering formulas, on their behalf. But the living had to be persuaded to do so. Passers-by reading the inscriptions on a funerary monument would be all the more inclined to pronounce these formulas if they judged its owner to have been a philanthropist; in the afterlife, those who had been philanthropic had the ear of the gods, and thus they could use their credit with them in favor of living persons who recited the formulas on their behalf. There was nothing like a flattering self-portrait to set the cycle of reciprocity in motion. This was the goal of an autobiography, which was usually preceded by the titles and name of the deceased.

Autobiographies were often limited to an accumulation of clichés that described an ideal character and the norms of conduct; examples are "I was one with a just heart," "a truly silent one, excellent of character," and "I gave bread to the hungry, water to the thirsty." Other repertoires were adapted to various sectors of professional activity; thus, a priest would boast of having "pure hands when carrying out the ritual," while a courtier took pride in having been "a confidant of the king before the Two Lands."

The term "cliché" should not mislead; wording and repertoires varied from one period to another, reflecting the spirit and the important trends of the times. Thus, in periods of disorder, accent was placed on exalting personal success, while when the monarchy was strong, the clichés included loyalist proclamations.

Sometimes, when its author considered the story of his life and career to be edifying and satisfying, an autobiography became a personal history. Such cases are providential for the historian, who often finds detailed information in them. Autobiographies are major sources for more than one period of history. What would Egyptology be without the autobiography of Weni for the Sixth Dynasty, that of Khnumhotpe for the beginning of the Twelfth Dynasty, or that of Ahmose, son of Ebana, for the birth of the

New Kingdom? Other valuable autobiographies include those of Bakenkhons, the Third Intermediate Period priests of Amun, Udjahorresnet, Sematawytefnakht, Djedhor-the-savior, and Petosiris of the Late Period.

M. Lichtheim, *Ancient Egyptian Autobiographies Chiefly of the Middle Kingdom: A Study and an Anthology,* Orbis Biblicus et Orientalis 84 (Freiburg and Göttingen, 1988); idem, *Moral Values in Ancient Egypt,* Orbis Biblicus et Orientalis 155 (Freiburg and Göttingen, 1997).

See Ahmose, son of Ebana; Sinuhe; Udjahorresnet; Weni.

Avaris

The translation of the word Avaris, *Hut-waret,* is "the mansion of the sloping plot of land." Avaris was a riverine port in the eastern delta on the Pelusiac branch of the Nile, at the margin of the cultivable land; its local god was Seth, lord of uninhabited areas. Given its location, Avaris controlled the outlet of the "Ways of Horus," a route leading to Asia, and in particular, to Byblos and the Phoenician coast. Avaris thus had both a strategic and a commercial function, and it attracted the interest of pharaohs who fortified it under the dynasties of Herakleopolis and made it their summer residence during the Middle Kingdom. Intensification of trade with Byblos led to the growth of a colony of Asiatics who took charge of working the copper imported from Cyprus. During the Thirteenth Dynasty, Nehesy made this city, with its considerable foreign population, the capital of the kingdom he had founded around 1720 B.C.E.; in the middle of the seventeenth century B.C.E., it would be overwhelmed by a new influx of Asiatics, the Hyksos. After taking Memphis, the Hyksos imposed their domination over all Egypt from their capital of Avaris, which was evidently pillaged when the land was liberated under Ahmose. But its location was so advantageous that Ramesses II chose to construct his new capital of Pi-Riamsese on its site. After the Pelusiac branch silted up, the site was abandoned. Modern archaeology has rediscovered Avaris around present-day Tell el-Daba.

M. Bietak, *Avaris and Piramesse: Archaeological Exploration in the Eastern Nile Delta* (Oxford, 1981).

See Ahmose; Ahmose, son of Ebana; Dynasties; Hyksos; Kamose.

Aya 1326–1323 B.C.E., Eighteenth Dynasty

Aya's career was closely connected with the royal house; he was a religious renegade who became king at the end of a dramatic era. We distinguish three stages in his career:

1. He was chief of the chariotry and one of the ministers whom Amenophis IV/Akhenaten instructed in his doctrine. Aya was undoubtedly a native of Akhmim. He had the rank of "god's father," for his wife Teye was the nurse of Queen Nefertiti. His tomb at Amarna expresses his total loyalty to Atenism and his devotion to the inspired royal couple.
2. One of Tutankhamun's viziers was none other than the same "god's father," who participated in the restoration of the traditional religion.
3. The "god's father Aya"—with his title and name enclosed in a cartouche—became king, and invested with that office, he presided over the funeral of Tutankhamun. His four years of reign were not enough time to create many monuments, although the speos (rock-cut chapel) of Akhmim, architraves associating the elderly king with his predecessor at Karnak, a huge funerary temple at Medinet Habu, and a rock-cut tomb in the Valley of the Monkeys were undertaken.

Aya's representations and names were mutilated, his sarcophagus was smashed, and his mummy has yet to be found. His successor Haremhab, and later tradition as well, endeavored to wipe out his memory.

See Amarna, Amenophis IV, Haremhab, Tutankhamun.

Berenike

Thanks to French dramatist Jean Racine, this women's name is famous as that of the young Jewish princess from the family of the Herods whom the Roman emperor Titus refused to marry. In fact, the name was popular throughout the areas of the Hellenized east that were at some time subject to the Ptolemies of Egypt; and Greco-Macedonian though it was, it became typically Egyptian. Borne by the mother of Ptolemy II, in whose honor the famous port of Berenike on the Red Sea was named, it passed from mother to daughter within the dynasty, and it was a common name among the people as well. There were four queens of Egypt and at least two famous princesses named Berenike.

The Greek poet Callimachus wrote of a miracle: Berenike II supposedly dedicated a lock of her hair to the divine while pronouncing a wish that her husband, Ptolemy III Euergetes, would return safely from war (246 B.C.E.), and the lock was transported into the northern sky, where it could be observed from then on as the constellation Coma Berenices, between Taurus and Leo. When her daughter died in her adolescence in 238 B.C.E., priests from all of Egypt convened in Canopus and proclaimed the apotheosis of this new incarnation of the Eye of Re, making detailed provisions for a national cult of this young Berenike. Another poetic touch, but in the pharaonic style: to adorn her commemorative statues, the priestly scribes conceived a crown made of four objects that were both hieroglyphs writing out the name Berenike and symbols of her divine power and the promise of youthful fecundity.

See Ptolemy, Queens.

Bocchoris 720–715 B.C.E., Twenty-fourth Dynasty

Son of the Saite prince (and possible king) Tefnakhte, this sole king of the historian Manetho's Twenty-fourth Dynasty continued his father's policies. For six years, Sais imposed its own pharaoh on Memphis, Tanis, and Herakleopolis. Shabaka, king of Kush, defeated Bocchoris and had him burned alive as a rebel. The unfortunate king is known from several monuments. Two of them are vases, one ancient and the other an eighteenth-century copy, that were discovered in Italy (hence the name "tomb of Bocchoris" given to an Etruscan tomb at Corneto). A rich fictitious tradition surrounded his memory: he was supposedly a legislator who was beneficent to the poor, and a wise judge as well, and it was in his reign that a lamb prophesied the misfortunes of foreign invasions and the ultimate redemption of Egypt. Herodotus' picturesque description of Mycerinus as the wise king who built the third pyramid probably draws on anecdotes about Bocchoris.

See Kushite (Dynasty), Sais, Saite (Dynasties), Third Intermediate Period.

Bubastis

Bubastis, a city in the eastern delta, was situated on the easternmost branch of the Nile at a point where the basin of this branch is immediately contiguous with that of the Tanitic branch and about twelve and a half miles west of the outlet of the Wadi Tumilat. The site, located near Zagazig, the modern metropolis of the region, retains its ancient name: Tell Basta. Bubastis was originally called Bast, from which the name of the goddess Bastet ("she of Bast") was derived; later, it was known as "the house of Bastet" (Greek *Boubastis,* Latin *Bubastis*). The city and its cult of the lion-headed goddess were founded during the earliest dynasties.

Bastet, who was in the sphere of influence of the Heliopolitan pantheon, was a local variant of Sakhmet, the feminine personification of the dangerous but pacifiable power of the sun. In the royal temples of the Old Kingdom, she was a patroness of the sovereign, and the cult of this "mistress of the life of the Two Lands" would later enjoy a long existence north of Memphis (the Bubastieion and the subterranean cat cemetery at Saqqara).

The importance of Bubastis in the Sixth Dynasty is attested at the site by the remains of buildings of Teti and Pepy I and by a private cemetery. The city's temple was embellished by a series of pharaohs, from Amenemhet I to Nectanebo II, and the prestige of its physicians and of its "house of life" was recognized under the Ramessides. The strategic position of Bubastis doubtless led to the settling of Libyan Meshwesh there during the Tanite era.

Shoshenq I and other members of his dynasty called themselves "son of Bastet," and the personal names of the Libyan Period reflect the growing popularity of this goddess. From that time on, animal worship would view cats as manifestations of Bastet, and we have wonderful Saite bronzes from the city's animal cemetery. Bastet was understood to be the "soul of Isis," and her worship became universal. According to Herodotus, her joyous festivals were the best attended of all those in Egypt.

Buto

As early as the Archaic Period, this city in the extreme north of the western delta, near the marshes, bore the double name Pe-Dep, which is probably a sign of the duality of its original organization. Its principal deity was the goddess Wadjit, who was simultaneously the uraeus (i.e., cobra) who adorned the pharaoh's brow, the goddess of the red crown of Lower Egypt, and a dangerous lion. Behind the Greek name Buto lies an Egyptian expression meaning "house of Wadjit." Horus of Pe, prototype of the king, also had a long-standing cult there. According to a tradition, Horus and his mother, Isis, took refuge in the thicket of Chemmis, located in a lake on the outskirts of Buto, from which he later emerged to win his throne. From the Old Kingdom on, ritual symbolism made Pe-Dep symmetrical with Upper Egyptian Hierakonpolis (Nekhen). The *pshent* crown resulted from the union of Wadjit and Nekhbet, "the White One of Nekhen," the goddess of the white crown of Upper Egypt, who was resident in the predynastic city of el-Kab. The divine "souls" of Buto were the counterpart of the "souls" of Hierakonpolis. These parallelisms clearly stem from the concept that the balanced union of the two lands was the realization of the plenitude of the power and harmony of the universe.

Nevertheless, several rituals that appear to be archaic—including the incantation for the censing of the uraeus, the mime of the royal funeral, and the consecration of the sanctuary—allude only to Buto and neighboring towns, as if they concerned only that region.

Historians no longer assert that at the end of the fourth millennium, there was a "kingdom of Buto" whose conquest by the south supposedly unified the land and inaugurated the historical period. But it would be incorrect to maintain that Buto was only a frontier dreamed up by dualistic thinking to serve as a counterpart to Hierakonpolis: recently, deep drillings demonstrated that human occupation at Buto went back to the beginning of the third millennium. A cardinal point in the imaginary organization of space and center of the immemorial cult of the royal uraeus, Buto was a part of the principality of Sais in the eighth century B.C.E. Herodotus reported that the oracle of its goddess was the one most venerated by the Egyptians. Founded anew by the Saites and despoiled under Xerxes, its great temple saw the landholdings that had been guaranteed by the rebel pharaoh Khababash restored to it by the satrap Ptolemy.

See Crowns.

Cachettes

Guarded by police and protected by a fort, the Valley of the Kings, where the royal tombs were excavated into the hillsides, was assuredly sacrosanct. Still, though the entrances to the sepulchers were walled and banked up, their location was no secret, at least to the administration and the workmen of the Tomb. Even tombs found inviolate in our own time were not entirely unscathed: objects were missing and disarray was evident in the tomb of Tutankhamun (no doubt consequences of a transfer), and precious objects had been removed from that of the in-laws of Amenophis III. Other enigmatic examples include the mysterious Tomb 55 (possibly of Smenkhkare) with its contents in disarray and the cache of forgotten jewels in Tomb 56. Tragically, attacks on the dead became routine toward the end of the New Kingdom. The outbreak of greed that culminated in the ravaging of all the royal and private tombs on the west bank of Thebes is well-known. Records describe inquiries that were conducted to detect, determine the extent of, and punish the acts of pillage carried out by the small gangs that had been formed among the personnel of the funerary temples and among the "workmen of the Tomb." The preserved reports deal with the cemeteries of the Eleventh and Seventeenth Dynasties (e.g., Dra Abu el-Naga), the Valley of the Queens, and the royal tombs and funerary temples. During the reign of Ramesses IX, the robberies occurred against a backdrop of poverty, strikes, Libyan incursions, and malfeasance in high places. The damage was considerable, but with the collusion of the vizier, the prefect of the west bank, who was responsible for the cemeteries, attempted to conceal its extent, much to the scandal of his colleague on the east bank. Under Ramesses XI, the pillaging took place in a context of famine, civil war, and struggles for power; the inquiry was more vigorous and successful, but the troubles persisted. Nearly all the burials of the kings and queens were broken into; their furnishings were trashed, and the tombs were stripped of metal objects and the precious jewels that adorned the dead.

With the rise of the Theban theocracy, Herihor was reduced to restoring the mummies of Sethos I and Ramesses II, which were placed in borrowed coffins. Confidence was not restored under this Twenty-first Dynasty, and the dead were grouped in collective burials (such as the second cachette of Deir el-Bahari, which contained the bodies of priests of Amun). The high priests of Thebes preoccupied themselves with saving at least the bruised hides of the "great gods" (that is, the royal dead). Many inspections were made under Pinudjem I, and a number of the royal mummies were rewrapped. After various attempts to group them together, the bodies of most of the New Kingdom pharaohs ended up in two cachettes, each of the pharaohs in a reused coffin and deprived of all burial goods:

THE TOMB OF AMENOPHIS II

This tomb had already been pillaged when it was opened by Victor Loret in 1898. Besides Amenophis II, it sheltered Tuthmosis IV, Amenophis III, Siptah, Sethos II, Ramesses IV, Ramesses V, and Ramesses VI, along with three anonymous individuals, one of whom might be Teye, the wife of Amenophis III, according to a much-debated medical assessment. This cache was sealed up under Pinudjem I.

THE "ROYAL CACHETTE" OF DEIR EL-BAHARI

This cachette, which was discovered by the Abd el-Rasul brothers in the 1870s, was emptied in 1881 by a team directed by Gaston Maspero. The burial place, which was sunk into a crevice of the rock wall on the margin of the bay of Deir el-Bahari, contained two series of inhumations:

(a) A collection of dead "vagabonds" of the Seventeenth through the Twentieth Dynasties: Seqenenre, Ahmose, Amenophis I (along with eight ladies and two princes who were closely related to him), Tuthmosis I, Tuthmosis II, and Tuthmosis III, Ramesses I, Sethos I, Ramesses II, Merneptah, Ramesses III, and Ramesses IX.

(b) The mummies (all in their original coffins and accompanied by varying quantities of burial equipment) of the high priest and king Pinudjem I, his successors the high priests Masaharta and Pinudjem II, and six queens and princesses of this pontifical family.

There is considerable debate regarding the chronology of the transfers that resulted in this double morgue. According to the latest theory, it was created by Pinudjem II, who desired to shelter his own and his relatives' remains, along with those of the sacred royalty of the past. The cachette received at least one final "guest" under Shoshenq I.

N. Reeves and R. H. Wilkinson, *The Complete Valley of the Kings: Tombs and Treasures of Egypt's Greatest Pharaohs* (London, 1996), pp. 194–207; K. Myśliwiec, *The Twilight of Ancient Egypt: First Millennium B.C.E.* (Ithaca, 2000), pp. 35–40.

See Valley of the Kings.

Caesar

For three centuries, the famous name of the conqueror of the Gauls, of the Julius who crossed the Rubicon, would have a fine career in the *Who Was Who* of the pharaohs. This career began in 43 B.C.E., when the child of the Roman dictator and Cleopatra VII ascended the throne in association with his mother, with the name "Ptolemy surnamed Caesar, beloved of his father, beloved of his mother." The poor lad, who was ridiculed by the nickname Caesarion, "little Caesar," was killed in 30 B.C.E. by the agents of another pharaonic Caesar: his half brother Octavian, whom the Divine Julius had adopted according to Roman law as his son and heir, and whose victory over Mark Antony and Cleopatra carried him to the throne of Egypt.

In 27 B.C.E., the Senate and the People of Rome sanctified the full powers of this *imperator* (military autocrat) by conferring on him the holy title of *augustus.* The emperor Augustus' Latin titulary was translated into Greek, which remained the administrative language of the eastern provinces; in both Demotic documents and hieroglyphic cartouches, this pharaoh is therefore called "Autocrator Caesar Sebastos." Beginning with Tiberius, the series of emperors who assumed the title of Caesar and the role of pharaoh would continue to employ this basic titulary on temple walls at Dendara, Kom Ombo, Philae, and other sites.

Cambyses 525–522 B.C.E., Twenty-seventh Dynasty

Cambyses was the second king of the Persians and the Medes. He ruled Egypt for two years, founding the Twenty-seventh Dynasty. His father, the illustrious Cyrus, had already united Iran, Anatolia, and the Babylonian empire under his scepter. In 525 B.C.E., the great Persian army defeated Psammetichus III near Pelusium and seized Memphis. Cambyses was crowned pharaoh by the clergy of Sais, the native city of the preceding dynasty. This immediate acceptance of a foreigner who had come suddenly from afar into the dynastic theology was a momentous event. It was as though the doctrine of the conquered, which postulated the cosmic omnipotence of the ruler, immediately took advantage of its chauvinistic sensibility to co-opt the effectively ecumenical power of the conqueror.

An Apis bull had just died; its splendid sarcophagus was carved with a dedication in the name of Cambyses. Nevertheless, Herodotus reported that the latter killed the animal with his own hand; Herodotus then described the excesses, the madness, and the cruelty of the son of Cyrus, as well as the failures he experienced in Nubia and in the Libyan desert. The supposed murder of Apis was one of the examples by which fifth-century Egyptians came to stigmatize their foreign rulers as profaners. Added to the bad press that Persian opinion gave to Cambyses under Darius, the rancor in Egypt toward the Asiatic occupiers fed Herodotus' caricature of a mad tyrant who was preceded and followed by two wise rulers, Cyrus and Darius.

See Cleopatra, Romans.

Cheops (*or* Khufu) 2538–2516 B.C.E., Fourth Dynasty

Second pharaoh of the Fourth Dynasty and son of Snofru and Queen Hetepheres, Cheops reigned for twenty-three years. He exercised as rigorous a control over the means of production as his predecessor, Snofru, both at home and abroad, in the Sinai and at the diorite quarry in Nubia. It was evidently thanks to this control that he was able to erect the Great Pyramid of Giza (height 481 feet, length at the base 756 feet), which he provided with a funerary complex that also included the pyramids of his queens (Meritites and Henutsen) and the tombs of his sons. He also reburied his mother, Hetepheres, after her original tomb was pillaged.

A monument like the Great Pyramid could be built only through sweat and suffering. Thus originated the bad reputation that was attached to the name of Cheops and which reached the ears of Herodotus; it contrasted with the popularity of his father, Snofru.

J. P. Lauer, *Le Problème des pyramides d'Égypte* (Paris, 1952); I. E. S. Edwards, *The Pyramids of Egypt,* rev. ed. (Harmondsworth, 1985); M. Lehner, *The Complete Pyramids* (New York, 1997).

See Fourth Dynasty.

Chephren (*or* Rakhaef) 2509–2484 B.C.E., Fourth Dynasty

Fourth pharaoh of the Fourth Dynasty and son of Cheops, Chephren reigned for twenty-six years. The pyramid he built at Giza (height 469 feet, length at the base 705 feet) is second in size only to that of Cheops. The funerary temple east of the pyramid is linked by a causeway to the valley temple, the massive, austere granite architecture of which remains impressive to this day. The Great Sphinx of Giza was created from a rocky outcrop near the causeway; posterity would regard this monument as an image of Re-Harmachis. A number of life-size statues of Chephren have survived.

C. Zivie-Coche, *Sphinx: History of a Monument* (Ithaca, 2002).

See Fourth Dynasty.

Chronology

Pharaonic civilization is lost in the darkness of the ages. The dates of the reign of a king of Egypt are among the questions that specialists most often pose. They must be forgiven, however, for usually being able to supply only a vague answer, situating a given king in terms of decades or half a century, or even a century for very early periods, or for being able to say with certainty only that a given pharaoh reigned for a minimum of *x* years. In the present work, the dates prior to 700 B.C.E. aim only at establishing plausible lengths for reigns, and there should be no reason for surprise if they differ somewhat from those in the chronological tables of other, excellent works on Egyptian history. In what ways can we approach, at least, the dating of events in Egyptian history, and, more important, arrive at the best estimate of the lengths of the eras of that history? We arrive at these goals by two successive steps: establishing a relative chronology, determining the order of kings and events, and then seeking an "absolute chronology," situating the events according to an agreed-upon calendar—in our case, the Common Era (that is, the era determined by the conventional date for the birth of Christ).

Each reign was a renewal of the original creation of the cosmos, and it constituted an era that ended with the death of the sovereign. The change of year was marked by the heliacal rising of the star Sothis (Sirius). In the Middle Kingdom, the year 1 of a king was officially postponed until the beginning of the "civil" year that followed his coronation. In the New Kingdom, year 2 began 365 days after the day of his coronation. In the Late Period, year 2 began on the day of the heliacal rising of Sothis that followed the coronation, which could thus entail the shortening of year 1 to only a few days. Knowing these specifics, it should be easy to establish a perfect chronology by adding the reign lengths of the sovereigns. But unfortunately, the documentation at our disposal fails to furnish us with the final date of the reign of every king, and there are even kings whom we know only by name. On the whole, the succession of kings is well established, but there were times when, because of coregencies that saw two monarchs associated on the throne or because of political rivalries, there were two or more of them at the same time.

One means of mitigating the gaps and obscurities in our sources lies in the few works of Egyptian historical writing that are known to us. Of the history composed in Greek by the priest Manetho, we have a summary that was used by chronologists of the Roman and Byzantine eras; it furnishes a list of kings, divided into thirty dynasties, with an indication of the length of each reign as a raw number of years. The work of this Greco-Egyptian historian, whose figures were unfortunately often altered in the process of copying, was derived from earlier king lists. By good fortune, we have a papyrus from the reign of Ramesses II, the Royal Canon of Turin, which lists the lengths of reigns almost to the day, but it survives to us only in tatters. The Palermo Stone and its fragments, a precious monument though it is also mutilated, lists the important events of each reign, from the beginning of history down to the Fifth Dynasty; even scholars who consider it to be an archaizing copy or compilation made during the Twenty-fifth Dynasty accept it as a trustworthy source. The data in these synthetic works can be cross-checked with those in the more or less exhaustive lists of kings carved, for religious reasons, in temples (Abydos) and tombs (Saqqara) and with those in occasional autobiographies of kings and commoners.

The individual reigns and dynastic sequences furnish a broad framework within which materials that do not bear an exact date can be approximately dated, with objects whose text or context includes a royal cartouche or a name dated to a reign serving as a typological reference point. The method can be used for all artifacts, from architectural remains to objects of daily use. The various products of the material culture can be dated ever more closely, period by period and sometimes with great precision. The results of relative chronology have been corroborated and illustrated by the study of the stratigraphy of occupation sites, of the additions and alterations made to monuments such as temples, of the growth in the size of cemeteries, and of changes in funerary practices.

To link this relative chronology to absolute chronology, Egyptology has a tool that is peculiar to it, one that derives from the calendrical system of the Egyptians. They counted only 365 days in a year, with the result that the calendar deviated progressively from the actual year by one day every four years and one month every 120 years. The season of the calendar called "Harvest" could thus fall in the midst of the "Inundation" season of the real year, and the official calendar would again coincide with the real year only after 1,456 years had passed. The Egyptians accommodated themselves so well to this shifting year and to this inaccurate calendar that Ptolemy III failed to induce them to accept the introduction of leap years, which the emperor Augustus would eventually impose on them. They did, however, note that the heliacal rising of Sothis coincided with the beginning of the inundation, and they made it a day of festival.

For us to be able to fix the astronomical date to within a four-year period, we need only one text stating that a "rising of Sothis" was celebrated on a particular day during the reign of a king, the givens of relative chronology being sufficient to avoid any hesitation regarding the cycle of 1,456 years in which the event took place. We have only five documents of this sort, one from the Middle Kingdom, and four from the New Kingdom.

Royal dates complemented by an allusion to a phase of the moon invite attempts to specify dates down to the day, but they involve a brief cycle, and the interpretation of the data is often debated. Application of the "Sothic theory" confronts theoretical criticisms, in addition to the uncertainties regarding matters of detail, such as the latitude at which the heliacal rising was observed.

The Sothic theory offers some solid steps toward a chronology whose validity can be confirmed by other kinds of information. One of these means is the approximate dating of objects by measuring the residual radioactivity of a carbon isotope that is in all organic material so as to determine how long an organism has been dead. This Carbon 14 dating, the methods of which have been refined to reduce margins of error (dendrochronological calibration), is especially valuable for the earliest periods. This last is also true for the dating of pottery by thermoluminescence.

Further means of cross-checking are furnished by two sets—one archaeological and the other textual—of synchronisms with neighboring civilizations. The archaeological synchronisms are the less precise. At first sight, the presence of Egyptian artifacts from an established dynasty at a site in western Asia or the Aegean suggests that this site is contemporary with the dynasty in question, and, vice versa, the discovery of Asiatic or Aegean objects in an Egyptian excavation site suggests that the latter existed when these objects were made. But an isolated object can at best furnish only a terminus ad quem for the presumed exchange.

When one finds a number of imported objects in a number of deposits belonging to the same chronologically determined culture, however, the contemporaneity of the importing and exporting cultures is clear. The results obtained by Assyriologists and Near Eastern archaeologists square with the conclusions of Egyptologists working with Sothic dates. Textual synchronisms are obviously more precise, but more localized in time. They are furnished mostly by historical accounts and diplomatic archives that explicitly inform us that a particular king of Egypt was contemporary with a particular Near Eastern monarch.

From 720 B.C.E. on, our dates are exact, or at worst, valid to within a year. Thanks to Sothic dates and to a number of synchronisms with foreign kingdoms, there is no doubt as to the chronological placement of the Eighteenth through the Twentieth Dynasties: recent readjustments according to a "short chronology" have brought Ramesses II's accession date of 1290 (that given in the *Cambridge Ancient History*) down to 1279 at the latest. The Twelfth Dynasty is solidly established at the beginning of the second millennium, thanks to Sothic dating. In any event, expected progress in physical technologies will bear on the third millennium, for which we have no precise synchronisms with foreign lands, or any Sothic dates. Adding the lengths of the reigns of the Thinite and Memphite periods, as best we know them from contemporary documents and from tradition, corresponds roughly with the total obtained by the Royal Canon of

Turin for this era (about nine and a half centuries). But even recently, a discrepancy of about three centuries has remained with regard to the date of Menes, the first king of Egypt.

See Dynasties, Sources for History.

Cleopatra

Among all the famous queens of Egypt, Cleopatra, the last representative of the Ptolemaic dynasty, was chronologically the fourth, after Hatshepsut, Teye, and Nefertiti. Of these four women, who lived through times of obscure political crises and thus belong as much to dreams as to history, it is she who has been the most vivid, both in memory and in the contemporary spotlight. In our own day, her sex appeal, which the Romans denounced, qualifies her to promote beauty products and items of finery.

But this torrid charmer of Caesar and Mark Antony also symbolizes the final moments of independent Egypt, the African land where civilization was born. Afrocentrists thus ask why painters and filmmakers have turned to white models and actresses to represent Cleopatra—notwithstanding the fact that she was the issue of an often incestuous line from the Balkans. On at least four occasions, Hollywood has incarnated her in the most illustrious stars of their day, in films with scripts derived from Shakespeare and with directors inspired by lurid paintings in the style of Egyptomania. The Renaissance, as well as the classical and Romantic eras, inherited what the Greek and Latin authors had written. Those authors included Plutarch, who collected the information of earlier writers in his *Lives,* and certain writers who were contemporary with the events, all of them representing the Roman point of view, as well as later historians who were even more hostile than they toward the Ptolemies.

Even in Egypt, Cleopatra's extraordinary personality was the stuff of dreams. Hermetists counted her among the magicians expert in the occult sciences. In Arab folklore, a small bay in Alexandria became "Cleopatra's Baths," and the two New Kingdom obelisks from Heliopolis that by chance were reerected on the site of the temple of the deified Julius Caesar in Alexandria were called "Cleopatra's Needles." Even at the end of the twentieth century, when underwater archaeology located the island of Antirhodos, where the heroine lived during her final weeks, the media announced the "discovery of Cleopatra's palace," though nothing remained there but the meager ruins of some buildings of Roman date.

For two millennia, only one Cleopatra has been the subject of dreams, literature, and speculation. But in fact, she was the seventh queen to bear that name (which means "of illustrious paternity"), which had been that of figures from the heroic age of Hellas, and which had long been fashionable among the ruling family of Macedonia. The destinies of the earlier Cleopatras of Egypt, and in particular, the family dramas and the political role of the first three, were anything but quiet and insignificant. When she became a widow, Cleopatra I, a Syrian princess who had married Ptolemy V Epiphanes (194/193 B.C.E.), exercised a judicious regency during the four years (180–176 B.C.E.) when her oldest son, Ptolemy VI (surnamed Philometor, "he who loves his mother"), was still a minor. The latter married his sister, Cleopatra II (173 B.C.E.), who bore him two boys named Ptolemy and two Cleopatras, one of them the future Cleopatra III. Not long thereafter, under Ptolemy VI to Ptolemy IX, there ensued a confused period of hatreds and reconciliations, of murders within the royal family, and of internecine warfare complicated by foreign wars. Cleopatra II and Cleopatra III—the latter married to her uncle, Ptolemy VIII Euergetes II—were redoubtable women, partisans, and sovereigns. Despite dynastic quarrels, social upheavals, and economic crises, Egypt continued to be administered tolerably well by its Greco-Egyptian bureaucracy.

Except for the period 205–186 B.C.E., when an insurgent Upper Egypt escaped the government of Alexandria, decorative programs were continued in the temples. In the mammisi (birth house) of Dendara, and at Edfu, Ombos, and other sites, we see the standardized images of pharaohs and sister-wives accompanied by the titularies of these Ptolemies and Cleopatras, though the cartouches were sometimes left blank when local notables were uncertain who the actual sovereigns were. Nevertheless, the situation invited the intervention of foreign powers: the Seleucids of Syria, from whom the Ptolemies tried in vain to wrest Palestine, and the Romans, who step by step pursued their subjection of the east. In 168 B.C.E., the authority of the Roman legate Popilius halted the Seleucid king Antiochus III at the gates of Alexandria. In 51 B.C.E., Ptolemy XII (called "the Flutist"), who was in debt to the Romans, called on them in his will to protect the joint reign of his children, Cleopatra VII and her younger brother, Ptolemy XIII. We know what finally became of this protectorate: twenty years later, the pharaoh was a Caesar, and Egypt was a province of his empire.

Though it had been troubled for a century and was supposedly ruined, the kingdom was nevertheless alive and still rich in resources in 51 B.C.E. In that year, it found itself drawn into the tumult of the Roman civil wars, while the disunited pacifiers of the Mediterranean world were directly involved in the customary Lagide and Alexandrian quarrels. In 48 B.C.E., after the great Pompey was treacherously murdered by the ministers of young Ptolemy XIII, Cleopatra, who was about twenty years of age, made her appearance before Julius Caesar and seduced him. In the Alexandrian war that ensued, the Roman general prevailed over the city and the army of the young pharaoh, who drowned as he attempted to flee. The queen persuaded her lover to visit Upper Egypt with her; she was already pregnant with a new Ptolemy, who would be named Ptolemy Caesar. From 46 to 44 B.C.E., she resided at Rome, where she was an ambassador of Hellenistic refinement, a representative of an unusual religion, and a disturbing symbol of the monarchic principle—a shocking triumph.

After Caesar's assassination in 44 B.C.E., Cleopatra retreated to her kingdom. Ptolemy XIV, her second younger brother and coregent, died in his turn—poisoned, it would be claimed, at her order.

From then on, the coregent was Ptolemy Caesar, who was aptly styled "beloved of his father and beloved of his mother." While Egypt remained neutral, the Caesarians defeated the murderers of the Divine Julius, and their leaders—Octavian, whom Caesar had adopted as his son, and Mark Antony—divided up the task of pacifying and governing the world. Antony, who received the Hellenized east and was imbued with a Dionysiac spirit, summoned Cleopatra to Cilicia in 41 B.C.E. The queen arrived at Tarsus by boat, in the guise of Aphrodite and surrounded by luxury. By way of paying homage, she invited him to feast on board her ship. Already in his forties, the general succumbed to the charms and the prestige of the heiress of the Ptolemies, who was only twenty-eight; he found himself drawn into the Alexandrian lifestyle and its Bacchic revelries. Thus began, at the highest level of power, an undisguised liaison that is difficult for historians to evaluate, for they have no information beyond the accusations of the Augustinian propaganda that made Antony into a good soldier who was depraved by a Levantine adventuress, and Cleopatra into a paragon of feminine wantonness and superficiality. The couple's monarchic ambitions, which balanced the Caesarian views of Octavian, and their practices inspired by Dionysiac ideology, which was ill received by Roman purists, were the basis of the accusation of this total debauchery that would be unleashed throughout the "Nights of Cleopatra." Of these famous nights, there were few enough in the ten years that followed. They were interrupted by the two pregnancies of the beautiful queen and by the double life of Antony, who was often carried away from Alexandria by the necessities of his military obligations and his politico-familial diplomacy. Antony was fighting on two major fronts. In the east, he had to protect Syria and control its Armenian borders, which were under constant threat from the Parthians of Iran; in fact, his efforts met with more failures than successes, and the latter were precarious. In the west, he needed to maintain his partisans in Italy and to negotiate a modus vivendi with Octavian, which led him into Roman family affairs: his Roman marriage to Octavia, the latter's sister, plunged him into a scandalous triangle.

These setbacks did not alter the political aspirations of Cleopatra VII. Immediately after their encounter of 37/36 B.C.E., she got her lover to eliminate her sister Arsinoe, who had presented herself as a rival in Caesar's day and had then taken refuge in Ephesus. At that time, they celebrated an Egyptian-style marriage that culminated in a grant to the queen of Coele-Syria and other domains in Asia. Later, in 34 B.C.E., Antony solemnly constituted, on behalf of "the new goddess" and what we could call the Roman branch of the Lagides, a domain consisting largely of the territories that had belonged to the Ptolemies and the Seleucids. The kingdoms and their revenues were divided among the queen, her son Ptolemy XV Caesar, the firstborn (in 40/39 B.C.E.) twins of Antony—Alexander-the-Sun and Cleopatra-the-Moon—and their third child, Ptolemy Philadelphus (born in 34 B.C.E.). The names received by the divine progeny of the "queen of kings"—Alexander, Philadelphus, Caesar, and Cleopatra—were themselves a program. Such a system of princely appanages, though on a much more modest scale, had already been in use under the Ptolemies. The couple's ambitious imperial dream could only be realized by force of arms, provided the ruler of the east could defeat his western rival. Once begun, their war ended with the disaster at Actium. We know the dramatic events that ensued: after the final frenzied revelries, the crisis of Antony and Cleopatra preparing her death; the suicide and agony of Antony and his misunderstanding regarding Cleopatra, who had shut herself up in her tomb; and the queen's death by means of a serpent's venom.

The Roman historians Polybius and Diodorus had not been kind toward the Hellenistic sovereigns, and the severity of historians' criticism would increase over time. On the whole, Cleopatra VII Philopator does not appear to have been any more vindictive, cruel, or rapacious than her Lagide predecessors, and it would seem that she was without the perversities of some of them. She was, after all, the loyal mistress of two successive lovers and an attentive mother toward her three royal children. Her charm was not due so much to her physical traits, according to contemporary writers. Her face, known from busts and coins, and which resembled that of her father, is not disagreeable, though her nose was a bit too aquiline. She owed her successes and her reputation as an enchantress to her eyes, her voice, her presence, her culture, and her intellect. If we must characterize Cleopatra VII, her genius is to be found in her audacious force of character and her regal political intellect. In the worst of circum-

FIGURE 3. *Far right, Cleopatra VII and her son Ptolemy XV Caesarion worshiping the pantheon of Dendara. Photo by Ragnhild Bjerre Finnestad.*

stances, she twice seized the occasion to make a reality, for herself and her children, of the ideal program of the Egyptian monarchy: divine rule over the entire world, as had been achieved by Darius and Alexander.

How did Egypt fare during the twenty years of Ptolemy XIII, Ptolemy XIV, and Ptolemy XV, when Cleopatra ruled the land? As chance would have it, there are few administrative documents on stone and few private archives to shed light on the internal situation. A decree (dated to 41 B.C.E.) guaranteeing tax exemptions to Alexandrians who owned land in two nomes seems at least to show that the government bureaus were functioning normally. A decree issued by the priests of Karnak in 39 B.C.E. alludes to a recent troubled period and to a famine, but determining the extent of this crisis is impossible. Documents from Thebes and other cities of the south expressing thanks to the *strategos* Callimachus attest to the extensive power of native dynasts, though we cannot speak of a disintegration of the state. As before, construction activity continued in some of the temples. At Dendara, the naos (shrine) of Hathor-Aphrodite and Isis, which was begun in 54 B.C.E., as well as the Osirian chapels on the roof of the temple, were largely built and decorated during Cleopatra's lifetime. The cartouches of the queen and of the Ptolemies with whom she carried out the rituals were left blank, except on the lofty exterior wall where she is depicted officiating behind Ptolemy Caesar (see figure 3). Also completed under Cleopatra VII and Caesarion was the mammisi of Hermonthis, which, like the other mammisis, served to celebrate the mystery of Hathor's eternal birthing of the divine child engendered by Amun, a mystery that assured the perpetuity of the office of kingship. Though Roman writers cruelly defamed this final Lagide ruler, the Roman authorities did not proscribe her memory or her statues in her own land. As before, many girls received her name: the Cleopatra whose once famous mummy ended up in the Bibliothèque Nationale in Paris was a young Theban girl who lived during the Roman Period.

M. Grant, *Cleopatra* (New York, 1972); E. Flamarion, *Cleopatra: The Life and Death of a Pharaoh* (New York, 1997); E.E. Rice, *Cleopatra* (Stroud, Gloucestershire, 1999); M. Chauveau, *Egypt in the Age of Cleopatra* (Ithaca, 2000), chapters 1 and 2; idem, *Cleopatra: Beyond the Myth* (Ithaca, 2002).

See Alexandria, Caesar, Ptolemy, Queens.

Clergy

When referring to pharaonic Egypt, the term "clergy" obviously does not cover precisely the same social realities as in our modern societies. There were basically three types of priestly activities, depending on who benefited from them:

1. On behalf of the pharaoh: According to the most ancient concepts, all care lavished on the physical person of the pharaoh, from providing his meals and ablutions to maintaining his wig and his false beard, were considered to be priestly offices. These offices became honorific duties that were awarded to members of his entourage or the elite of the courtiers. Additionally, many priestly offices were attached not only to the king's funerary cult, but also to the institutions of which he was the eponym.
2. For the post-mortem benefit of a private person: To assure chances of survival in the hereafter, the deceased had to be the object of a cult entailing the recitation of formulas, as well as libations and the consecration of offerings. During their lifetimes, Egyptians often drew up contracts with priests for the perpetuation of their mortuary cult.
3. For the benefit of deities: The maintenance of the order of the cosmos required that the hypostases (effigies, statues, sacred animals) of the deities who represented its principles receive a cult in the temples. A daily cult ritual consisted of clothing and anointing the image, libations, fumigations with incense, and the presentation of

offerings (especially food offerings). On the occasion of festivals, the statue of a deity would leave the temple in procession, visiting way stations and the sanctuaries of associated deities.

In the funerary temples of the pharaohs, and especially in the temples of deities, the organization of the clergy could be complex. If the temple was of some size, the clergy was organized into a hierarchy and specialized according to function, from the simple "pure"-priest (*wab*) to the "prophets" (who spoke in the name of the deity; they did not predict the future). The clergy was sometimes divided into four classes, from "ritual priest" and "god's fathers" down to specialists of all sorts (scribe of the divine writings, astronomers, musicians, etc.). In principle, priestly service was organized into four (later, five) staffs, called "phyles," that rotated on a monthly basis.

The three types of priestly service were in no way exclusive. Moreover, they involved the same basic principles, including the fact that the service was compensated, in general by a share of the offerings after they were consecrated, but often also by the usufruct of fields or by statutory revenues. This was an important matter in pharaonic history: a priestly office entailed both a sacerdotal duty and the advantages that constituted its compensation, and frequently more the latter than the former. For an example, an architect named Minmes boasted of having received the offices of prophet and pure-priest (*wab*) in the temples where he had worked, which were in locales stretching from Upper Egypt to the eastern delta. It is evident that he had a right to the benefits tied to these offices, while the actual services for which these were the compensation were surely subcontracted. The Egyptian clergy was thus a class of holders of material privileges.

The clergy could hope to control more, as well. The temples were in fact economic units; they had fields, cattle, precious materials (including gold), boats, equipment, and numerous personnel—in short, a whole complex that was often large, or even immense in the case of temples such as those of Re of Heliopolis, Ptah of Memphis, and especially Amun of Thebes. The administration of these complexes was the object of competition between the pharaohs, who aimed to entrust them to loyal men through whom they could control the temple administrations, and the clergy, who regarded this responsibility as their own prerogative. This conflict, which was endemic, is illustrated in particular by the history of the high priests of Amun during the New Kingdom; the theocratic concept that was imposed under the Twenty-first Dynasty was the ideological sanction of a balance of power that ultimately favored the clergy of

Amun. From then on, the oracle of Amun, and through it the clergy who manipulated it, became the supreme decision-making authority, to which even the pharaoh submitted his political program. The region that belonged to this theocracy was coextensive with the territory that was mostly controlled by the domain of Amun—that is, Upper Egypt and Middle Egypt as far as el-Hiba. In earlier periods, Egyptian history had been punctuated by the alternation of phases. During some phases, the central power managed to subject the administration of the temple domains to its own representatives (as in the Middle Kingdom, when the nomarchs were also "overseers of prophets"). At other times, this administration escaped them, as when royal decrees guaranteed the autonomy of temples, or a balance of power enabled the clergy to take charge of their domains.

Thus, the clergy held a double advantage: the material compensation associated with every priestly office, and the possibility—which was often a reality, according to the political situation—of controlling and thus profiting from the administration of the goods belonging to the temple. But what category of the population constituted the clergy?

During much of the history of pharaonic Egypt, the conditions for access to priestly service were not very restrictive: literacy, undoubtedly, and when it was necessary to officiate, a state of ritual purity (shaved head, sexual abstinence, linen clothing, no fish consumption). Neither an act of faith nor a spiritual commitment was a prerequisite. Down to the New Kingdom, at least, we often see an accumulation of priestly, military, and administrative offices in the hands of the same family, or even a single person. Priestly offices could be bought or sold, in whole or in part, or acquired by co-optation, heredity, or royal nomination, for the king retained a say in their transmission, which he exercised to the extent he could in regard to the most important ones. In any case, the caste spirit, which made its appearance here and there, became predominant in the Late Period. From then on, heredity became a condition of access to priestly office, and it was proclaimed as such: among the arguments they invoked to obtain the favor of deities, priests pointed out that they were the sons of priests. Herodotus, who visited Egypt during the first Persian domination, explicitly described the Egyptian clergy as a closed caste, and everything leads us to believe that he observed correctly.

S. Sauneron, *The Priests of Ancient Egypt* (Ithaca, 2000); G. Lefebvre, *Histoire des grands prêtres d'Amon de Karnak jusqu'à la XXIe dynastie* (Paris, 1929).

See High Priest of Amun.

Colossi

Measurable achievements materialized the divinity of the pharaoh, as recalled by the incredible pyramids of Cheops and Chephren. The making of royal effigies 40 feet tall, or even more than 65 feet, carved in granite or metamorphosed sandstone (quartzite), reached its apogee under Amenophis III and Ramesses II. These hypostases of the monarch were proportionate in size to the immense royal and divine temples, and they were set up in the parts of the sacred enclosures that were open to the people, so that they could adore the statues, which were defined by specific epithets: "ruler of rulers," "ruler of the Two Lands," or "beloved" of this or that deity. The most spectacular colossi still standing are the so-called Colossi of Memnon at Thebes and the "small" colossi of Amenophis III at Luxor, along with that of Ramesses II originally from Memphis and now in front of the railroad station in Cairo. We can also calculate the sizes of the collapsed colossi of Memphis and the Ramesseum. Two fragments reused at Tanis once belonged to the largest known example, which was nearly 89 feet high. The rock-cut statues of Abu Simbel are beautiful examples of this oversized statuary, though their creation did not pose the same problems of transport and erection as their movable relatives at Thebes, Memphis, and Pi-Riamsese.

Conspiracy

The pomp, the luxury, and the power inherent in the office of the pharaoh could not have failed to arouse ambitions, and they were multiplied as the size of the royal family grew through polygamy. In the atmosphere of eastern courts, they blossomed into so many intrigues and cabals. This culture of conspiracy found sanction in the ultimate principle of royal legitimacy, the free choice of the sun god, which facilitated after-the-fact justifications. In fact, in the Late Period, the theme of conspiracy had become so familiar that it served as the basis for the prologue of a wisdom text known as the Instruction of Ankhsheshonqy.

For earlier periods, the existence of conspiracies is especially detectable through conflicts over succession or through changes in dynasty, though our sources are rather reticent regarding such matters. In any case, three conspiracies are known to us; the amount of surviving detail differs, but all three originated or were developed in the harem.

Weni was named judge in an exceptional inquiry that was initiated to judge an unnamed queen under Pepy I of the Sixth Dynasty.

The first king of the Twelfth Dynasty, Amenemhet I, faced strong opposition; the last of the plots fomented against him, when his son and coregent was returning from an expedition in Libya, ended in his assassination. News of this assassination provoked the flight of Sinuhe, in the story that bears his name, not because he had taken part in the plot, but because it had been prepared in the harem, to which he was attached.

The harem was also the center of a conspiracy hatched by one of the wives of Ramesses III, Teye, who planned to assassinate the king and to replace him with her son, Pentaweret. She was joined in her attempt by a number of high officials: a chamberlain, an overseer of pure-priests of Sakhmet, a general, the commandant of troops in Nubia, and others. The conspirators resorted to drastic measures—that is, drastic measures for that era—for they planned to cast a spell on the guards to gain entry to the palace of Medinet Habu. It is quite probable, though not definitively proven, that the conspiracy led to the death of Ramesses III. In any case, the reaction was severe. The principal conspirators were condemned to commit suicide, while others had their nose and ears cut off. Other punishments were less bloody, but nevertheless feared by ancient Egyptians: names were changed to make their meanings unfavorable, with the result that one of the principal conspirators, the chamberlain, was from then on called Mesedsure, "Re hates him"; and retrospectively, mentions of the offices they had exercised so unworthily were eradicated by invoking an appropriate formula.

P. Vernus, *Affaires et scandales sous les Ramsès* (Paris, 1993), chapter 5.

See Amenemhet I, Ramesses III, Sinuhe, Weni.

Coregency

As in most ancient Near Eastern civilizations, royal succession in pharaonic Egypt was a tricky matter: ambitions, intrigues, and plots would spring up, all the more so in that there was no formal rule, the succession from father to son having only the force of custom. Pharaohs thus had to take steps to strengthen the position of their chosen successor.

Among the means at their disposal was coregency; during the lifetime of a king, his successor was associated with him on the throne as a pharaoh in his own right and with all the attributes of the office, in particular, a complete titulary. Moreover, events could be dated to the two partners simultaneously by juxtaposing the year dates of their respective reigns.

Coregency was not easy to reconcile with fundamental royal dogma, in that the pharaoh was supposed to be the earthly representative of the creator god, whose uniqueness was his principal characteristic. To avoid the difficulty, ideology drew on the corpus of available representations. The younger partner was assimilated to the god Horus-who-protects-his-father, a reference to the myth of Osiris, or he acted as a "staff of old age," a custom according to which a man who had reached old age shared his office with his son. In practice, the younger partner often assumed the more active duties, such as leading military expeditions. An example is Senwosret I, whom scholars consider the "dynamic" element of the coregency that associated him with his father, Amenemhet I, though he recognized the latter's theoretical superiority by "making reports" to him.

This type of coregency is clearly attested during the Twelfth Dynasty, but it was not the only type. Besides parallel reigns during periods when Egypt was politically divided, we know of forced coregencies. Thus, prior to year 7 of Tuthmosis III, and against his will, Hatshepsut had herself crowned as a pharaoh, associating herself fictively with her father, Tuthmosis I, and reigning jointly with Tuthmosis III until her death.

Aside from reasonably well-established coregencies (e.g., Tuthmosis III and Amenophis II), many remain uncertain and debated; one of the favorite pastimes of Egyptologists, in fact, is to propose or to disprove one or another coregency involving some pharaoh or other. The succession from Amenophis III to Amenophis IV, for example, annually inspires a host of dense and ingenious scholarly studies. We may smile, but it must be admitted that our sources remain unusually vague regarding coregencies, for as effective as this institution could be in practice, it was difficult to integrate into the traditions and phraseology of royal documents.

W. J. Murnane, *Ancient Egyptian Coregencies,* Studies in Ancient Oriental Civilization 40 (Chicago, 1977).

See Amenemhet I, Pharaoh, Senwosret I, Sinuhe.

Crowns

Accession to royal office was principally marked by the assumption of crowns, and when he entered a temple to officiate, a king was first crowned by its deity. Different headdresses revealed the divine quality of the sovereign, who shared the headdresses, for the most part, with certain major gods. The simplest and most convenient and doubtless the most common, were the head covering of pleated fabric (called *nemes* in Egyptian, and formerly called *klaft* by Egyptologists) and the diadem of precious metal with two strips of cloth that hung down behind the neck. The white crown, a tall miter with a bulbous top, and the red crown, which was topped by a stiff, stalk-like appendage and one that was thin and spiraling, were perennial symbols of kingship over Upper and Lower Egypt, respectively. The former enclosed in the latter formed the *pshent,* the "Two Pow-

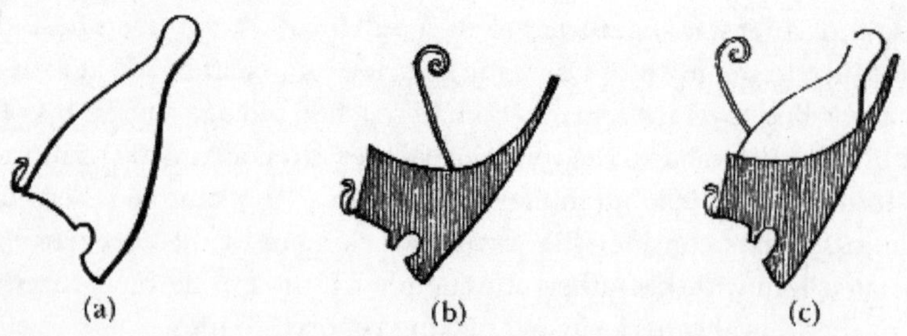

FIGURE 4. *(a) white crown, (b) red crown, (c) double crown (also called pshent). From Adolf Erman,* Life in Ancient Egypt, *trans. H. M. Tirard (London, 1894), p. 60.*

ers" that, joined together, expressed the beneficent advent of peacemaking power (see figure 4). The *khepresh,* a blue cap covered with little circles, appeared at the end of the Middle Kingdom. The list includes many other headdresses, from the simplest and oldest, such as the bag-shaped head covering, to extravagant concoctions like the *henu* and the *hemhem,* on which feathers, sun disks, serpents, falcons, and horns were combined. The common and nearly indispensable feature of all royal headdresses was the uraeus (i.e., cobra) attached to the front. These symbols of royal power, which were handled by initiated chamberlains, priests of the goddess "Great-of-magic," all seem to have contained the same redoubtable power: each headdress provided with a uraeus was itself the uraeus, which was in its turn identified with the Eye of Re. The latter shared in the nature of the blazing goddesses Sakhmet, Wadjit, and Nekhbet. To the extent that the theological equivalence of the crowns seems obvious, it is difficult to make out the mythologies and practices that were specific to each of them.

A. M. J. Abubaker, *Untersuchungen über die ägyptischen Kronen* (Glückstadt, 1937).

Darius I 522–485 B.C.E., Twenty-seventh Dynasty

Darius, son of Hystaspes the Achaemenid, was the second of the Persian pharaohs. Master of the empire after the death of Cambyses, he easily reconquered Egypt, which had revolted (possibly under Petubastis III). He eliminated the satrap (governor) Aryandes, who was behaving like an independent sovereign, and on at least one occasion, he visited his rich possession in Africa. He demonstrated his concern for the deities of Egypt, and he had the "house of life" at Sais restored. At his command, a project begun by Necho II was completed: connecting the eastern branch of the Nile to the Red Sea by a canal dug through the Wadi Tumilat and the Isthmus of Suez. Large stelae with inscriptions in three languages (Egyptian, Old Persian, and Babylonian) were set up along the watercourse. Economically and strategically, this undertaking integrated the satrapy into the empire.

Because Darius ordered a written compilation of the customs of Egypt, he was later counted as one of the great lawgivers of the land. In an atmosphere of peace, the traditional arts, and statuary in particular, flourished in the best Saite tradition. A monumental portrait of a standing Darius, sculpted in Egypt of graywacke from the Wadi Hammamat, was dug up by archaeologists in a palace at Susa. According to its trilingual dedication in cuneiform, this statue commemorated the emperor's conquest of Egypt, but its lengthy hieroglyphic titulary proclaims that Atum and Neith conferred the role of maintaining the order of the universe on the son of Hystaspes. Darius' clothing is Persian, but his pose is Egyptian. On the base, the symbolic image of the Uniting of the Two Lands introduces a pictorial listing of the peoples of the empire, from India to Ionia.

In Egypt, Darius would later be considered a model pharaoh: the frontiers that late historiography attributed to the conquests effected by the legendary Sesostris were none other than those of the Achaemenid empire.

K. Myśliwiec, *The Twilight of Ancient Egypt: First Millennium* B.C.E. (Ithaca, 2000), pp. 136–54.

See Persians, Udjahorresnet.

Diplomacy

Warfare, both defensive and offensive, was inherent in the pharaoh's role as incarnation of the creator god. In principle, diplomacy was not, for there was no common ground between this god, who was son of a god and the sun on earth, and the rulers of foreign lands. When scribes write that the king granted the "breath of life" to "rebel" princes who came to him bearing their goods, they do not tell us whether this peace was negotiated or whether these gifts were trade goods. Of course, even when his partners from Khatti, Babylon, or Assyria accorded him an official primacy, the pharaoh negotiated at least as often as he battled. Egypt sent and received ambassadors, interfered in the affairs of others, combated the intrigues of rival empires, distributed the gold in which it was so rich, loaned royal physicians to other courts, and signed treaties. Pharaohs and their foreign colleagues exchanged official letters, and as needed, the ladies and princes of their respective families showered one another with epistolary civilities. It is improbable that Egypt contributed much to the development of international law, which was the work of rival and allied states in the Fertile Crescent. The correspondence informing us of pharaonic diplomacy in the fourteenth and thirteenth centuries was written in Babylonian (on cuneiform tablets from Amarna, Ugarit, and Boghazköi, among others).

Exceptionally, Ramesses II had the text of a treaty carved on the walls of the temple of Karnak and of the Ramesseum. The hieroglyphic translation of a Babylonian text, this fully reciprocal document provides for peace and mutual assistance, as agreed upon with the Hittite king. Nevertheless, in a preamble, the king of the Hittites is presented as requesting this peace, for it was always maintained that Egypt's "Bull of Rulers" could set his boundaries where he wanted!

Diplomatic marriages were a common practice among the great powers of the second millennium. Amenophis III's boast, in a letter to the king of Babylon, that the king of Egypt never gave his daughters in marriage seems in fact to have corresponded to reality. Amenophis III took Babylonian and Mittanian princesses as wives, and among his wives, Ramesses II counted two daughters of the Hittite king Hattusilis. Times had changed when King Solomon of Israel obtained the daughter of a Tanite king as his bride!

Djoser 2617–2599 B.C.E.

Djoser was the second king of the Third Dynasty; his Horus name was Netjerykhet. He ruled for nineteen years. We know almost nothing of his reign, except that he was undoubtedly the first pharaoh to place the Sinai peninsula and its mineral resources (copper, turquoise) under Egyptian control. His monuments are few, but the quality makes up for the quantity. It was he, in fact, who erected the great monumental complex at Saqqara to which tourists still flock: a niched enclosure wall with a perimeter of 5250 feet shelters a series of buildings that are models of palaces and jubilee structures, and which complement the royal tomb. The tomb, in turn, comprises a network of subterranean galleries and rooms surmounted by a six-stepped pyramid that is nearly 197 feet high. The architecture, which was explicitly conceived as the transposition into stone of buildings of light materials (wood, reeds), attained perfection; Djoser's statue is the first known life-size statue. These advances in technology are attributed to Imhotep.

Djoser left behind such a prestigious memory that two and a half millennia later, during the Ptolemaic Period, an apocryphal work was written in his name. This account, carved on the island of Sehel and known as the Famine Stela, was intended to use events of his reign to justify possessions in Nubia that belonged to the temple of Khnum in the Ptolemaic era.

See Imhotep, Pyramids, Third Dynasty.

Dreams

Sleep was considered both a delicate and a privileged phase, in which one could enter into contact with the dead and with the gods in dreams, both spontaneous ones and dreams solicited by the practice of incubation (spending the night in the funerary chapel of a deceased person or in the sanctuary of a deity). What was true for ordinary private persons was obviously true for pharaohs, to whom the gods revealed themselves in dreams, as they otherwise revealed themselves by means of miracles and oracles, or even by direct inspiration. The message transmitted in the dream was political or historical. For example, the god might request the king to restore his sanctuary, which had fallen into ruin—such was the justification for Senwosret I's work in the temple of Elephantine—or promise victory on the eve of battle, as in the cases of Amenophis II and Merneptah, or inform the future pharaoh that he had chosen him for the royal office, as in the case of Tantamani. That dream, once explained, revealed that Tantamani would hold power over Kush and Egypt. In a dream of Tuthmosis IV, Harmachis was said to have promised the throne, provided that Tuthmosis IV clear the Great Sphinx of Giza, one of his hypostases, from the sands.

S. Sauneron, *Les Songes et leur interprétation,* Sources Orientales 2 (Paris, 1959).

See Famine, Tuthmosis IV.

Dualisms

In all its manifestations, ancient Egyptian kingship was conceived as a dual institution by means of which the north and the south of the land were united. By turns, the king wore the white crown of Upper Egypt or the red crown of Lower Egypt; he could also wear both of them together, the double crown known as the *pshent.* He was "lord of the Two Lands," the "king of Upper Egypt and Lower Egypt," protected by the "Two Ladies," that is, Nekhbet, the vulture goddess of el-Kab in Upper Egypt, and Wadjit, the cobra goddess of Buto in Lower Egypt; he was also protected by Seth as lord of Upper Egypt. We could make no end of listing the string of dualistic expressions and representations that formulated the dogma of kingship and culminated in rituals like that of the coronation or the *sed*-festival (a sort of royal jubilee).

These frequent proclamations of dualism have not failed to strike Egyptologists. One of them, Kurt Sethe, developed a complex theory according to which this dualism reflects political events that occurred in prehistoric times (*Urgeschichte*), episodes in which kingdoms of Lower and Upper Egypt supposedly took turns exercising hegemony over the entire land.

Contemporary Egyptology has distanced itself from this theory, which somewhat naively and mechanically postulates a political event behind each dualistic image in pharaonic ideology. In fact, it was characteristic of Egyptian civilization to express a reality as the union of two opposites; thus, "to comport oneself" was "to sit and stand up," while "totality" was "that which exists and does not exist." This form of thinking was surely at work in the dualisms of royal dogma. As a political unity of which the pharaoh was both symbol and guarantor, the Egyptian state was the union of Upper and Lower Egypt, primarily because the geographical distinctness of the two regions was obvious to a style of thinking that invoked contrasting pairs. Cultural distinctions also could have corresponded to this geographical opposition when the pharaonic state was born. In addition, this birth was the culmination of an extension into the north of an already organized society in the south (which is not the same as saying a conquest of a Lower Egyptian kingdom by an Upper Egyptian kingdom).

Generally speaking, the pairs utilized by royal ideology had a basis in reality; after all, a small kingdom in the northern delta, centered on Buto, could have existed at a certain point in prehistory, while Nekhbet's city of el-Kab was important in predynastic times. But systematic thought in ancient Egypt worked in such a way as to make pairs of such realities, forcing them into an artificial symmetry based on analogies that were formal rather than historical or political.

H. Frankfort, *Kingship and the Gods: A Study of Ancient Near Eastern Religion as the Integration of Society and Nature* (Chicago, 1948).

See Crowns.

Dynasties

Egyptologists group the kings of ancient Egypt into dynasties numbered from one to thirty. This classification is borrowed from Manetho, an Egyptian priest who wrote a history of Egypt in Greek during the reign of Ptolemy II; his work has come down to us only in fragments. Manetho characterized each dynasty by referring it to a city, or, in the case of foreign kings, by giving them ethnic designations: Hyksos, Ethiopians (i.e., Kushites), Persians. The geographical adjectives refer to the nome whose forces imposed a new power, to the city whose deity was the patron of that power (which amounts to the same thing), or to the place where the tombs of the kings in question were located.

But it is uncertain whether the notion of "dynasty" meant, for Manetho, the concept of hereditary succession within a family that is familiar to us. His dynastic divisions take appropriate account of certain actual discontinuities in Egyptian political history, such as the transition from the Seventeenth to the Eighteenth Dynasty, which corresponded to the expulsion of the Hyksos, but without a change in family or city, or the successive triumphs of cities of the delta from the Twenty-first Dynasty on. But it is clear that the framework of these dynasties cannot be applied to all of the socioeconomic and cultural developments that occurred during the pharaonic period.

See Chronology.

Eighth Dynasty

The Eighth Dynasty, which sprang from the struggles over dynastic succession after the death of Nitocris, was incapable of restoring order during the little time it managed to remain in power (2140–2130 B.C.E.). Though filled with uncertainties, the list of the kings who composed it is as follows:

Neferkare the Younger
Neferkamin
Ibi, reign: two years and one month
Neferkaure, reign: four years, two months
Neferkauhor, reign: two years, one month
Neferirkare (Horus name: Demedjibtawy), reign: one and a half years

To the extent they could, these kings perpetuated the model of the Old Kingdom; the pyramid of one of them, Ibi, is located at Saqqara. They resided at Memphis, while Abydos functioned as the administrative center of Upper Egypt, and they promulgated decrees that employed the traditional formulas. But they had to deal with a powerful family of Koptos, that of the vizier Shemay, who had power over the first seven nomes of the south in his capacity of governor of Upper Egypt. Shemay married Nebet, the daughter of King Neferkauhor, and he secured a number of advantages for his own funerary cult and for those of his sons, one of whom was named Idy. Those advantages included personnel devoted to the maintenance of their cult foundations, chapels in most of the sanctuaries, and the pharaoh's special protection of these monuments.

See First Intermediate Period, Nitocris.

Eleventh Dynasty

The ancestor of the Eleventh Dynasty, who was honored as such by his posterity, was a "prince" and "governor" named Inyotef, son of Iku; Inyotef was a contemporary of the last kings of the Eighth Dynasty. He breathed ambition into a region that until then had been snoozing in provincial obscurity. Under the Ninth Dynasty, Thebes and Koptos formed an alliance that was opposed by Akkhtifi, potentate of the extreme south of Egypt, though he did not succeed in destroying it. Quite the contrary, Thebes' power and influence increased under Mentuhotpe and his son Inyotef to the point that the latter proclaimed himself pharaoh and the former was retrospectively promoted to that supreme office as the first king of the Eleventh Dynasty, though he had in fact never reigned. But the new dynasty had to reckon with another one, that of Herakleopolis, which controlled the delta and a part of Middle Egypt; the region of Thinis and

Abydos, which the two parties conquered and lost by turns, constituted the frontier zone. Hostilities continued, and a king of Herakleopolis counseled his son Merykare to pursue a policy of peaceful coexistence. This advice was useless in the face of the irrepressible ambition of Thebes, however. This ambition succeeded in triumphing over the dynasty of Herakleopolis and reunifying Egypt during the reign of Mentuhotpe II, at a date that remains uncertain (c. 2022 B.C.E.).

From that time on, the Eleventh Dynasty disposed of natural and cultural resources that enabled it to revive the traditional policies of great pharaohs: expeditions to the mines and quarries, as well as to foreign ports, restoration of temples, and construction of huge funerary monuments. But scarcely had the Eleventh Dynasty eliminated its Herakleopolitan rival than a pretender to a new legitimacy arose in its ruling class: Amenemhet, the vizier of Mentuhotpe IV, took advantage of the weakness of the pharaoh, who was in fact not recognized as such in the later annals, to seize power in a civil war. The list of the kings of the Eleventh Dynasty is as follows:

Mentuhotpe I and Inyotef I, 2130–2115 B.C.E.
Inyotef II, 2115–2066 B.C.E.
Inyotef III, 2066–2059 B.C.E.
Mentuhotpe II, 2059–2009 B.C.E.
Mentuhotpe III, 2009–1997 B.C.E.
Mentuhotpe IV, 1997–1991 B.C.E.

See Ankhtifi, Henenu, Inyotef, Mentuhotpe, Ninth and Tenth Dynasties.

Erasures

"Annihilating" persons by destroying their names in all accessible inscriptions was a means of cursing both the living and the dead, and it was one of the sanctions that accompanied the death penalty. The effacing of the names and sometimes the images of disgraced dignitaries or hated family members occurred in tombs in all periods of Egyptian history. Erasures of the names, and sometimes the destruction of the effigies, of kings are obvious indications of political crises. The names of a sovereign consigned to oblivion were often replaced by the titulary of the later king who censored his memory. Certain usurpations do not indicate hostility, but simply the appropriation or restoration of a monument, however. The most famous cases of erasure are:

Tuthmosis III persecuted the memory of the pharaoh Hatshepsut.
Akhenaten's name was mutilated and his buildings were dismantled when the traditional religion was restored.

Haremhab substituted mentions of himself for those of Tutankhamun.
Memory of the usurper Amenmesse was persecuted by Sethos II.
Sethnakhte did the same to Siptah, Twosre, and the treasurer Bay.
The memory of the six Kushite kings of the Twenty-fifth Dynasty was retrospectively proscribed by the Saite Psammetichus II, who waged war against their Sudanese successors.
Amasis suffered the same fate under the Persian Cambyses.

This type of postmortem damnation by eradicating the memory of disavowed rulers is attested in many other societies. More particular to the Egyptian mentality is the elimination by erasure of divine persons. The two known cases are different:

Akhenaten had the names and images of Amun chiseled out. His intention was to communicate the god's futility (and perhaps, since Amun means "hidden," to indicate that the mystery of divine identity was eliminated by the revelation of Aten, the visible sun).
From the ninth century on, the names and images of the god Seth were effaced on older monuments. The idea was to combat a real being who, since he was no longer venerated as a naturally necessary agent of the divine order, was now considered merely a demon, the murderer of Osiris and the enemy of gods and men.

Famine

For its staples, particularly grains, Egyptian agriculture depended entirely on the Nile inundation, which was often irregular. Too low an inundation—or worse, several years of them—would result in a lack of grain, food shortages, and famine, the latter sometimes leading to acts of cannibalism. A well organized state could at least partly ward off such disasters by means of judicious stockpiling, but famines were especially bad during periods of disorder. At such times, amid the general suffering, a local potentate who had been astute enough to lay aside reserves would succeed in feeding his city, and even allied cities as well.

An apocryphal stela, dated to Djoser but in fact carved during the Ptolemaic Period, reports that for seven years—surely a significant figure—Hapy (that is, the Nile inundation) did not arrive on time; grain was thus in short supply, the people were hungry, and disorder set in. Imhotep went in search of the reasons for this disaster, and the god Khnum announced to him that he would use his influence with Hapy—and this influence was substantial, for the sources of the Nile were located near Khnum's city of Elephantine. This text, called the "Famine Stela," was intended to justify the rights of the temple of Khnum to territory in Nubia, but it is based on one of the sad realities of pharaonic Egypt.

J. Vandier, *La Famine dans l'Égypte ancienne,* Recherches d'archéologie, de philologie et d'histoire 7 (Cairo, 1936); K.W. Butzer, *Early Hydraulic Civilization in Egypt: A Study in Cultural Ecology* (Chicago, 1976); W. Schenkel, *Die Bewässerungsrevolution im alten Ägypten* (Mainz, 1978).

See Djoser, Imhotep, Strikes.

Fifteenth Dynasty

See Hyksos.

Fifth Dynasty 2450–2321 B.C.E.

A myth demoted to a popular tale (Papyrus Westcar) explains the dynastic change from the Fourth to the Fifth Dynasty: the god Re, assuming the form of a pure-priest of Horus of Sakhebu, impregnated Ruddjedet, the priest's wife, with three children who would be the first three kings of the Fifth Dynasty, contrary to the wishes of Cheops. Behind the person of Ruddjedet undoubtedly lies Queen Khentkaus, mother of the first three pharaohs of the Fifth Dynasty. The kings of this dynasty were:

Userkaf (2450–2444 B.C.E.); he built his pyramid at Saqqara, not far from that of Djoser, while his sun temple was at Abusir

Sahure (2444–2433 B.C.E.)

Neferirkare Kakai (2433–2414 B.C.E.)
Raneferef, son of the preceding, whose funerary complex he completed (2414–2408 B.C.E.)
Shepseskare (2408 B.C.E.); perhaps a son of Userkaf, he scarcely managed to maintain his legitimacy for more than a few months
Neuserre Ini (2407–2384 B.C.E.); perhaps a son of Neferirkare
Menkauhor (2384–2377 B.C.E.)
Djedkare Izezi (2377–2350); he built his pyramid between Saqqara and Dahshur
Wenis (2350–2321)

An extremely important change took root in the Fifth Dynasty. Pharaoh, who had previously been the supreme power, ceded this role to the god Re, with whom he entered into a relationship of filiation; in fact, the title "son of Re" would from then on appear regularly in the royal titulary. As a monumental expression of this change, the pharaohs of the Fifth Dynasty, except for the last two, built temples to the sun. At the heart of these sacred complexes was a platform representing the primordial mound, upon which an obelisk was erected; around it, there was a vast open-air esplanade containing an altar for the celebration of a cult inspired by nature (an inspiration that can be observed in Neuserre's "chamber of the world"). The sun temple was closely related to the funerary temple, to which it forwarded offerings after they were consecrated.

An important sociological change can also be discerned in the Fifth Dynasty, one that was either the cause or the effect of the king's (relative) loss of ideological status: the highest offices were no longer reserved exclusively for members of the royal family. Thus, the office of vizier fell to private persons with no blood tie to the king. An increasing number of private autobiographies stress personal merit, even if exercised in the service of Pharaoh. Finally, in the course of the dynasty, we see the first great lineages of high officials, as the hereditary principle began to counterbalance the free choice of the kings.

Otherwise, the kings continued to build pyramids, but much smaller in size than those of the Fourth Dynasty. They also continued to send expeditions to the diorite quarries of Nubia, to the Sinai, and to Byblos, and they assured the security of the borders by means of operations against the Libyans, the Nubians, and the bedouins. A high level of artistic technique was maintained during the Fifth Dynasty, as is especially evident in bas-relief and statuary.

M. Lichtheim, *Ancient Egyptian Literature: A Book of Readings*, vol. 1: *The Old and Middle Kingdoms* (Berkeley, 1973), pp. 219–21; I. E. S. Edwards, *The Pyramids of Egypt*, rev. ed. (Harmondsworth, 1985), p. 150.

See Khentkaus, Neferirkare Kakai, Neuserre Ini, Ptahwash, Sahure, Wenis.

First Dynasty

See Archaic (Period).

First Intermediate Period

The period beginning with the collapse of the Old Kingdom at the end of the Sixth Dynasty (2140 B.C.E.) and ending with the definitive victory of the Theban dynasty and the reunification of Egypt during the reign of Mentuhotpe II (2022 B.C.E.) is called the First Intermediate Period; the reunification marked the beginning of the Middle Kingdom. The First Intermediate Period thus includes the Seventh, Eighth, Ninth, and Tenth Dynasties, and part of the Eleventh.

The unity of this period consists in some sense in the dismemberment of the unity of Egypt at the end of a progressive decline of royal power in the face of local separatism and the assertion of the principle of hereditary transmission of offices, a process that was aggravated by the consequences of climatic change. In fact, the nomarchs, who viewed their office as family property, behaved like potentates in their nomes, relying on a clientele whom they maintained and rewarded just as Pharaoh did his courtiers. They ignored the feeble sovereign of the moment, or acknowledged only his purely nominal sovereignty. They accumulated civil titles ("governor," "great nome chief") and religious titles ("overseer of prophets," implying control of temple property), and they often also took the title "overseer of the south," which originally indicated supervision of the nomes of Upper Egypt, or at least a part of that region. Evidently, many of these nomarchs allowed themselves to be tempted by ambition: in one way or another, they associated themselves with other nomes to form a bloc that was likely to dispute with a neighboring one, alliances forming and dissolving by turns. The consequence of these quasi-feudal rifts was the multiplication of famines, which the inscriptions mention almost obsessively; a powerful nomarch could deal with such problems, but woe to the region that did not enter the sphere of influence of a coalition favored by the balance of power at the moment! Little by little, antagonism polarized a Herakleopolitan monarchy that controlled the delta and part of Middle Egypt by relying on the powerful family of nomarchs at Asyut, and the ambitious dynasty of Thebes, which had subjugated Upper Egypt with the aid of Koptos. This Theban dynasty would succeed in imposing its power on the entire land, putting an end to the First Intermediate Period.

This period left a profound mark on the civilization of Egypt, not only physically through damage and destruction, but above all, intellectually and ideologically. It gave birth to a pessimistic vision of the world, one that would nourish a current of thought that would remain part of the cultural patrimony of the literate. A "democratization" of funerary beliefs also occurred: from then on, ordinary private persons would lay claim to the solar postmortem destiny that had been the exclusive privilege of Pharaoh. Texts describing this destiny were written on their behalf; these were the Coffin Texts, which were largely inspired by the corpus of texts from the royal pyramids.

See Ankhtifi, Eighth Dynasty, Eleventh Dynasty, Inyotef, Mentuhotpe, Merykare, Ninth and Tenth Dynasties, Seventh Dynasty .

Fourteenth Dynasty

The Fourteenth Dynasty actually encompassed at least two kingdoms located in different areas of Lower Egypt, in part contemporaneously:

One kingdom was ruled by pharaohs at Xois who controlled part of the western delta. We know almost nothing about them, except that they might already have been ruling contemporaneously with Sebekhotpe IV (1730–1723 B.C.E.).

The other kingdom was founded in the eastern delta by Nehesy around 1720 B.C.E.; its capital was Avaris, a riverine port that served as a conduit for trade with Asia. Its kingship was Egyptian in style, though the territory was densely populated by Asiatics. This kingdom was swept away by the wave of Hyksos who extended their domination over Egypt from their base in its territory.

See Avaris, Hyksos, Xois.

Fourth Dynasty

The reasons for the transition from the Third to the Fourth Dynasty, and the conditions under which it occurred, remain obscure. The succession of pharaohs is more or less as follows:

Snofru (2561–2538 B.C.E.)
Cheops, his son (2538–2516 B.C.E.)
Radjedef, son of Cheops, buried at Abu Rawash (2516–2509 B.C.E.)

Khephren, son of Cheops (2509–2484 B.C.E.)

Two lines of pretenders: on the one hand, two kings, one of whom was named Baka (Bicheris), son of Radjedef, and on the other hand, Mycerinus, who reigned contemporaneously until he succeeded in imposing himself as the legitimate pharaoh (2484–2467 B.C.E.).

Shepseskaf, son of Mycerinus (2467–2464 B.C.E.); he completed his father's funerary complex at Giza, but for himself, he built a curious monument in the shape of a sarcophagus (the Mastabet el-Faraun), located between Saqqara and Dahshur.

The end of the dynasty was dominated by the quarrels of pretenders; only one name emerges, that of Ptahdjedef (Manetho's Thamphthis).

The Fourth Dynasty was above all the dynasty of the builders of the Great Pyramids. What better symbol of a period when Pharaoh was the supreme value around whom all of society was organized? In fact, not only did he drain the resources of the land for his own benefit, but also high administrative and religious offices were entrusted only to members of his family. It is an easy but doubtless justified cliché to feel sorry for the Egyptian people, "who crushed the granite for the hemmed-in Cheops," according to the verse of Sully-Prudhomme.

The art of the period, in particular the royal statuary, reflects the massive and overwhelming perfection attained by the institution of kingship. The Fourth Dynasty represented the culmination of a logic that was born in the Archaic Period and already highly evolved under the Third Dynasty. But at the very moment when this evolution reached its acme, we discern the first signs of a new development that would challenge the pharaoh's ideological status.

See Cheops, Chephren, Hardjedef, Metjen, Mycerinus, Snofru.

Funerary Temples

In the Old and Middle Kingdoms, each pyramid was accompanied by a temple composed of two buildings: a building at the foot of the pyramid (called the funerary temple) and a building in the valley (called the valley temple) that received the body of the deceased king. In these buildings, the king is depicted serving the gods, carrying out real and/or symbolic acts linked to his office, and receiving offerings. Endowments of land supplied the altars and nourished a numerous clergy, along with the inhabitants of the "pyramid town." These "funerary" monuments, the size of which testifies to the divine status of the sovereign, began to function while the king was still alive. As far as we know, in these same periods, the temples of local deities were much smaller. In addition, there is reason to think that the temples erected for the gods in the New Kingdom largely inherited the architectural forms and the iconographic mechanisms with which the king had once communicated with the divine in his own temple, both in this life and the next, so as to maintain the order of the universe.

For the Old Kingdom, the best known funerary complexes are those of Snofru (Dahshur), Chephren (with the adjacent Sphinx of Giza), Sahure (Abusir), Wenis (Saqqara north), and Pepy I and Pepy II (Saqqara south). From that of Neferirkare (Abusir), we have many fragments from papyrus archives, giving us a glimpse of the functioning of these institutions, which were the principal cult places of the kingdom and important elements in the economic development of the Memphite region. The remains of the funerary temples constitute nearly the only source enabling us to form a picture of what the divine kingship was like in the age of pyramids. The remains include statues of the sovereign, rows of deities, and scenes depicting jubilees, hunts, triumphs in war, parades on land and in boats on the river, processions of personified domains, and statues representing bound foreign peoples. The funerary temples were the place shared by the permanent (the king) and the evanescent that corroborated the permanent. In them, we see the commemoration of exemplary deeds and experiences: the arrival of Sahure's fleet, returning from Asia; the transport by boat of palmiform columns of granite from Aswan; or the misery of starving bedouins in the temple of Wenis. But the representation of a triumph over Libyan princes, repeated with the same details on the walls of at least four successive funerary temples, became an atemporal sign of the king's effectiveness in war, just like the depictions of the smiting of groups of enemies or those of a griffin attacking barbarians.

From the Middle Kingdom, the only well-known funerary complexes are that of Senwosret I at Lisht and that of Senwosret II, with its workmen's village, at el-Lahun. The vast and complex monument that serviced one of the pyramids of Amenemhet III at Hawara was known to Greek travelers by the name Labyrinth and classified as one of the Seven Wonders of the World. Demolished, it is today barely recognizable.

At Thebes in the New Kingdom, the royal tombs in the Valley of the Kings were separate from their funerary temples. With the cliffs as backdrop, each king erected his own "mansion of millions of years in the house of Amun in the west of Thebes." Each temple was above all a temple of Amun-Re, with whom the king's spirit more or less merged. In it, the king had a chapel of his own, and the funerary deities were present there, along with a court for the worship of the sun. Each year, on the "Festival of the Valley," Amun left Karnak to visit these royal temples. Their cults were already functioning while their founders were still alive, and the great Ramessides also had "mansions of millions of years" at Memphis, "in the house of Ptah," and at Heliopolis, "in the house of Re." These temples of eternity, whose decoration was similar to that of contemporary divine temples, were thus much more than funerary monuments. They differed radically from the chapels in the tombs of officials. In these royal monuments, as in the temples of gods and goddesses, life on earth was reduced to representations of the great festivals presided over by Pharaoh and to textbook commemorations of actual exploits, such as the expedition dispatched by Hatshepsut to Punt or the wars of the Ramesside kings. Administered by a *sem*-priest, the royal temple was surrounded by a palace, workshops, storerooms, and offices, and was provided with much landed property; the complex constituted a complete enterprise that was fiscally attached to the house of the god with whom it was theologically related.

The best preserved of the funerary temples of Thebes are those of Hatshepsut (Deir el-Bahari), Sethos I (Gurna), Ramesses II (Ramesseum), and Ramesses III (Medinet Habu). The hugest of all was the "mansion" built by Amenophis III and placed under the joint patronage of Amun-Re and the funerary god Sokar; nothing of this temple survives except the Colossi of Memnon. On the east bank, the hypostyle hall of Karnak was itself part of the "mansion of millions of years" of Sethos I, and the lateral temple of Ramesses III and the bark shrine of Sethos II in front of it were classed in the same category of perpetual foundations.

G. Haeny, in Byron E. Shafer, ed., *Temples of Ancient Egypt* (Ithaca, 1997), pp. 86–126.

See Pyramids.

Hardjedef

Hardjedef, son of Cheops, was buried at Giza. He might have been caught up in the struggles over the dynastic succession. His fame did not result from politics, however, but from his abilities as a man of letters. The wisdom text he wrote, the Instruction of Hardjedef, led him to be counted among the great writers and thus a paragon of culture, along with Amenhotpe, son of Hapu; Khaemwese; and Imhotep. One of the stories in a cycle of tales (Papyrus Westcar) shows him contacting a famous magician named Djedi and taking him in charge. So great was his prestige that tradition selected him (no doubt fictively) as the finder of several chapters of the Book of the Dead, at Hermopolis, which he discovered on the occasion of tours of inspection and inventorying in the temples.

M. Lichtheim, *Ancient Egyptian Literature: A Book of Readings*, vol. 1: *The Old and Middle Kingdoms* (Berkeley, 1973), pp. 58–59.

Harem

In wealthy homes, the wife (there was normally only one) and her servants had living quarters of their own. But Egypt never had the equivalent of a Turkish harem or of the *gynecea* in which women lived separately, more or less in seclusion. In New Kingdom temples, noble ladies formed groups of musicians and singers that we call, using a highly approximate term, the "harem" of the god.

In the New Kingdom, institutions that housed a large number of women also existed. (The Egyptian term for these means "enclosure," a place where persons are kept.) Administered on behalf of queens who resided in them, these were not mere instruments of the pharaoh's sexuality. Located at Thebes, Memphis, and Gurob, these "royal harems" drew income from fields and from the yield of certain taxes. In them, young foreign captives were given an Egyptian education, while large numbers of women worked on textile production. These enterprises were administered and served by a large corps of masculine functionaries (overseer, deputy, scribes, men who collected and delivered fish, salesmen, guards), but we have no evidence that this staff included eunuchs.

E. Reiser, *Der königliche Harim im alten Ägypten und seine Verwaltung*, Dissertationen der Universität Wien 77 (Vienna, 1972).

Haremhab 1323–1293 B.C.E., Eighteenth Dynasty

A native of Hut-Nesut in Middle Egypt, this royal scribe had a career whose first stages recall those of Amenhotpe, son of Hapu (scribe of recruits and overseer of work in the quartzite quarries). After he became generalissimo and high steward, we find him at Memphis under Tutankhamun, honored with the title of prince (*erpa*), which had also distinguished the wise minister of Amenophis III. In the future, this title, which indicated a higher rank than that of vizier, would serve to distinguish the prince and deputy whom the king destined to succeed him. It was at this time of his life that Haremhab dedicated his beautiful scribal statues at Thebes and Memphis, and that he built his huge funerary monument, which was recently rediscovered at Saqqara. Among the lively reliefs commemorating his activities in the north and the south, we find a presentation to the king of tribute and captives from Syria and Nubia. This evidence could be interpreted to mean that he led military operations for the purpose of consolidating what remained of the empire.

At the death of Tutankhamun, Haremhab accepted the aged Aya as sovereign, but it was not the *erpa* Nakhtmin, surely the latter's son, who succeeded him on the throne. At the instigation of Horus, the *erpa* Haremhab went to Thebes, where he was crowned by Amun. He had his own names carved over those of Tutankhamun, including those on the stela proclaiming the general restoration of the traditional order and those on the effigies of Amun to which the young king had lent his visage. An important decree proclaimed measures to protect private property and means of transportation against racketeering, as well as to restructure the military districts and administrative councils in the provinces. The enlargement of Karnak was resolutely undertaken: the Ninth and Tenth Pylons were added on the south, and on the west, the Second Pylon, which would be left to the first Ramessides to decorate. To build these pylons, Haremhab began to dismantle the Aten temples and to reuse the *talatat* (small stone blocks) of which they were made.

Haremhab appropriated and enlarged the funerary temple of Aya. His large and beautiful tomb in the Valley of the Kings contains our earliest copy of the Book of Gates, a symbolic depiction of the regeneration of the sun. In his Memphite tomb, a uraeus was added to the brow of his nonroyal images; Mutnodjmet, his chief wife, was buried there.

Haremhab rebuilt the clergies with men chosen from the army, a policy that seems to indicate the elimination of the heirs of the Amarna courtiers and the promotion of new men. As his vizier and heir presumptive, this military man chose a colleague in the military, Ramesses. The latter succeeded him, and Ramesses quickly associated his son Sethos, who was also a soldier, with his rule. By usurping the works of Tutankhamun (whose tomb he nevertheless respected), by posthumously proscribing Aya and Nakhtmin, and by his own acts, Haremhab brought an end to an era and presented himself as the initiator of a new one. He was recognized as such by the Ramesside dynasty, which he basically created. Under Ramesses II, he was counted as the direct successor of Amenophis III.

C. Lalouette, *Thèbes ou la naissance d'un Empire* (Paris, 1958), pp. 573–84; G. Steindorff and K. C. Seele, *When Egypt Ruled the East,* 2d ed. (Chicago, 1957), pp. 242–47.

See Aya, Erasures, Tutankhamun.

Harkhuf

Harkhuf was overseer of dragomen and overseer of all the foreign countries of the south under Merenre and Pepy II. He was buried at Elephantine. By virtue of his offices, Harkhuf participated actively in the policy of expansion in Nubia conducted by the pharaohs of the Sixth Dynasty. He participated in and then led several expeditions—either departing from Elephantine or via the oasis road (more or less the modern Darb el-Arbain)—to various lands, including Yam, a principality that was probably located near Kerma in the Dongola region. Harkhuf returned from these expeditions laden with exotic products: incense, ebony, panther skins, elephant tusks, and even a dancing pygmy. While the expedition was returning home, Pepy II learned of the pygmy and was unable to contain his impatience. He addressed a decree, which is reproduced in Harkhuf's autobiography, commanding him to drop everything and conduct the pygmy to the capital, taking great care regarding this precious person: "If he takes a boat with you, place competent men who will be around him on both sides of the boat, lest he fall in the water. If he sleeps at night, place competent men who will sleep around him in the cabin!" Even pharaohs could be trivial!

A. Roccatti, *La Littérature historique sous l'ancien Empire égyptien* (Paris, 1982), pp. 200–7; M. Lichtheim, *Ancient Egyptian Literature: A Book of Readings,* vol. 1: *The Old and Middle Kingdoms* (Berkeley, 1973), pp. 23–27.

Hatshepsut 1471–1456 B.C.E., Eighteenth Dynasty

Hatshepsut was the daughter of Tuthmosis I and Ahmose and wife of Tuthmosis II, to whom she bore only a daughter, Nefrure. At the death of Tuthmosis II (1478 B.C.E.), succession to the throne fell to a son he had had by a concubine named Isis; but this son, Tuthmosis III, who was married for the occasion to Nefrure, was still a young boy. Hatshepsut was therefore called to exercise the regency, according to an often attested custom, in particular at the beginning of the dynasty (Ahmose-Nofretari). But, driven by ambition, she transformed this regency into a formal coregency. In fact, a little before year 7 of Tuthmosis III, she had herself crowned, assuming the titulary, the regalia (including the false beard), and the epithets (including that of "bull") proper to a pharaoh. Her legitimacy was supported by oracles and was justified by invoking the wishes of her father, Tuthmosis I, through whom the choice of Amun himself was supposedly manifested (theogamy). This was not really a usurpation of the throne; events were dated to the regnal years of Tuthmosis III, who was duly included in displays of royal power. Nevertheless, in formal mentions of the two monarchs, Hatshepsut was always accorded the primacy, whether by a subtle detail indicating her preeminence, or by giving only a minimal reference to the young king. Clearly, Hatshepsut benefited from significant support, in particular that of the upper clergy of Amun and his high priest Hapusonb, and she was able to win the devotion of loyal men such as Senenmut. She maintained the bulk of the power until her death, under obscure circumstances, around year 22 of Tuthmosis III. The latter had been displeased at having been kept in the background for such a long time, and after the queen's death, he had her cartouches erased and replaced by those of Tuthmosis I and Tuthmosis II, and by his own.

Though Egypt's influence now extended beyond the Third Cataract in Nubia, the reign of Hatshepsut was not distinguished by great conquests. It did, however, see the completion of the policy of restoration that had begun after the expulsion of the Hyksos. The first kings of the Eighteenth Dynasty had concentrated their restoration efforts in the Theban region, somewhat neglecting the remainder of the land. Hatshepsut rebuilt and renewed the cults of sanctuaries that had been virtually abandoned since the Hyksos, such as the Speos Artemidos.

Obviously, she did not neglect Thebes, the dynastic city. The temple of Montu and the processional route from Luxor to Karnak were objects of her care. Even more so was the temple of Karnak, where she built, among other things, a barque sanctuary (the "red chapel") and erected two pairs of obelisks (the transportation of the first pair is represented in her temple at Deir el-Bahari). Building materials and the products necessary for the temples to function were available thanks to intense exploitation of quarries and mines, and to commercial relations with exotic trade partners, in particular Punt. (The texts and images of the famous reliefs of Deir el-Bahari record an expedition she sent there.)

Beyond the purely material aspect of these accomplishments, Hatshepsut's attempt to restore the primordial order entailed the beginning of a new classicism based on imitation of Middle Kingdom works. The last traces of Second Intermediate Period style were now eliminated from art and literature.

That Hatshepsut's funerary temple was built at Deir el-Bahari, near that of Mentuhotpe II, indicates her choice of the Middle Kingdom as a model. This temple rises in two superimposed terraces bordered by porticos and is ascended via a ramp that is the continuation of a lengthy causeway. On the upper terrace, a colonnaded court leads to the sanctuary, which was excavated into the rock wall that overhangs the monument; the design of the temple was thus suggested by the site itself. Aside from a tomb that had been prepared when she was the wife of Tuthmosis II, Hatshepsut had a tomb excavated for herself as pharaoh; it is in the Valley of the Kings, near that of her father, Tuthmosis I.

S. Ratié, *La Reine Hatchepsout: Sources et problèmes,* Orientalia Monspeliensia 1 (Leiden, 1979); J. A. Tyldesley, *Hatchepsut: The Female Pharaoh* (London, 1996).
See Erasures, Senenmut, Tuthmosis I, Tuthmosis II, Tuthmosis III.

Heliopolis

In Egyptian, Heliopolis was called *Iunu,* which was the origin of the name *On* in the Bible. This "city of the sun" (the meaning of the Greek name) was located near the eastern desert, slightly downstream from the apex of the delta. It was undoubtedly founded at least as early as the Archaic Period. Its increase in religious importance seems to have paralleled the growth in political and agricultural importance of the nearby Memphite region, in the time of the builders of the pyramids. Although the "kingdom of Heliopolis," which supposedly unified predynastic Egypt, is but a figment of scholarly imagination, there is no doubt that the city was the origin of the mythology that identified the sun as the creator of the universe and was the keystone of all Egyptian religion and the basis of royal ideology.

Imhotep, the architect who invented the Step Pyramid and thus architecture on a monumental scale, was also "greatest of seers," the high priest of Heliopolis. Legend would recount that the founder of the Fifth Dynasty, whose kings built temples to the sun, held this same office before assuming the throne.

The Pyramid Texts gave the deceased king access to the perpetual destiny of the sun. The mysteries and offerings of Heliopolis became a major theme in funerary magic. Heliopolis was the high place par excellence from which Re created the world. Creation occurred on the soil of Heliopolis, and obelisks would reproduce the city's *benben* stone, the manifestation of the emergence of light. The bird who was eternally reborn made his appearance in the "Mansion of the Phoenix." The lawsuit pitting Osiris and Horus against Seth, which resulted in the survival of Osiris and the pacification of the kingdom, took place in the "House of the Magistrate."

The Ennead of deities who participated in creation resided in the "Great Mansion."

We could make no end of listing the archetypal myths and ritual models that tradition attached to Heliopolis. The sun was worshiped under various names and images: Re-Harakhty, an identification of the daytime sun with a celestial Horus, depicted as a falcon crowned with a sun disk; Atum, "lord of the Two Lands," crowned with a *pshent* and identified with the setting sun; and Khepri, "the one who comes into being," a rather abstract entity, the reborn sun symbolized by the scarab. A form of Hathor named Nebet-hetepet or Iusaas represented the desire of the creator god and the hand that stimulated this desire. A sacred bull, Mnevis, was the representative of Re on earth.

The "House of the Sun," the primordial residence of Re, was the theological cradle of the monarchy. From Djoser to Ptolemy II, considerable royal construction activity occurred at Heliopolis, especially under Senwosret I, Tuthmosis III, and Ramesses II; the latter's political theology and personal foundations honored Re more than Amun. The solar monotheism of Amenophis IV seems indeed to have had its origin in the reflection of Heliopolitan priests. Greeks would extol this City of the Sun as a seat of learning and wisdom. The heroes of various stories (including Potiphar of the Bible) were learned men from this city.

The premier holy place in religious representations and the second metropolis after Thebes in the New Kingdom, Heliopolis is better known from texts than from the dismembered remnants of its once sumptuous edifices and the now dispersed vestiges of its vast cemeteries. Many of its obelisks and statues were exported in the age of the Caesars. In the Middle Ages, dismantled temple walls were used in the construction of Cairo, which has grown to the extent that it now includes the very soil occupied by the prestigious ancient capital. All that remain above ground are an Arabic place name, Ain Shams (source of the sun), and an obelisk of Senwosret I, now enclosed in a little garden serving as a museum, along with a stunted tell from which beautiful bits of Ramesside temples and houses still project and several obelisks in Rome, London, and New York.

See Imhotep, Old Kingdom.

Henenu

Henenu was a chief steward in the reigns of Mentuhotpe II and Mentuhotpe III; he was buried at Deir el-Bahari. He was first charged with administering the newly conquered regions between Thinis and the area north of the nome of Aphroditopolis. After earning the king's esteem through his effective administration, he was entrusted with the leadership of major expeditions to the quarries. Mentuhotpe III renewed this trust, and in year 8 of the king's reign, Henenu was in charge of an extremely important mission. Departing from Koptos, he crossed the Eastern Desert via the Wadi Hammamat to the coast of the Red Sea. There, he constructed seagoing ships and set out for Punt, on the Sudanese coast, from which he brought back precious items that were indispensable but unavailable in Egypt. On his return journey, he took advantage of the proximity of the quarries to extract stone needed for temple statues.

See Eleventh Dynasty.

Heqaib

Heqaib was the surname of Pepynakht, an overseer of foreign countries and of dragomen under Pepy II; he was buried at Aswan. He was so effective at defeating and pacifying Nubian lands that posterity considered him a paragon of a warrior. Several centuries after his death, the surname of this great man would again be given to children of families at Elephantine.

His tomb became a place of pilgrimage, and when it got to be too small, a chapel was built for him on the island of Elephantine, next to the temple of Satis. During the Eleventh, Twelfth, and Thirteenth Dynasties, kings and commoners left monuments (naoi, statues, stelae, offering tables) inscribed with their names in the enclosure of this chapel, reckoning that such a great man would be an excellent intercessor with the gods. Thus, like Izi, Imhotep, and Amenhotpe, son of Hapu, Heqaib was one of the "deified" men of pharaonic Egypt.

See Amenhotpe, son of Hapu; Imhotep; Izi.

Herakleopolis Magna

Herakleopolis Magna, the capital of the twentieth nome of Upper Egypt, was slightly south of the place where the Bahr Yusuf flows into the Faiyum, at the site of the modern village of Ihnasya el-Medina. The name of the village derives from the Egyptian name of the ancient city, *Hut-nennesu,* "the mansion of the royal child."

Its principal deity was Herishef (in Greek, Harsaphes), originally a ram in front of a pond; in this form, he was already worshiped during the First Dynasty. But it was not until the First Intermediate Period that Herakleopolis Magna assumed an important role in history, as the native city of the pharaohs of the Ninth and Tenth Dynasties.

After a return to more ordinary status, Herakleopolis again rose to prominence in the Third Intermediate Period because of its strategic position on the political map of the time. In fact, the city commanded the zone bordering the territory of the theocracy of Amun (Upper Egypt and Middle Egypt as far as el-Hiba). Libyan chiefs took control of the fortresses and bases of operations that had been established in the region since the Ramesside Period; after they seized power (Twenty-second Dynasty), they were careful to appoint their sons to the high local offices, including the pontificate of Harsaphes and the command of the district founded by Osorkon I at the entrance to the Faiyum. The holders of these offices would manage to elevate themselves to pharaohs (e.g., Peftjauawybast) at the time of the Kushite conquest.

Under the Saites, Herakleopolis was the fief of a powerful family of admirals who were charged with collecting the royal tax. The family was founded by Sematawytefnakht.

Another Sematawytefnakht (the name is derived from a local god, Sematawy) of Herakleopolis had a rather interesting claim to fame. According to the so-called Naples Stela, he participated in the battle of Arbela, in the army that Darius III deployed against Alexander the Great.

M. el-Din Mokhtar, *Ihnâsya el-Medina (Herakleopolis magna),* Bibliothèque d'Étude 40 (Cairo, 1983).

See Ninth and Tenth Dynasties, Third Intermediate Period.

Herihor

In Upper Egypt, a vizier (one of two) was in charge of administrative, fiscal, and judicial matters. In Nubia, a viceroy commanded the garrisons, levied auxiliary troops, and directed the exploitation of the gold mines. The first prophet of Amun headed the personnel and the domains of the god who had become by far the richest landowner in the country and who was, through his oracle, the obligatory arbiter of every decision. In addition to these offices, a generalissimo served at the head of all the military forces.

Under Ramesses XI, at the end of the Twentieth Dynasty, a single man was invested with all these offices for the first time: Herihor, without doubt one of the greatest power grabbers in history. Master of all the resources of the south, he was the "guide of the army of all Egypt." In Lower Egypt, a certain Smendes was more or less his homologue, and the two men maintained cooperative ties in matters of cultural undertakings and commercial relations.

Though he recognized his own human condition and the sacral supremacy of the ghostly Ramesses for a time, at least, Herihor soon usurped the pharaoh's supernatural privileges. He was "son of Amun"; his name and his title of high priest were enclosed in cartouches. In place of the king, and dressed as a king, he officiated on the walls of the temple of Khons at Karnak and restored the famous hypostyle hall of Amun. Under his leadership, measures were taken to restore and to protect the mummies of Sethos I and Ramesses II.

This extraordinary career seems to have been brief (1080–1064 B.C.E.), however, and Herihor's legitimacy was sometimes contested: his image and name were effaced on a stela he had dedicated at Abydos. But he founded a regime that would last more than three centuries. Upper Egypt would be a politically sovereign principality governed by a high priest who was also head of the armed forces. Herihor's astonishing personality remains a mystery. His pompous inscriptions never name his parents, as was normal for pharaohs (and only for pharaohs), but mentions of him in administrative and private sources also ignore the customary indications of parentage, suggesting a rather obscure origin. His own name was Egyptian, but several of his sons had typically Libyan names, leading us to think that he was a scion of the military colonists or newly Egyptianized invaders who at that time constituted the majority of the armed forces. His wife, Nodjmet, who died long after him and whose burial was found in the cachette of Deir el-Bahari, passed away bearing the title "king's mother." This circumstance has led some scholars to think that the couple were the parents of Smendes, the founder of the Twenty-first Dynasty, though another hypothesis is possible. Recently, the unexpected appearance of a bracelet inscribed with the name of Herihor on the art market served as a reminder that the burial place of the creator of the Theban theocratic state remains unknown, though this piece of jewelry could have been one of the objects removed from the cachette of Deir el-Bahari during the 1870s.

K. Myśliwiec, *The Twilight of Ancient Egypt: First Millennium B.C.E.* (Ithaca, 2000), pp. 17–22.

See High Priest of Amun, Twentieth Dynasty.

Hermopolis Magna

This city was the capital of the fifteenth nome (called the Hare nome), located in the heart of Middle Egypt, in the vast plain bordered on the east by the Nile and on the west by its arm, the Bahr Yusuf. The remains of its temples are visible near the modern village of el-Ashmunein, whose name is derived from *Shmun,* the ancient Egyptian name of the city. About six miles away, its cemetery of Tuna el-Gebel lies at the foot of the desert hills. Hermopolis was one of the most famous religious centers, thanks to the prestige of its principal deity, Thoth, whom the Greeks identified with Hermes (hence the name Hermopolis). The city dominated a region that was economically important because of its rich fields, and because of the proximity of the alabaster quarries of Hatnub. These material advantages sometimes led those who controlled it to set themselves up as independent potentates when the central power was weak; thus, at the end of the Seventeenth Dynasty, the region fell under the control of Tetian, an Egyptian collaborator of the Hyksos, who ruled from the neighboring town of Neferusy. During the Third Intermediate Period, several local chiefs, including a certain Djehutiemhet, again assumed the attributes of a pharaoh.

Akhenaten himself included the region of Hermopolis in the territory of his new retreat, Akhetaten. But aside from these brief episodes and others like them (such as during the First Intermediate Period, when local nomarchs exercised their power), Hermopolis opened up to history at a relatively late date. In the Ptolemaic and Roman eras, the fascination that Thoth exerted on the Greeks brought many of them to Hermopolis, where an original synthesis of pharaonic civilization and Hellenistic culture developed; the famous tomb of Petosiris is the most spectacular evidence of this phenomenon.

Hierakonpolis (Nekhen) *and* **Eileithyiaspolis** (Nekheb)

These cities were the capitals of the third nome of Upper Egypt, situated on each side of the Nile, facing each other; Hierakonpolis (Kom el-Ahmar) was situated on the west bank, and Eileithyiaspolis (el-Kab) on the east bank. This area is distinguished by its traces of very early eras: the prehistoric, the predynastic, the protodynastic, and the Archaic Period. At Kom el-Ahmar, archaeologists discovered a very early decorated tomb, and in several cachettes of a temple erected within a vast enclosure wall, they found votive objects such as the Narmer Palette and the mace heads of Narmer and Scorpion.

The prominent role that these two cities played in the formation of pharaonic civilization explains the use of their cultic traditions in Egypt's fundamental symbolism. Nekhen and Nekheb were the southern pendants of the twin cities of the northern delta, Pe and Dep (Buto), thus forming one of the dualisms expressing the unity of the land through the association of Upper and Lower Egypt; Nekhbet, the vulture goddess of Nekheb, was paired with Wadjit, the cobra goddess of Buto.

See Buto, Dualisms, Narmer, Scorpion.

High Priest of Amun

The literal translation of this priestly title is "first god's servant of Amun-Re, King of the Gods," and it is often rendered as "first prophet of Amun." In the Ptolemaic Period, Greek nomenclature in fact applied the word "prophet" to the highest rank of priests—ahead of the "god's-fathers" and the "pure-priests" (*wab*)—undoubtedly because it fell to them to express the oracular will of the gods. In the Seventeenth and Eighteenth Dynasties, sovereigns from Thebes expelled the Hyksos and then put together a vast and prosperous empire. Amun, the patron god of their city, supposedly sired these kings, and he sometimes confirmed them through his oracles. His providential effectiveness was both acknowledged and reinforced by additions to his temple complex, by the celebration of his annual festivals, and by donations, proportionate to his primacy, of fields, livestock, gold mines, and workshops. His revenues furnished his altar and maintained a numerous clergy. A large bureaucracy was put in place to administer his goods. Many secular officials received benefices of "prophets of Amun," while their wives were "songstresses of Amun." With time, and despite the Atenist interlude, the "house of Amun" became an economic and social power comparable to the "king's house," and far richer than those of the other gods and goddesses. Outranking the second, third, and fourth prophets, the high priest ruled an immense cultic enterprise that was both spiritual and temporal. The position was filled by royal appointment (Ramesses II named Nebwenenef, who had been head of the clergy at Dendara, as well as a former military officer, Bekenkhons).

During the Eighteenth and Nineteenth Dynasties, it was rare for the office to pass from father to son. In Dynasty Twenty-one, a process was set in motion that would make the high priest of Amun an autonomous political power for about half a century. Theological reflection and devotion to the primordial and omnipresent organizer of the universe increased the king's (and everyone's) dependence vis-à-vis Amun-Re and his oracle. As specialization in sacred knowledge and ritual techniques grew, a privileged group of priests of Amun was formed through heredity and marriage. From Ramesses IV to Ramesses XI, several generations of a single family monopolized the pontifical seat itself, and with it, temporal rule over the domain of Amun. Then, an upstart generalissimo named Herihor became first prophet of Amun and inaugurated a "theocratic" regime. Under the Twenty-first Dynasty, which emerged from this Theban theocracy, and then under the princedoms of the Twenty-second and Twenty-third Dynasties, the high priest was an independent ruler who governed Upper Egypt under the sanction of oracles, though not without having to take account of the agitation of priestly lobbies. After the Kushite Haremakhet, son of Taharqa, this dangerous pontifical office gave way to the spiritual and regal power of the "adoratrice," daughter of the Saite pharaoh.

See Adoratrice, Clergy, Herihor, Pinudjem.

Hittites

Even in imperialism, competition exists everywhere. As they extended their domination over Syria-Palestine, the pharaohs of the New Kingdom encountered greed equal to their own. It was during the reign of Akhenaten that the Hittite empire—a state with an Indo-European population whose center was in Anatolia—began to complicate the power struggle between Egypt and Mitanni. After some direct confrontations, as well as indirect ones through allied states, the Hittite king Suppiluliumas judged it convenient to establish a provisional modus vivendi with Egypt so as to leave him free to pursue the defeat of Mitanni. The weak pharaohs of the day were delighted not to have to wage war against so redoubtable a sovereign; at the death of Tutankhamun, an Egyptian queen even offered to marry a Hittite prince. But of course, this peaceful coexistence scarcely survived the collapse of Mitanni, which left the appetites of Egypt and Hatti to face one another. The conflicts that began under Sethos I culminated in the famous battle of Qadesh, which Ramesses II, in year 5 of his reign, "lost victoriously" to the Hittite king Muwatallis. In his year 21, after further indecisive conflicts, this pharaoh signed a peace treaty with Hattusilis, Muwatallis' successor. Both the Egyptian and the Hittite versions of the treaty text have survived. It appears to sanction a division of influence, which could not have satisfied Ramesses II, though he was obliged to make do with it; the treaty established a lasting peace that was later sealed by his marriage to a daughter of Hattusilis in year 34. During the reign of Ramesses III, the Hittite empire suffered gravely from the invasion of the Sea Peoples, though whether it disappeared entirely under their blows is uncertain.

C. Lalouette, *L'Empire des Ramsès* (Paris, 1985), pp. 123–38; G. Steindorff and K. C. Seele, *When Egypt Ruled the East,* 2d ed. (Chicago, 1957), chapters 14–16.

Hurrians

Originally from the region of Lake Van, Hurrians spoke a language that was neither Semitic nor Indo-European, but related to Urartian. They spread through Mesopotamia and then through Syria during the second millennium B.C.E., and some of them undoubtedly were among the Hyksos who invaded Egypt. But it was at the beginning of the Eighteenth Dynasty that Egyptians took them into account by creating the name *Kharu,* at first to designate the Hurrians settled in Palestine, and later as a geographical term not only for Syria-Palestine, but for all of western Asia north of Egypt. Hurrians were a major component of the population of the kingdom of Mitanni, which the Egyptians also called Naharin, a Semitic name meaning "(the land of the) two rivers"; during the Eighteenth Dynasty, Mitanni was the principal power the Egyptians had to confront in their expansion into Asia.

Revue hittite et asianique 36 (1978).

See Hyksos.

Hyksos Fifteenth Dynasty

"Hyksos" is the Greek form of the Egyptian expression *heqa khasut,* which originally meant "ruler of foreign lands"; later, it was reinterpreted as "shepherd kings." We use the term to designate the Asiatic people, mostly Semitic but with Hurrian elements, who overran the eastern delta kingdom that had been founded by Nehesy and was already densely populated by Asiatics. From Avaris, the capital of this kingdom, a Hyksos chief named Salitis established his domination over Egypt by having himself crowned at Memphis (1650 B.C.E.). This domination was exercised in various ways: absolute control over the eastern delta; relinquishment of the remainder of Lower Egypt to Asiatic vassal chieftains; installation of Egyptian collaborators in Middle Egypt; surveillance of Upper Egypt and its Theban dynasty by garrisons installed in strategic places (e.g., Gebelein); and alliances with Nubian potentates. Additionally, a part of Palestine bowed under Hyksos rule. All these territories were subject to tribute collected by an administrator with the Egyptian title "overseer of the treasury."

It appears that Egyptian tradition blackened the Hyksos occupation to an extreme degree, imputing barbarism and impiety to these foreigners. The documentation, however, requires a more nuanced approach. It is true that the Hyksos imposed their own culture in Avaris and its region: house burials, donkey sacrifice, cults of Canaanite deities (and the Canaanization of the local god Seth); and it is true that they pillaged

Egyptian cemeteries and cities, with the result that many monuments were transported from Memphis to Avaris and reused there. But otherwise, they did not scorn Egyptian civilization, and their kings adopted the titulary and the traditional apparatus of pharaohs, to the point of entrusting Egyptian hirelings with the task of writing texts in praise of them. The Hyksos erected monuments in the temples (and usurped many others!), and they patronized culture and the sciences, as witnessed by a copy of a mathematical treatise that was made under Apophis. Finally, they introduced new weapons (axe and dagger) into Egypt, and perhaps the horse as well.

The Hyksos dynasty reigned in Egypt for about a century (1650–1539 B.C.E.), and they were defeated only at the end of an arduous struggle that cost the life of at least one of the nationalist Egyptian pharaohs (Seqenenre Tao). Kamose began the war of liberation, but it was Ahmose who finally eradicated Hyksos domination by taking Avaris and the city of Sharuhen in Palestine. The list of Hyksos pharaohs (not without uncertainties) is as follows:

Salitis (Sharek)
Bnon
Apachnan
Apophis
Khamudi

M. Bietak, "Avaris and Piramesse: Archaeological Exploration in the Eastern Nile Delta," *Proceedings of the British Academy* 65 (1979): 225–90.

See Ahmose; Ahmose, son of Ebana; Apophis; Avaris; Kamose; Second Intermediate Period; Sequenenre Tao; Seventeenth Dynasty; Sixteenth Dynasty.

Imhotep (*or* Imuthes)

During the reign of Djoser, Imhotep was high priest of Heliopolis, the capital of priestly learning. For this reason he was chosen by the king to oversee the construction of his monumental complex. This was a difficult task, because at that time, there was no solidly established tradition of stone architecture for such a large construction. For a trial run, this was a masterful stroke. Posterity made no mistake in according Imhotep a glorious destiny.

A wisdom text written by him (or attributed to him) was included among the classics of literature, and he was considered to be the patron of scribes. He also became part of the pantheon of Memphis as the son of Ptah and a mortal woman, Kherduankh. Other cities of Egypt made him the architect of their temple, contrary to all historical fact. Sanctuaries were erected to him, especially at Thebes, often in association with Amenhotpe, son of Hapu; persons who were ill would go to these temples to seek a remedy for their suffering by consulting his oracle or through incubation. Under the Greek name Imuthes, he was sometimes identified with Asclepius.

D. Wildung, *Egyptian Saints: Deification in Ancient Egypt* (New York, 1977).

See Amenhotpe, son of Hapu; Djoser; Famine.

Inyotef Eleventh, Thirteenth, and Seventeenth Dynasties

Like Mentuhotpe, the name Inyotef was borne by kings of the Eleventh Dynasty, as well as by kings of the end of the Middle Kingdom and of the Second Intermediate Period.

ELEVENTH DYNASTY

Inyotef I (Horus name Sehertawy) was undoubtedly the first of the Theban potentates to proclaim himself king, though the title was retrospectively attributed to his father, Mentuhotpe I (2115–2068 B.C.E. for the two of them). He was buried in the Asasif.

Inyotef II (Horus name Wahankh) had a lengthy reign (2115–2066 B.C.E.) marked by war with the kingdom of Herakleopolis. The two armies confronted each other in the region of Abydos, and by turns, they seized and lost the city of Thinis. When all was said and done, Inyotef extended his realm slightly farther north, to the borders of the nome of Hypselis. In his tomb, which was already pillaged during the Twentieth Dynasty, a stela was discovered on which he is represented along with his pet dogs, who are designated by their names (which are of Berber origin).

Inyotef III (Horus name Nakhtnebtepnufer) was the son of the preceding king. During his brief reign (2066–2059 B.C.E.), he endeavored to consolidate the gains of his predecessors.

END OF THE MIDDLE KINGDOM AND SECOND INTERMEDIATE PERIOD

Along with an obscure Inyotef IV of the Thirteenth Dynasty, certain kings of the Seventeenth Dynasty bore the name Inyotef, undoubtedly a conscious reference to the Inyotefs of the Eleventh Dynasty, near whose tombs they built their own at Dra Abu el-Naga. The reason was that they, too, intended to restore the unity of Egypt from their base in Thebes.

Inyotef V (throne name: Nubkheperre) might well have been the founder of the Seventeenth Dynasty (c. 1650 B.C.E.). He married Sebekemzaf, a woman from a powerful family of governors of Edfu who were themselves allied by marriage to the preceding pharaohs. In doing so, Inyotef V intended to assure the loyalty of the provinces of the Thebais in order to form an alliance capable of keeping the Hyksos power at bay. Koptos and Abydos were members of this alliance. He dismissed a high official of the temple of Koptos for a grave offense (perhaps embezzlement), and he built at the temple of Abydos. He no doubt had to wage war to obtain his epithet "victorious."

Inyotef VI (throne name: Sekhemre-wepmaat) and Inyotef VII (throne name: Sekhemre-herhermaat) were sons of Sebekemzaf II. These kings had very short reigns and are known only by what remains of their tombs.

See Eleventh Dynasty, First Intermediate Period, Mentuhotpe, Second Intermediate Period.

Inyotefoqer

Inyotefoqer held the office of vizier at least from the coregency of Amenemhet I and Senwosret I, and during a large part of the sole reign of the latter. Because of his high office, he supervised all major undertakings, such as the construction of an edifice at Abydos, expeditions to the amethyst mines of Wadi el-Hudi, and still others to the shores of Punt on the Sudanese coast. Additionally, Inyotefoqer took part in military operations in Nubia and had a fortress built in a strategic location. His glorious career was clouded by the sad fate of his son, also called Inyotefoqer; for having committed a serious crime, he underwent not only physical punishment but also a magical punishment in the form of the execration of a figurine bearing his name. Vizier Inyotefoqer built a mastaba at Lisht, as well as a tomb at Thebes, the latter undoubtedly intended for his mother, Senet, and his wife.

Izi

Nomarch of Edfu, Izi was appointed to this position by Teti after spending the first part of his career in the central administration at Memphis during the reigns of Djedkare Izezi and Wenis. Posterity treated him as a model administrator, posthumously calling him "vizier," an office he never held. Moreover, like Heqaib at Elephantine, he became a patron saint at Edfu. His name enriched the stock of local proper names, and his mastaba in the cemetery of Edfu became a chapel. During the Eleventh, Twelfth, and Thirteenth Dynasties, private persons deposited their funerary monuments (shawabtis, naoi, statues, stelae, offering tables) there, convinced that because Izi's prestige had brought him into contact with the world of the gods (hence his epithet "the divine, the living"), he would be an effective intercessor.

See Heqaib.

Jubilee (*Sed*-Festival)

The *sed*-festival, or "jubilee," was a complex ceremony intended to reaffirm and to renew the pharaoh's powers. The notion that it concealed a ritual execution, as in certain monarchies of Africa, remains a pure hypothesis. Though they do not allow a clear reconstruction of the ceremonies, representations allow us to discern its main points. Dressed in a characteristic short mantle, the king went on procession to meet the "royal children," who were carried on litters. Afterward, in the jubilee pavilion, as king of the south and then as king of the north, he received the homage of the officials and the people of Upper and Lower Egypt while gazing upon the tribute that was brought for this occasion—in particular, cattle. He ran a ritual course wearing a kilt with a false tail. He offered to the deities and visited their primitive sanctuaries, preceded by a cortege of priests carrying standards. Finally, he shot arrows toward the four cardinal points, affirming his assumption of power over the universe. The elements of the ceremony date back through the Archaic Period into protohistory.

Ideally, the jubilee marked the end of a cycle of thirty years. But although it indeed occurred in the thirtieth year of the reigns of a number of kings, the cycle was far from regularly respected. Some kings celebrated a second or third jubilee only a few years after the first one.

In any event, preparations for the *sed*-festival mobilized the people and the resources of the land well in advance, perhaps inspiring military expeditions to procure the necessary cattle. Statues and obelisks were set up, and rooms in temples or even pavilions, such as the famous "white chapel" of Senwosret I, were constructed for the *sed*-festival. The officials most favored by the king participated as officiants in the jubilee rituals; others received commemorative objects, often vases, which at their death became the pride of their funerary equipment.

As an event, the *sed*-festival was simultaneously religious, political, social, and economic—when it was in fact celebrated. There were very few kings who we are certain or can reasonably suppose actually had a jubilee. Among the approximately ten were Pepy I, Pepy II, Senwosret I, Amenemhet III, Tuthmosis III, Amenophis III, Ramesses II, and Ramesses III. Otherwise, the many mentions of the *sed*-festival refer only to an isolated act from the entire ritual or are mere wishes that a king might celebrate jubilees. Moreover, pharaohs were believed to celebrate them as part of their postmortem destiny; thus, the false buildings in the enclosure of the Step Pyramid of Djoser were intended to assure the king the possibility of celebrating his jubilees in the hereafter.

E. Hornung and E. Staehelin, *Studien zum Sedfest*, Aegyptiaca Helvetica 1 (Geneva, 1974).

Kagemni

Kagemni was a vizier who began as an administrator under Wenis and reached the apogee of his career under Teti, near whose pyramid his mastaba was found. In addition, we have an instruction addressed to a Kagemni, who is appointed vizier by Snofru in its conclusion. It is possible that this is the same person, and that posterity, playing with history, displaced the beneficiary of the instruction into the blessed reign of Snofru in order to bestow the aura of this most popular of kings on the text.

A. Roccati, *La Littérature historique sous l'Ancien Empire égyptien* (Paris, 1982), p. 139; M. Lichtheim, *Ancient Egyptian Literature,* vol. 1: *The Old and Middle Kingdoms* (Berkeley, 1975), p. 59.

See Snofru, Teti.

Kamose 1542–1539 B.C.E., Seventeenth Dynasty

Kamose, the last king of the Seventeenth Dynasty, ruled at least three years. During his third year, he began the war of liberation against the Hyksos by seizing Neferusi, a city held by their collaborators, and then pressing forward to the environs of Avaris, though he did not capture it. Threatened from his rear by the ruler of Kush, who was allied with the Hyksos king Apophis, he turned back. The ruler of Kush in fact had serious grievances with Kamose, who had earlier attempted the reconquest of Nubia by retaking Buhen. Like other pharaohs of the Seventeenth Dynasty, Kamose was buried at Dra Abu el-Naga.

See Apophis, Avaris, Hyksos, Second Intermediate Period, Seventeenth Dynasty.

Khaemwese

Fourth son of Ramesses II and second born of his chief wife, Isetnofret, Khaemwese was appointed by his father to the office of high priest of Ptah at Memphis. During his long pontificate, he displayed great care for the deceased Apis bulls, opening the smaller gallery at the Serapeum, where his own tomb would be located. Khaemwese, who would be remembered often, and sometimes in highly original ways, was interested in theological rarities and in the monuments of the past. He had restoration work done on Old Kingdom pyramids and on the statue of one of the sons of Cheops. This lettered prince passed into legend as a magician who was curious about ancient inscriptions and who kept the company of ghosts, for better or for worse.

See Ramesses II.

Khasekhemwy 2660–2635 B.C.E., Second Dynasty

The name of this pharaoh, who ruled at the end of the Second Dynasty, proclaims an era of reconciliation. It does so by its wording, "appearance of the two powers (*khasekemwy*), in whom the two gods are reconciled," and by the way it is written, with the usual palace facade in fact surmounted by the images of Horus and Seth facing each other (thus replacing the image of Horus alone, or the image of Seth alone in the case of Peribsen). This king aimed to put an end to the political conflicts between one movement, which had taken Horus as its emblem, and an opposing one symbolized by Seth. The restoration of national unity was reinforced by the defeat of Nubians in the south and Libyans in the north.

With order established both internally and externally, Egyptian civilization took the qualitative leap that brought it from the Archaic Period into the Old Kingdom. Technological development benefited not only metallurgy—from that time on, artisans knew how to cast statues of copper—but especially architecture. Stone was no longer confined to marginal uses, but began to be used and worked with mastery, as demonstrated by the chamber fashioned of limestone in Khasekhemwy's tomb at Abydos and by his carved granite doorjamb from Hierakonpolis. The way was prepared for the genius of Imhotep.

W.B. Emery, *Archaic Egypt* (Baltimore, 1961), pp. 101–3.

See Archaic (Period), Djoser, Imhotep, Peribsen.

Khentkaus

Khentkaus was queen at the beginning of the Fifth Dynasty. Her exceptional importance is shown by several indications: her sarcophagus-shaped tomb north of the causeway of the pyramid of Mycerinus, her funerary temple, her titulary designating her as mother of two kings (Userkaf and Sahure). Her third son, Neferirkare Kakai, came to the throne only after her death, and he established a cult for her near his own tomb. This queen inspired one of the tales from the cycle of stories known from Papyrus Westcar: it recounts how Re created a new dynasty by impregnating the wife of a priest of Sakhebu with three sons. The destiny of this queen also partly nourished the Greek legend of Rhodopis, who was considered to be the builder of the third pyramid at Giza (as was Nitocris).

See Fifth Dynasty, Neferirkare Kakai, Sahure.

Kush

Kush was originally the name of a small region of Nubia, south of the Second Cataract. First attested under the Twelfth Dynasty, the term was later extended to all the territories of the south. During the Second Intermediate Period, a powerful kingdom, Sudanese in culture and with Kerma as its capital, extended from Dongola to the Second Cataract. Its chief was called "ruler of Kush" by the Egyptian scribes in his service and by the chancery of the pharaoh in Thebes. The first Tuthmosids destroyed this state and pushed still further south.

During the New Kingdom, all the territory from el-Kab to the Fourth Cataract was administered by a viceroy who bore the title "king's son of Kush" (the filiation being purely honorific). This vast domain was subdivided into two zones, each one entrusted to a lieutenant: Wawat, north of the Second Cataract, and Kush proper to the south. As chief military, religious, and civil leader, the "king's son" organized the collection of tribute by the mayors of towns and the Nubian chiefs, conducted punitive raids on the rare occasions of frontier rebellion, and supervised the exploitation of the gold mines and the construction of monuments.

What remained of the sedentary native population was rapidly Egyptianized during the Eighteenth Dynasty. Black peoples from the southern steppes delivered cattle, panthers, giraffes, and other products of the African interior. In the colonial towns, numerous temples and speoi (rock-cut chapels) were constructed in the king's name to the major deities of Egypt and to the local Horuses and Hathors. A number of these have survived almost intact: Amada and Buhen under the Tuthmosids; Soleb, Sedeinga, and Sesebi under the Amenophises; and especially the prestigious series of temples under Ramesses II, including Abu Simbel, el-Derr, Wadi el-Sebua, Gerf Hussein, Beit el-Wali, and many others. These sumptuous viceroys dedicated many monuments in Nubia, but since they were loyal administrators dispatched by the king, not regional potentates, they made their tombs at Thebes or in their hometowns. The Theban tomb of Huy at Qurnet Murai is known especially for its colorful representation of Nubians bearing tribute for Tutankhamun. Though classified as a foreign land, just like Kharu (i.e., Syria-Palestine), Kush was directly ruled as a single domain and thus almost as subject to the royal administration as the provinces of Egypt itself.

After the Ramessides, Egypt lost nearly all its foreign empire, maintaining fairly continuous control over only the pastoral and mineral resources of a nearly depopulated Lower Nubia. In the Twenty-first Dynasty, the title "king's son of Kush" was awarded as a benefice to the wife of Pinudjem, the high priest of Amun, and in the Twenty-second Dynasty, it was borne by a grandson of Osorkon II resident at Elephantine; this city was once again the Nubian frontier. In the eighth century B.C.E., Kush was once more a state, one whose history was determined by the successive dynasties of Napata and Meroe. Like the Assyrians and the Persians, the Hebrews would retain the name of Kush ("son of Ham," according to them) to designate the kingdom the Greeks called Ethiopia.

W. A. Adams, *Corridor to Africa* (London, 1977); B. G. Trigger, *Nubia under the Pharaohs* (Boulder, Colo., 1976); *Histoire générale de l'Afrique,* vol. 2: *Afrique ancienne* (UNESCO, 1980), pp. 239–94.

See Kushite (Dynasty), Meroe, Napata, Nubia.

Kushite (Dynasty)

The ancient Greek word Ethiopia was a vague term for the immense area including all the lands south of the First Cataract of the Nile, corresponding to what the Arabs call Sudan. This is why Manetho used the term "Ethiopian" to designate the Twenty-fifth Dynasty from Napata in Nubia, which ruled both its native Sudan and Egypt for five decades. Earlier still, in his *Histories,* Herodotus had described "King Sabacos" (i.e., Shabaka), who personified the entirety of his dynasty, as an "Ethiopian." Today, the term Ethiopia is the name of a multiracial nation above the eastern horn of Africa; forged by the Abyssinian dynasty founded by Tewodros II, its territory includes none of the area ruled by the ancient kings of Napata and Meroe. It is thus convenient to calls these pharaohs Kushites, a term derived from "Kush," which was their own name for their native land.

After the Twentieth Dynasty, Nubia, which had become extremely Egyptianized during the New Kingdom, was abandoned by the Egyptian garrisons; later "viceroys of Kush," contemporary with the Tanites and the Libyans, do not seem to have been able to exercise power over very much territory. In the distant and fertile Dongola, a local power took root during the ninth and eighth centuries; this series of princes, anonymous to us, were buried at el-Kurru, near Napata.

Napata, site of a major cult of Amun, had been the southernmost metropolis of Egyptian rule, and although the culture of the Napatan domain picked up the thread of its Sudanese patrimony, a pharaonic cultural tradition nevertheless remained. The ruler of Napata adopted pharaonic titles and regalia, putting him on an equal ideological footing with the rival Libyan kings among whom Egypt was divided. We cannot say whether the adoption of this prestigious model was the cause or the result of the northward expansion of the Kushites.

Toward 750 B.C.E., Kashta was recognized at Elephantine. Under his son Piye, all the Thebais, where the Shoshenqide line had been eliminated, was annexed. Despite the efforts of Tefnakhte, ruler of the west, Piye extended his protectorate to all the principalities downstream. Shabaka, Piye's brother, eliminated King Bocchoris, Tefnakhte's son: there was now only one pharaoh between the Sudanese Sahel and the Mediterranean. It is with this Shabaka (716–702 B.C.E.) that Manetho begins his Twenty-fifth Dynasty. Under this king, the custom of placing two uraei (cobras) on the front of the royal diadem made its appearance; this innovation corresponded to the ancient theme of the unification of the Two Lands, a theme that now expressed the joining of two vast kingdoms. Shabaka was succeeded by two sons of Piye, Shabataka (702–690 B.C.E.) and Taharqa (690–664 B.C.E.), and then by Tantamani, Taharqa's nephew (664–656 B.C.E.).

The policies and the construction activity of the Kushites differed in size and range, depending on whether we are considering the Sudan or the two parts of Egypt. From the *gezira* of Meroe to the Third Cataract, urban and rural life prospered in the habitable portion of the Sudan. At Napata, Sanam, Kawa, and Pnubs (Kerma), the importation of Egyptian artisans endowed the sanctuaries of Amun with small but magnificent temples. As Egyptianized as it was, the kingship remained deliberately Sudanese. The transfer of the kingship from brother to brother was not Egyptian, and the pyramids of the kings were located in the ancestral cemetery of el-Kurru, except for that of Taharqa, who chose Nuri, a short distance from Napata. But there were few exotic elements in the raiment of these rulers: a special diadem, jewels of an original type that represented the head of the ram of Amun.

In the Thebais, the local priestly families rallied to the Napatan pharaoh. This devotee of Amun from the distant south recognized the autonomy that the Tanite and Libyan high priests had gained for this polity. Kushite adoratrices—Amenirdis, daughter of Kashta, and Shepenwepet, daughter of Piye—took up the torch of their Shoshenqide predecessors. The temples of Thebes benefited from remarkable embellishments carried out in the name of the king or the god's wife. Generally small and styled with restraint, these monuments represented an archaizing renaissance in temple decoration.

The Twenty-fifth Dynasty seems to have had an almost permanent hold on Memphis. Its control of the delta was weaker; the kingdom of Sais, which proclaimed a new dynasty, the Twenty-sixth, constituted a tenacious obstacle for a conqueror come from so far, and there were also "great chiefs" and minor Tanite pharaohs. To judge from his building activity and the memory he left behind, Taharqa ruled supreme for some years over his outsized Nilotic empire. Around 700 B.C.E., the Egypto-Sudanese proved unable to prevent the Assyrian emperor Sennacherib from ravaging Palestine. Under Esarhaddon, and then Assurbanipal, the Assyrian war machine forced its way into Egypt: Memphis (671 B.C.E.), then Thebes (666 B.C.E.) were captured. This intervention ended by reinforcing Sais and the independent realms in the north. A counterattack by Tantamani unleashed the return of Assurbanipal, which ended in the spectacular sack of Thebes (663 B.C.E.). Subsequently, the Saite Psammetichus drove the Napatan dynasty back beyond Assuan (656 B.C.E.).

N. M. Serif, J. Leclant, and A. Hakem, *Histoire générale de l'Afrique,* vol. 2: *Afrique ancienne* (UNESCO, 1980), pp. 259–346; K. Myśliwiec, *The Twilight of Ancient Egypt: First Millennium B.C.E.* (Ithaca, 2000), pp. 68–109.

See Adoratrice.

Leontopolis

The city called *Taremu* (land of the fishes) by the Egyptians became Greek Leontopolis, "city of the lions," because of the tawny beasts that were kept there; they were sacred to Mahes, the "Terrifying Lion," son of the goddess Bastet. This obscure city in the eastern delta became important under the Osorkons of the Twenty-second Dynasty, who were devotees of these deities. Toward the end of the Libyan anarchy, a minor king, the pharaoh Iuput II, had his principal residence there, but the hypothesis that the entire Twenty-third Dynasty was Leontopolite is highly debatable. This Leontopolis, present-day Tell el-Muqdam, should not be confused with the like-named city, present-day Tell el-Yahudiya, located in the Heliopolitan nome, where the Jewish high priest Onias built a temple during the Ptolemaic Period.

Libyans

In the Sixth Dynasty, a people called *Tjemehu* were noted as being in the margin of Lower Nubia, "toward the western corner of the sky." From the Archaic Period on, we have mentions of the name of the *Tjehenu,* who are to be located in Marmarica, just west of the delta. The scenes of "Libyan booty" in funerary temples of the Old Kingdom represent these Tjehenu as anthropologically similar to the Egyptians, but ethnographically different: the men have long hair, and they wear crossed shoulder straps and penis sheaths. At that time, Mediterranean Marmarica and the grassy steppes of the Sahara were much better watered than they are today, and the Tjehenu devoted themselves to cattle raising and arboriculture. The original differences (racial, ethnic, or geographical) between the Tjehenu and the Tjemehu remain indeterminate. One specious theory holds that the former were a brown-skinned people and the latter were light-skinned, blond-haired Libyans who were first attested in the Twelfth Dynasty. From the Middle Kingdom on, these two terms for Egypt's western neighbors were practically synonymous. Until the middle of the second millennium—and in spite of the progressive desiccation that began around 2400 B.C.E.—these impoverished populations were of scant bother to Pharaoh. Compared with Asiatics and Nubians, the Libyans occurred rarely in mentions of hostile peoples during this period. Raids were conducted against them, and they furnished warriors. Religious imagination associated them with the cult of Hathor-Sakhmet, mistress of the confines of Libya.

Around 1400 B.C.E., groups called the Meshwesh and the Libu (the origin of the name Libya, which comes to us via Greek) appeared in Marmarica. Their domain covered the hilly seashore and the hinterland steppes between the corner of Lake Mariut and the present-day border of Egypt and Libya. Unified under great chiefs, they increasingly left their homeland, moving their camps and their herds ever closer to the oases, and especially to the delta. These were white-skinned savages, both tattooed warriors and archers whose "uniform" included a war feather and a finely plaited lock of hair on the side of the head. They delivered cattle and fat as tribute to Amenophis III, who listed them by name among the dangerous lands. In the twelfth and eleventh centuries, these barbarians entered the international arena, weakening and finally destabilizing Egypt. Already aggressive and combated by Sethos I, they were dealt with vigorously by Ramesses II, who constructed a series of fortresses between el-Gharbaniyat and Marsa Matruh to keep an eye on them. Equipped with light chariots and bronze weapons, and reinforced by Mediterranean pirates, the Libu, along with the Meshwesh, were barely stopped by Merneptah, and Ramesses III was obliged to expel both of them and other related ethnic groups from the western delta. These victorious pharaohs transplanted captured Libyan warriors to the east, where they aided in the defense of the eastern borders of Lower Egypt.

Under the increasingly weak rule of the later Ramessides, these colonists—and, undoubtedly, fresh waves of Libyans—achieved military domination over the delta and the north of Middle Egypt. Bubastis in the east and Herakleopolis to the south became bastions of the supreme chieftainship of the Meshwesh, from which the Twenty-second Dynasty would emerge; meanwhile, the Libu overran the western confines of the delta, while other peoples settled in various locales. After they seized power, these conquerors retained their tribal structure: the title "great chief of the Meshwesh" was proudly borne by the ruling families of Shoshenqide blood, and it also designated the chiefs of local population groups.

The Libyans' most visible contribution to the history of Egypt was their monopolization of the military profession in the north, along with a lack of discipline that deviated from Egyptian ideals and practices and led to anarchic decentralization in the seventh century B.C.E. Intentionally subjected to linguistic Egyptianization since Ramesside times, and rapidly assimilated to the superior culture of the conquered, the Libyans introduced almost nothing of their own culture. Their few introductions included personal names that would be handed down to the Saite Period and beyond, in particular names that had belonged to Meshwesh pharaohs and princes; a feather stuck in or flattened against the hair of the "great chiefs"; some mysterious titles, perhaps pertaining to clans; and perhaps the enigmatic goddess Shahdedet.

In Marmarica, the Meshwesh and the Libu were replaced by other peoples, whom the Egyptians collectively designated Tjemehu, Tjehenu, or Pyut. At first posing a threat that was repelled by Osorkon II and Psammetichus I, and then contained by the Saite garrison of Marea, they eventually aided the Egyptians as auxiliaries under Tefnakhte and during the Twenty-sixth Dynasty. In the fifth century, resistance to the Persians would owe much to the Libyans Inaros (whose name was Egyptian) and his son Ithanyras (a Libyan name).

A. Leahy, ed., *Libya and Egypt c. 1300–750 B.C.* (London, 1990).

Lisht

Near the village of Lisht stretch the remains of the capital founded by Amenemhet I. Its name, *Amenemhet-itj-tawy,* "Amenemhet is the one who seized the Two Lands," was abbreviated to *Itj-tawy.* The pharaohs of the Twelfth Dynasty wanted a capital that was strategically located at the juncture of Upper and Lower Egypt, while escaping the direct influence of Memphis, some twenty miles to the north. Though only Amenemhet I and Senwosret I built their funerary complexes there, Lisht remained the capital into the Thirteenth Dynasty. The city was again a strategic location in the Third Intermediate Period. The prestige of the Middle Kingdom capital was such that at a later date, the hieroglyphs for Itj-tawy were read as the word *khenu,* "residence, capital."

See Amenemhet I, Middle Kingdom, Senwosret I.

Loyalism

As the earthly representative of the creator god, Pharaoh was the keystone of the physical and social universe of Egypt. He made no secret of it; on the stelae and the statues he set up, on the walls of the temples, a thousand inscriptions trumpet the omnipotence of his office and sing a stony hymn to his glory.

Of course, his humble subjects adhered to this vision of the world, on which ancient Egypt based its identity—or at least they behaved as if they did. Still, the intensity with which they participated in the pharaoh's gigantic panegyric varied from period to period. In troubled times, the exaltation of personal merit and individualism prevailed. But when the monarchy was strong, loyalist proclamations blossomed on the monuments of private persons who could afford them, that is to say, the ruling class. In their autobiographies, they vaunted Pharaoh's perceptiveness and benevolence, and their largely rhetorical praise credited the pharaoh with elevating them from rags to riches. As though reciting a rosary, they intoned the favors they received from the sovereign, dissolving their pride in sycophantic behavior. Private inscriptions sometimes turned to overt thanksgiving ("I wish to adore Pharaoh, so great is his power"), to which readers were invited to associate themselves ("give praise to the king"), with extravagant praises taking the place of reasoned statements.

This loyalistic phraseology was rooted in the education given to the sons of the ruling elite. In fact, the pharaohs of the Twelfth Dynasty hired writers to produce works (the Loyalist Instruction, the Instruction of a Man for His Son) that took the form of wisdom texts and inculcated in students the notion that their conduct on earth should be loyalty and faithful service to the king. In such conduct, the noble found his honors, and the sons of the middle classes their prosperity, while the dissident was condemned to annihilation without burial. Though these works were dictated by the difficulties of the Twelfth Dynasty in imposing its legitimacy, they were still judged worthy of interest—that is to say, capable of producing loyal and docile subjects—in the New Kingdom.

See Middle Kingdom, Twelfth Dynasty.

Macedonian (Dynasty)

The name "Macedonian" is sometimes applied to the Argead dynasty, which must be distinguished from that of the Ptolemies, though both were of Macedonian origin. This Thirty-first Dynasty of Egypt consisted of three kings. The first was Alexander III of Macedonia (Alexander the Great), whom the Egyptians recognized as a legitimate universal lord, child of the creator god, a sovereign destined by the latter to rule the world, as was every pharaoh. This divine quality was automatically transmitted to his successors, his half brother, Philip Arrhidaeus (323–317 B.C.E.), and his posthumous son, Alexander Aigos (317–311 B.C.E.), who were called on to rule, if only nominally, Macedonia and the empire built by Alexander. "Pharaoh Alexander (I)" spent less than six months in Egypt. "Pharaoh Philip" and the second Pharaoh Alexander never visited the land; they were mere puppets dangling between Asia and Europe, hostages in the hands of the *diadochi* (successors), and were quickly eliminated. Philip, a mentally disabled youth, and Alexander II, a little boy, were depicted on the walls of Egyptian temples as adult, virile pharaohs making offerings to the gods. In those days, what was important was to inscribe the name of the predestined lord of the inhabited world.

See Alexander the Great, Ptolemy.

Memphis

Capital of the first nome of Lower Egypt, Memphis was located below the apex of the delta, about twelve miles from the modern city of Cairo, on the west bank of the Nile. The name Memphis derives from that of the pyramid of Pepy I: (*Meryre*)*-men-nefer,* "Meryre is enduring of beauty." The original name of Memphis, however, was *Ineb-hedj,* "the white wall." The urban area and its temple quarter, which was delimited by an enclosure wall, are located near (and under) the modern village of Mit Rahina. In the desert to the west, its immense cemetery area extends more than eighteen miles, from Abu Rawash in the north, via Giza, Zawyet el-Aryan, Abusir, and Saqqara, to Dahshur in the south.

The city owed its brilliant history to its strategic location at the junction of Upper and Lower Egypt; hence its epithet *Mekhat-tawy,* "balance of the Two Lands." Is it not in fact significant that Memphis was founded by Menes, the pharaoh who unified Egypt? Once their supremacy extended over all of Egypt, the kings of the Archaic Period, who were from Upper Egypt, wanted an administrative center from which they could easily manage the landed estates they established in Lower Egypt. Thus, they appointed high officials who resided in Memphis and whose tombs were located at Saqqara. As early as the Second Dynasty, certain kings were buried there. But it was with the Third Dynasty and the beginning of the Old Kingdom that Memphis was promoted to capital and official residence (*khenu*) of the pharaohs. Though the Twelfth Dynasty founded a new capital, Lisht, farther to the south, the political and strategic advantages of Memphis' location imposed themselves again in the New Kingdom, all the more so because Asia had become the prime objective of Egyptian imperialism. Thus, from the beginning of the Eighteenth Dynasty, the crown prince resided there; the pharaohs often stayed there, and it was there that Amenophis II was born. Haremhab made the city his principal residence. Though Ramesses II moved his capital to Pi-Riamsese in the eastern delta, Memphis would remain one of the principal cities throughout the New Kingdom. The city retained its prominence during the upheavals of the Third Intermediate Period and the Late Period. When pharaohs chose other cities as capital, they displayed special devotion to the temples and ceremonies of Memphis, and some of them (Bocchoris, Khababash) even reigned there.

Throughout all political fluctuations, Memphis weighed heavily in Egyptian history for three main reasons. First, a great deal of economic activity was concentrated there, not only around its temples and major cemeteries, but also in the city itself. Crafts, and especially metalworking, were an ancient tradition at Memphis, and in the New Kingdom the city had a large shipyard. The city's function as port commanding the complex network of Nile branches and canals in Lower Egypt was enlarged in the early Eighteenth Dynasty by the establishment of the port of Perunefer, where a large workforce from Asia was concentrated. This opening of Memphis to the outside world, and its resulting cosmopolitanism, were renewed in the reign of Amasis with the settling of Greek and Carian colonists there.

Throughout the history of Egypt, Memphis was also a center of culture, art, and intellectual activity. Its libraries, its temple laboratories, and its workshops preserved the manuals, treatises, canons, and know-how related to monuments that were regarded as sacred. If a part of Egypt was cut off from Memphis, it experienced a decline in artistic technique and hieroglyphic writing; this was especially the case during the Second Intermediate Period.

Finally, and especially, Memphis was the greatest religious center in the land. Its original god was Ptah, who was later associated in a triad with Sakhmet and Nefertem. Among the many other deities of the city were Hathor, "mistress of the sycamore"; Sokar, god of the necropolis, who was identified with Osiris; and the Apis bull, whose hypostases were buried in the Serapeum amid displays of popular fervor. Moreover, the great ceremonies that lent religious sanction to the kingship took place at Memphis; in this connection, it is revealing that annalistic tradition began the Hyksos domination with the coronation of Salitis in this city, and that Alexander the Great was crowned there. Furthermore, some pharaohs (Ramesses II, Ramesses III) chose to celebrate their jubilees at Memphis, or to locate funerary temples (Amenophis III, Shoshenq I) there, far from their burial places. In short, Memphis was the place par excellence of ideological legitimation.

That Memphis was the very essence of Egyptian civilization explains how the words "Copt" and "Egypt" derive from the Egyptian expression *Hut-ka-Ptah,* "mansion of the *ka* of Ptah," one of the ancient names of the city.

H. Kees, *Ancient Egypt: A Cultural Topography* (London, 1961), chapter 6.

Mendes

This brief name, the Greek version of the pronunciation *P-bended,* stands for a lengthy Egyptian toponym meaning "the house of the Ram, lord of Djedit"; the ancient name survives in that of the village of Tmaï el-Amdid. A city in the eastern delta, on a secondary branch of the Nile, Djedit is attested from as early as the Old Kingdom. Its patron god took the form of a ram (or, in later periods, a billy goat). From the Middle Kingdom on, he was considered to be a manifestation of Re and Osiris; later, he was believed to incarnate the four gods of the elements (Re/fire, Shu/air, Geb/earth, Osiris/water) and to be the driving force behind animal reproduction, "the male who covers the females." The latter function earned this local god a small place in the royal pantheon when Ramesses II boasted of having been engendered by him.

The city retained its prestige throughout the ages. It was the capital of a vigorous principality during the Libyan anarchy, and it was honored by the Saites (naos of Amasis). Its importance grew as military might and economic prosperity became concentrated in the north of the delta, and it gave Egypt its Twenty-ninth Dynasty.

See Mendesian (Dynasty).

Mendesian (Dynasty)

A military blow inaugurated the Twenty-ninth Dynasty, from Mendes. Amyrtaios of Sais, the sole king of the Twenty-eighth Dynasty, had driven the Persian garrisons out of nearly all of Egypt. A certain Nepherites of

Mendes (398–392 B.C.E.) overthrew him and completed the work of liberation. After the death of Nepherites, Psammuthis' succession to the throne was disputed by Hakoris; the latter became king, proclaiming himself "the chosen one of the Ram, lord of Mendes." His successor, Nepherites II, was in turn overthrown by General Nectanebo of Sebennytos (378 B.C.E.). The Mendesian dynasty's rise to power, its turmoil, and its fall undoubtedly reflected the undisciplined ambitions of the military leaders who held the principal cities of the delta in the wake of the expulsion of the Persians. Hakoris (390–386 B.C.E.) is the least badly known member of the dynasty, thanks notably to a small chapel at Karnak that he usurped from Psammuthis and where his Cypriot mercenaries left their signatures. Hakoris' foreign policy included the hiring of Greek soldiers, alliances with Hellenic cities and with the Pisidians, and interventions in Phoenicia and Salamis. In its efforts to preserve the land from reconquest by the Persians, the policy prefigured that of the Sebennytic dynasty.

See Mendes, Sebennytic (Dynasty).

Menes 2950 B.C.E., First Dynasty

From the New Kingdom on, Egyptian tradition (and later, the Greek authors who drew inspiration from it) held that the first pharaoh to rule over a unified Egypt was called Menes. This name has been sought in the documents from the First Dynasty, and there is indeed an attested name Men, which could be the origin of the Greek form Menes, but it occurs on a seal of Narmer and a tablet of Aha. Everything thus depends on the status of Men on these objects, and scholars have postulated identifications of both Narmer and Aha with Menes. The debate is highly technical, but it seems clear that Men is the name of a private person (a prince) on the seal of Narmer, while on the tablet of Aha, it is a royal name, perhaps that of a deceased king who was honored by his successor. It has been conjectured that the name Menes simply comes from the Egyptian word *men*, "so-and-so," a designation forged by tradition to evoke a king whose name had been forgotten.

Menes supposedly inaugurated dynastic history by founding Memphis and the cult of Ptah, a claim that nothing has invalidated. But because he was the first king, tradition also credited him with cultural inventions (writing) and religious innovations. Either ignorance or the desire to justify a local tradition by assigning it a prestigious founder surely played a role in this tendency.

Manetho records that Menes was killed by a hippopotamus. Though we cannot be certain of the accuracy of this claim, we can note that there are mentions of hippopotamus hunting in the annals of the kings of the Archaic Period.

W. B. Emery, *Archaic Egypt* (Baltimore, 1961), pp. 32–37.
See Archaic (Period), Narmer.

Mentuhotpe Eleventh and Thirteenth Dynasties

Like the name Inyotef, the name Montuhotpe was borne both by pharaohs of the Eleventh Dynasty and by pharaohs of the end of the Middle Kingdom and the Second Intermediate Period.

ELEVENTH DYNASTY

Mentuhotpe I (2130 B.C.E.) did not actually reign, but posterity counted him among the pharaohs because he was the father of the first two kings of the Eleventh Dynasty, Inyotef I and Inyotef II. His Horus name "Ancestor" clearly hints that his titulary was concocted after his death.

Mentuhotpe II (throne name Nebhepetre), son of Inyotef III, reigned from 2059 to 2009. During his reign, he achieved a decisive victory over the dynasty of Herakleopolis, reunifying Egypt and thus putting an end to the First Intermediate Period and inaugurating the Middle Kingdom. The exact date of this reunification is uncertain; it seems to have been a bit earlier than year 39 of his reign, no doubt around 2022 B.C.E. The king marked the event by adopting a new Horus name, "He who reunites the Two Lands," and by making certain changes in the writing of his throne name, Nebhepetre. With Egypt once again unified, and with the borders secured by operations in Nubia, Mentuhotpe proceeded to the restoration of the temples of Upper Egypt, at such sites as Gebelein, Tod, Hermonthis, Dendara, and Abydos. To accomplish this restoration, and to assure the functioning of the cults, he sent numerous expeditions to the mines and quarries (in Hatnub, Wadi Hammamat, Aswan, and Nubia) and to exotic trading centers (Punt and the Syro-Lebanese coast). When the reunification made it possible for him to do so, he also drew on Memphite cultural tradition, which was undoubtedly the reason for changes in the original concept of his funerary temple at Deir el-Bahari. Located at the foot of the cliff there, the temple consisted of a terrace that stood at the far end of a causeway connecting it to the king's valley temple. On the terrace, there was an edifice surrounded on three sides by a columned ambulatory, and atop the edifice was a construction representing the mound on which the sun rose when the world was created. Integrated into the temple were six burial places for women of the royal family. At a short distance from the cliff, the king honored sixty of his soldiers who had fallen in battle with a collective burial.

Mentuhotpe III (throne name Sankhkare) reigned from 2009 B.C.E. until 1997 B.C.E. The son of Mentuhotpe II, he pursued his father's policy of restoring the temples; he was active at Hermonthis and Abydos, and he dispatched an expedition to Punt. He planned a funerary temple at Deir el-Bahari, not far from that of his father, but he died before it was completed.

Mentuhotpe IV (throne name Nebtawyre) reigned from 1997 to 1991 B.C.E. Egyptian annalistic tradition did not recognize this pharaoh, though monuments clearly indicate that he did indeed rule for at least two years. But Egypt was soon caught up in a civil war, which the vizier Amenemhet ended by founding the Twelfth Dynasty.

THIRTEENTH DYNASTY

At least three pharaohs of the Thirteenth Dynasty bore the name Mentuhotpe. We know practically nothing about two of them. The third, Mentuhotepi (throne name Sankhenre), has been placed in the Seventeenth Dynasty, but it is more likely that he ruled at the end of the Thirteenth Dynasty, when weak Theban pharaohs bowed before the Hyksos advance. A stela of this king seems to allude to campaigns he conducted against the Hyksos.

See First Intermediate Period, Second Intermediate Period.

Merneptah 1213–1204 B.C.E., Nineteenth Dynasty

Thirteenth son of Ramesses II and his chief wife, Isetnofret, he ascended the throne at an already advanced age and ruled for only eight years. His accomplishments obviously cannot be compared with those of his father, but his legacy is reflected in his funerary temple and his tomb at Thebes, a palace and work at the temple of Ptah in Memphis, and rock-cut chapels at el-Siririya and Gebel el-Silsila. In addition, his name is to be found added to the walls of earlier monuments at many sites in Egypt. The events of Merneptah's reign show that Egypt's military might and external security had diminished during the final years of Ramesses' reign.

In year 5 of Merneptah, the powerful Libu tribe, assisted by the related Meshwesh and Kehek and by contingents of pirates from the Aegean, moved eastward. As they headed toward Memphis, the invaders were stopped at Perire on the edge of the delta, at the price of a hard battle. The Libu chief was deposed, and the booty in arms, captives, and cattle was considerable. Merneptah also had to suppress a serious insurrection in Lower Nubia.

To assure a continued Egyptian presence in Palestine, actions were carried out against three Canaanite cities, Askalon, Gezer, and Yenoham, and against the people of Israel. One of the inscriptions lauding the victory over the Libyans and briefly mentioning these interventions in Asia is the only Egyptian text containing the word Israel, which is by far the most ancient mention of this name. This "Israel Stela" has contributed to the fame of Merneptah, but contrary to a distressingly persistent old idea, this king cannot be considered as the pharaoh under whom the Exodus took place. Merneptah's mummy was found in the cachette in the tomb of Amenophis II.

C. Lalouette, *La Gloire des Ramsès* (Paris, 1985), pp. 265–95.
See Libyans, Nineteenth Dynasty.

Meroe

"Meroe" is the Greek transcription of the Sudanese term *Merua,* the name of the capital of the kingdom of Kush (which the Greeks called "Ethiopia") between 550 B.C.E. and 350 C.E. It was located slightly downstream from present-day Shendi in the Butana steppe, above the confluence of the Nile and the Atbara. From the end of the eighth century B.C.E. on, the region was part of the Egypto-Nubian empire of Napata. Meroe seems to have been one of the residences of the sovereign of Kush at the beginning of the sixth century B.C.E. The transfer of the principal seat of the kingship from Napata to this southern city took place at the end of the same century, according to Herodotus, but the royal cemetery was not shifted from Nuri (near Napata) to Meroe until around 300 B.C.E.

The reasons the Sudanese kingdom shifted its center upstream could have been strategic (the threat posed by the Saites, and then by the Persians) or, more likely, economic and demographic (settlement of the populations of the Sahel at a crossroads between the Red Sea, the upper Nile, and Chad). In any case, it led to the growth of important cities in the Butana, to something of a start of iron working (slag heaps at Meroe, whose pan-African importance cannot be exaggerated), and to the extension of agriculture (retention basins for rainwater at the mouths of the large wadis).

A new civilization took form and spread, combining the native and the Egyptian heritages and taking in luxury products and even influences from the Hellenized world. Its governance was characterized by the moral influence of the god Amun (and sometimes his priests) and the eminent position of the mothers and wives of the king, the Candaces, which is so apparent in the temples and the cemeteries. There was sometimes a veritable coregency of the pharaoh (Meroitic: *kor*) and the queen (Meroitic: *ketke*), but there was no matriarchal devolvement of the throne, as a long-fashionable theory once held, much less an exclusively female dynasty, as the Romans believed.

The sanctuaries of Amun throughout the realm (Napata, Sanam, Kawa, Pnubs, Amara) received solemn visits from the sovereigns, who considerably embellished them. Osiris, Isis, and Anubis were still the gods of the dead, but temples were built for certain strictly Meroitic deities, such as Apedemak and Sbomeker. Small, elegant (but rather steep) pyramids of queens, princes, and kings filled the vast cemeteries of Meroe (and Sedeinga), while temples large and small multiplied in the Butana, at Meroe itself, and at Basa, Wad Ban Naqa, and Musawwarat el-Sufra. The images of deities and sovereigns were inspired by Egyptian style, and their repertoire of ritual poses and attributes on the whole conformed to Egypto-Kushite prototypes (double uraeus, rams of Amun). But the extravagant clothing, the enormous and baroque items of jewelry, and in particular, the fleshy corpulence of the human figures make for an original style of relief sculpture that can be called "Meroitic." Relations continued to be close between the Kushite clergy and that of contemporary Egypt, as shown by Ptolemaic-style hymns to the gods. The most surprising innovation was the creation, in the second century B.C.E. at the latest, of an alphabet for writing the Sudanese language. The alphabet has been deciphered, and the structures of the language have been to some extent elucidated, but its relationship to the modern tongues of the region is hotly debated. The alphabet borrowed its principle from the Greek writing system, but its twenty-three signs are Egyptian; it had both a monumental (hieroglyphic) form and a cursive (Demotic) version.

In the Ptolemaic Period, the northern boundary of the Meroitic realm lay between the Third and the Second Cataracts. But north of the uninhabited regions, some kings, such as Ergamenes, exercised a sort of religious condominium that extended as far as the ramparts of Lagide Egypt, as evidenced at the temples of el-Dakka, Dabod, and Philae; they also installed Kushite garrisons in some locales downstream from Wadi Halfa (Primis). Meroe reached its apogee around the turn of the era, in the time of King Ketakamani and Candace Amanitere. It was scarcely troubled by a military clash with Rome, which had recently become mistress of Egypt: in 23 B.C.E., the Kushites took Philae, and the Romans launched a retaliatory raid that pushed south as far as Napata. The frontier was finally fixed at el-Maharraqa, where it had been under the Ptolemies.

Defeated in warfare, the Kushites took their revenge. During the second and third centuries of our own era, Lower Nubia was intensively resettled, and agriculture was resumed there. The inhabitants adopted the language and culture of Meroe and declared themselves vassals of the distant sovereign of the south, as did the priests of Isis on the island of Philae. During the fourth century, the settlements of the Butana somehow fell under the blows of the Nuba and the Axumites, while the Ballana culture of Lower Nubia collapsed in the wake of raids by the Blemmyes of the eastern desert. The last pagan rulers of Lower Nubia, who were contemporary with the first Byzantine emperors, were buried with jewel-encrusted silver crowns similar to those of the kings of Meroe; these crowns were the final manifestations of pharaonic iconography.

W. Y. Adams, *Nubia: Corridor to Africa* (London, 1977), pp. 294–429; *Histoire générale de l'Afrique*, vol. 2: *Afrique ancienne* (UNESCO, 1980), pp. 295–346.

See Kush.

Merykare c. 2090 B.C.E., Tenth Dynasty

Merykare was a pharaoh of the second half of the Tenth Dynasty. Aside from other mentions, he is known from a text, the Instruction for Merykare, that was addressed to him by his father, who might have been a king named Khety. The poor quality and the lacunae of the preserved manuscripts are all the more to be regretted in that the work is exceptional. It is less one of those many pedestrian and conformist wisdom texts that have come down to us from pharaonic Egypt than an authentic treatise on governance. It contains pieces of political advice based on the royal author's personal experience and is thus an assessment of his reign. The author also admits his own errors, such as the sack of Abydos by his victorious troops. He advocates peaceful coexistence with the south—that is, with the Theban principality—and more generally, humane and even benevolent conduct toward ordinary mortals, his subjects. Because the creator god watches over the world order that he instituted, he doles out just deserts for human actions, even the pharaoh's. This work is undoubtedly apocryphal: Merykare ascribed his own ideas to his father to lend prestigious support to the new policy he intended to carry out.

M. Lichtheim, *Ancient Egyptian Literature: A Book of Readings*, vol. 1: *The Old and Middle Kingdoms* (Berkeley, 1973), pp. 97–109.

See First Intermediate Period, Ninth and Tenth Dynasties.

Metjen

Metjen was a high official whose career spanned the end of the Third and the beginning of the Fourth Dynasty; he is famous for the inscriptions in his tomb at Saqqara, which are undoubtedly the earliest private inscriptions with autobiographical content. They consist of a series of excerpts from official documents confirming Metjen's promotions and the revenues attached to them during his career as an administrator of royal domains in Lower and Middle Egypt. The emphasis is mostly on the estates or the sources of income that could be used to set up and provision his funerary cult. Thus, the content of what can be called the most ancient autobiography from pharaonic Egypt was already conditioned by the nature of the monument in which it was located—the tomb.

A. Roccati, *La Littérature historique sous l'Ancient Empire égyptien* (Paris, 1982), pp. 82–88.

See Autobiography.

Middle Kingdom

Scholars agree in beginning the Middle Kingdom with the reunification of Egypt under Mentuhotpe II (2022 B.C.E.). But although there is no consensus as to the date when it ended, it is reasonable to consider the Hyksos capture of Memphis (1650 B.C.E.) as marking its end and the beginning of the Second Intermediate Period. The event is all the more significant in that it led to a clean break in monumental style. Thus defined, the Middle Kingdom includes:

the end of the Eleventh Dynasty
the Twelfth Dynasty
most of the Thirteenth Dynasty, down to the pharaohs who lost Memphis
the Fourteenth Dynasty, which in fact includes two realms that were partly concurrent with the Thirteenth Dynasty

It was thus a period of more than 350 years, and it contributed much to Egyptian civilization.

First, a reorganization of the habitable environment occurred. Internally, careful planning led to the reclamation of part of the Faiyum, which had been covered with marshes and thus devoted solely to the pleasures of fishing and fowling (which is the title of a literary work of the Middle Kingdom). Compared with that of the Old Kingdom, foreign policy changed in scope. To the south, the valley of Lower Nubia was integrated into the territory of Egypt. To the north, traditional relations with Byblos intensified to the point that the local rulers were Egyptianized. The world of Syria-Palestine ceased to be confined to the role of an exotic trinket and initiated a dialogue with Egyptian civilization, if only via a massive influx of Asiatic immigrants beginning in the Twelfth Dynasty; the Middle Kingdom sowed the seeds of the New Kingdom expansion into Asia. Finally, Egypt also had trade relations with the Mediterranean world (Cyprus, the Aegean).

A restructuring of society also occurred. With the reform of the royal administration, there was a qualitative leap that entailed the end of "regional feudalism." The literate elite increased, and correlatively, a petty bourgeoisie arose that managed to acquire what had been a privilege of the upper ruling class, the setting up of inscribed votive monuments. In a parallel development, since the funerary beliefs that centered on Osiris were widespread in Egypt, this god's city of Abydos became an enormous religious metropolis where pilgrims and travelers came to leave ex-votos, and the city's political influence increased accordingly.

The new distribution of centers of influence also saw the rise of Thebes, which was either the capital of the Eleventh Dynasty or simply its city of origin. Patronized by the pharaohs of the Twelfth and Thirteenth Dynasties, Thebes played an influential role in politics and ideology from that time on. Administrators of Theban origin rose to high office, the domains of its temples were enlarged, and during the Twelfth Dynasty, one of its deities, Amun, took on national dimensions.

By synthesizing the legacy of the Old Kingdom and what had been gained from historical evolution, the Middle Kingdom founded a new classicism that would serve as a model, and even a cultural and artistic norm, at the beginning of the Eighteenth Dynasty and in the Saite Period. Even so, the vestiges of the Middle Kingdom seem far less impressive than those of the Old Kingdom: of the pyramids of the Twelfth Dynasty, there remain only the unattractive masses of their mud brick fill, for their limestone casings have long since been removed. The funerary temple of Mentuhotpe II cuts a poor figure because of the destruction it has experienced, but Hatshepsut drew inspiration from it in building her own. Yet the Middle Kingdom has left us some masterpieces, such as the White Chapel of Senwosret I at Karnak. Moreover, the Middle Kingdom introduced certain innovations, such as block statues (see figure 5), and in particular, it invested portraiture with a sense of individualization, which the Late Period would again exploit.

But it was especially in literature that the Middle Kingdom produced classics that would become constitutive of Egyptian culture. The Middle Kingdom breathed new air into an old genre, such as wisdom texts, by putting it in the service of political commitment (e.g., Loyalist Instruction, Instruction of Khety, Instruction of Amenemhet I). It drew on the horrors of the First Intermediate Period to nourish the so-called pessimistic litera-

FIGURE 5. *Block statue of Yamunedjeh. Dynasty 18. Luxor Museum. Photo by Nancy J. Corbin.*

ture, with its highly original tone: the Dispute between a Man and His *Ba,* the Admonitions of Ipuwer, and the Complaints of Khakheperresonb. The literature of the Middle Kingdom abounds in works of various sorts: poems, like the Hymn to the Nile, and rhetoric, like the Tale of the Eloquent Peasant. And it shines most radiantly in works of narrative fiction like the Tale of the Shipwrecked Sailor and especially the Story of Sinuhe, which might be one of the masterpieces of world literature.

M. Lichtheim, *Ancient Egyptian Literature: A Book of Readings,* vol. 1: *The Old and Middle Kingdoms* (Berkeley, 1973); D. Wildung, *De l'Âge d'or de l'Égypte: Le Moyen Empire* (Fribourg, 1984).

See Amenemhet, Ankhu, Eleventh Dynasty, Inyotefoqer, Senwosret, Sinuhe, Thirteenth Dynasty, Twelfth Dynasty.

Mycerinus (*or* Menkaure)

2480–2462 B.C.E., Fourth Dynasty

Son of Chephren, Mycerinus established his legitimacy only after turning back challenges from other pretenders who perhaps ruled contemporaneously with him. Of his activity as pharaoh, there remains essentially the third pyramid of Giza. It was much smaller (height 218 feet, length 354 feet at the base) than the other two, but sumptuously conceived, for it was intended to be covered with a casing of granite, of which only the lower courses remain.

Dyads and triads also remain, our earliest examples of group statues. They depict the king accompanied by his queen or by a goddess and a personification of a nome. Mycerinus' tomb was restored in the Twenty-sixth Dynasty.

See the bibliography of the entry Cheops.

See Fourth Dynasty.

Napata

Napata is the name, Sudanese in origin, of a territory in which present-day Kareima is located, in a zone where the Nile flows from north to south, slightly downstream from the Fourth Cataract. This territory includes several magnificent sites: Gebel Barkal, Sanam, and the cemeteries of el-Kurru and Nuri. At the foot of the enormous butte of Gebel Barkal (which the ancient Egyptians called the "Pure Mountain"), the Eighteenth Dynasty founded a temple to "Amun, lord of the thrones of the Two Lands," which the Ramessides then embellished; finds at the site include stelae of Tuthmosis III and Sethos I, as well as lions and sphinxes of Amenophis III. Dedicated to the premier patron of the Theban monarchy, Napata marked the southernmost point of his expansion into Kushite territory.

At some point after the withdrawal of the Egyptian administration toward the end of the Twentieth Dynasty, the region became the seat of an obscure native principality. The tombs of thirteen chiefs, whose burials were of Sudanese type—recumbent on a bed (and not in a coffin) under circular tumuli—have been excavated at el-Kurru. The material found in them reveals the loss and then the resumption of communications with Egypt, and the historical sequel suggests a continuity of the local cult of Amun. During the eighth century B.C.E., under Kashta and Piye, this dynasty of Napata extended its domination north of the First Cataract, assumed the attributes of pharaohs, gave Egypt its Twenty-fifth (Kushite) Dynasty, and Egyptianized its homeland.

Piye and then Taharqa lavishly embellished the temples of Amun at the foot of Gebel Barkal, from which we have stelae of the former king and beautiful effigies of the latter. At Sanam on the left bank of the river, Taharqa founded a city and a temple dedicated to "Amun, bull of Nubia." At el-Kurru, and then at Nuri, where the pyramid of Taharqa was the center of a new royal cemetery, the tombs of kings and queens took the form of pyramids endowed with funerary texts, sarcophagi, shawabtis (funerary figurines), and other typically Egyptian means of survival in the afterlife. This Egyptianization and the monumental use of the Egyptian language would continue after the loss of Egypt, when a second dynasty of Napata continued to dominate the Sudan: from about 650 to 300 B.C.E., a good twenty kings were buried at Nuri. Until the fourth century B.C.E., an evolved form of Late Egyptian served to write official inscriptions.

Amun, whose temple of Barkal would preserve statues bearing important inscriptions of Atlanarsa, Senkamanisen, Harsiotef, and Sastesen, remained the patron of the monarchy, even after the capital was moved to Meroe. The Meroitic kings traveled to Napata to receive the insignia of their power; two pyramid fields behind the Pure Mountain date to their era. In 23 B.C.E., the Romans drove the Kushites out of Lower Nubia and sacked Napata.

W.Y. Adams, *Nubia: Corridor to Africa* (London, 1977), pp. 246–93.
See Kush, Kushite (Dynasty).

Narmer c. 3000 B.C.E.

The name of this king occurs on a fairly large number of objects, some of them as far away as Palestine (where they were evidently taken as trade goods). His schist palette, the fame of which is deserved both for the perfection of its style and the interest of its decoration, evokes a victory over what seems to be a people dwelling in the marshes, perhaps in Lower Egypt; but does it commemorate an actual event, or is it a theme that had already become conventional? In any case, Narmer alternately wears the crowns that were those of Upper and Lower Egypt in the historical period. Otherwise, not only are the composition and the themes pharaonic, as on the mace head of King Scorpion, but the name of the king is also enclosed in a representation of a palace façade, according to a usage attested earlier but that would now become standard. Many scholars have identified Narmer with Menes, the first pharaoh, in particular because the two names are associated on a seal, though in a manner that offers no assurance that only one person is involved. Those who reject this identification do not deny that Narmer was at least the immediate predecessor of the first pharaoh.

See Menes, Scorpion.

Necho II 610–595 B.C.E., Twenty-sixth Dynasty

Though rather few monuments of his reign have survived, the Bible and Herodotus inform us of a number of spectacular events during his reign. By sending contingents to the Euphrates, he tried in vain to prevent the Babylonians from putting an end to Assyria and expanding into Syria. In the course of an operation that he led personally, he crushed the pious King Josiah of Judah at the Battle of Megiddo. For three years, Egypt dominated Palestine, Phoenicia, and Syria, as it had under Tuthmosis III, but Necho's army was defeated at Carchemish by Nebuchadnezzar, who extended the Babylonian empire as far as the border of Egypt. According to Herodotus, Necho (otherwise called Necôs) undertook the digging of a canal connecting the Nile to the Red Sea (which archaeology seems to confirm), but he supposedly did not complete this undertaking. He is also said to have dispatched a Phoenician fleet to the Red Sea, which, via a lengthy, coast-hugging journey, circumnavigated Africa—a fine tale of exploration that is undoubtedly a fable. This pharaoh, who resolutely opened Saite Egypt to the outside world, seems to have encountered opposition: his name was erased in many of his inscriptions.

Herodotus, *Histories,* book 2, 158–59 and book 4, 42; see A. de Sélincourt, *Herodotus: The Histories,* rev. ed. (Harmondsworth, Middlesex, 1972), pp. 193 and 283–84.

See Saite (Dynasties).

Nectanebo Thirtieth Dynasty

By habitually using this Greek name, Egyptologists confuse two different Egyptian names: Nakhtnebef (Greek Nectenebes), which was the name of the founder of the Thirtieth Dynasty, and Nakhtharemhebit (Greek Nectanabo), which was that of his grandson. The former (378–360 B.C.E.) donated a tenth of the imports and products of the Greek trading city of Naukratis to the temple of Neith at Sais. The intense resumption of architectural activity in the temples, from Philae in the south to Behbeit and Tanis in the north, illustrates the material wealth of the land and indicates a deliberate policy of recourse to divine providence. Stopped by the fortifications of Pelusium, a Persian attack perished in the flooded marshes of the Mendesian branch of the Nile: Egypt was saved for a quarter of a century. The works of Nectanebo II (359–341 B.C.E.), who deposed his uncle Teos, were comparable in number to those of his grandfather. His confrontation with the Great King Artaxerxes III, who tried from 351 B.C.E. on to reconquer Egypt, ended in a Persian victory and invasion. The Egyptian king managed to remain in Upper Egypt for eighteen months before taking refuge in Nubia.

In truth, we do not know the ultimate fate of this last great sovereign of native blood, who became the stuff of legend. National pride was pleased to recount that this king, a magician disguised as a god, actually procreated Alexander the Great. Under the Ptolemies, Egyptians continued to adore the beautiful falcon statues that he had caused to be carved in order to assimilate him to the god Horus. The magnificent sarcophagus that Nectanebo II had prepared for his burial was found in Alexandria, where until recently it passed in local folklore for the tomb of Alexander.

See Sebennytic (Dynasty).

Neferhotep I 1740–1730 B.C.E., Thirteenth Dynasty

Neferhotep I (throne name Khasekhemre) was the twenty-first king of the Thirteenth Dynasty. Of common origin—his grandfather was a mere militiaman—he managed to remain on the throne for eleven years and to establish the legitimacy of his line firmly enough that his two brothers, Sihathor and Sebekhotpe IV, were also able to assume the crown. He paid special attention to Abydos, the holy city of Osiris, putting the temple there back in order and reorganizing its ceremonies to conform with tradition as recorded in the sacred archives. At Byblos, the Egyptianized local dynasty continued to pledge him its allegiance. His reputation made him so significant a symbol that later, the Hyksos took the trouble to mutilate his images on consecrated objects that they appropriated in the course of their conquest.

See Hyksos, Sebekhotpe, Thirteenth Dynasty.

Neferirkare Kakai 2433–2414 B.C.E., Fifth Dynasty

Third king of the Fifth Dynasty, Neferirkare built a sun temple, the exact location of which remains unknown. He also built a funerary complex with a pyramid (height 226 feet) that was completed by his successor. Neferirkare owes his fame in particular to the hazards of discovery: archaeologists found part of the archives reflecting the activity of his funerary temple during the Fifth and Sixth Dynasties. These documents have proven to be a windfall for Egyptologists, providing insights into the organization and functioning of these funerary temples (lists of rituals, inventories of temple furnishings, accounts of income, receipts for allocations, etc.), which had earlier been known only from archaeological remains and titles borne by individuals.

See Fifth Dynasty, Khentkaus, Ptahwash.

Nefertiti

Nefertiti was the wife of Amenophis IV/Akhenaten, to whom she bore six daughters. She had her name preceded by the qualifier *Nefer-neferu-aten,* designating her as the one in whom "the perfections of the sun disk are perfected." She formed a sort of triad with her husband and the Aten, who was depicted bestowing his blessings. Charming details in the Aten temples of Thebes, and in particular, in the private tombs of Amarna, bring the tender relationship of the royal couple to life. In a bizarre twist, however, artists endowed the queen and her daughters with anatomy that was identical to that of Akhenaten. But the busts discovered at Amarna, the quartzite trial pieces, and the famous polychrome bust now in Berlin (for some reason, it has only one eye) reproduce a marvelous visage. This beauty, along with Nefertiti's close association with the world's first monotheistic prophet, have made her a renowned figure. Her actual personality is as unknown as her symbolic function is striking: she was the terrestrial incarnation of the feminine aspect of the divine creation.

See Amenophis IV, Queens.

Nekhebu

Nekhebu, who was also called Merptahankhmeryre, belonged to a family of overseers of construction works who were active during the Fifth and Sixth Dynasties; their family tomb complex was constructed at Giza, west of the pyramid of Cheops. In his rather detailed autobiography, Nekhebu recounts how, after completing his apprenticeship and making his way up the hierarchy in the shadow of his brother, he became overseer of all works and acquitted himself brilliantly in challenging assignments entrusted to him by Pepy II. These projects included the construction of royal *ka*-chapels in Lower Egypt—which necessitated a difficult procurement of wood for carpentry—the digging of canals in the region of Chemmis (at the marshy edge of the seashore) and in the region of Cusae (in Middle Egypt), and the construction of royal monuments at Heliopolis. His activities took Nekhebu as far as the quarries of Wadi Hammamat, where his name occurs in graffiti.

A. Roccati, *La Littérature historique sous l'Ancien Empire égyptien* (Paris, 1982), p. 181.

Neuserre Ini 2407–2384 B.C.E.

This pharaoh of the Fifth Dynasty built a pyramid (height 170 feet) at Abusir and a sun temple not far from there, at Abu Ghurab. Bas-reliefs decorating certain parts of the latter represent the *sed*-festival, a sort of royal jubilee. Other reliefs depict his era's doctrine of nature; thus, the "chamber of the world" is devoted to the three seasons of the year (inundation, winter, and summer). In each case the art depicts the life forms with which the god Re had filled Egypt: the growth of vegetation, animal reproduction and habits, and human activities. Today very much damaged, these bas-reliefs demonstrate the Egyptians' keen sense of observation: they even noted the annual migration of mullets from the brackish water of the marshes along the seashore to the fresh water of the First Cataract at Elephantine. Various indications suggest that the reign of Neuserre Ini was the culminating point of the Fifth Dynasty.

See Fifth Dynasty.

Nile

The Nile was called *iteru* (the pronunciation changed over time to *ior*), a word that could be applied to any permanent river. The plural form of the word, *na-iore,* which designated the branches that flow through the delta, was probably the origin of Greek *Neilos* and Latin *Nilus.* Surprisingly, the Nile played no central role in political theology. In the New Kingdom, the famous Hymn to the Nile lent choice expression to popular fervor, but it did not derive from official rituals, and there was scarcely any true religion of the Nile prior to the Greco-Roman Period. The ancient Egyptians did not deify the watercourse itself, but rather Hapy, the mysterious subterranean being whose dynamism manifested itself once each year, when the waters rose. Hapy, who was consubstantial with Nun, the primordial waters, was depicted with the appearance common to fecundity figures—a god dressed in the short loincloth of a fisherman and endowed with a bloated belly and pendulous breasts. Two habitats were ascribed to this god, from which he was thought to gush forth at the beginning of each year: one was at the apex of the delta, at the locale of present-day Old Cairo, and the other was near Elephantine. The cult of this cosmic figure remained localized, and as an auxiliary to major deities, Hapy was a relatively minor figure in temple iconographies.

Some misconceptions about the Nile persist. Though the rapid development of a high culture in Egypt was undeniably conditioned by the fertility of the silt-laden valley, which was renewed annually by its river, the birth of the pharaonic state did not result from any necessity for collective management of the distribution of the water. The earliest evidence for irrigation by means of basins—the result of desiccation—dates to around 2000 B.C.E., long after the Old Kingdom and the mighty builders of the pyramids.

The pharaoh was not a magician who brought the inundation, like rain-making sorcerers, nor even a direct mediator between the river and those who worked the land. Hapy's activity resulted from the providential will of a supreme deity. The arrival of the flood was the manifestation of a regular order assured by ritual acts performed for the gods, in particular, libation offerings of nourishing, purifying water. Bad years were one of several aspects of a disorder that resulted from subversion, ignorance, or negligence. In fact, kings displayed little concern for the Nile itself, though there were offerings to Hapy at Gebel el-Silsila and Heliopolis. The kings took practical steps, and they also rendered thanks to Amun at the arrival of a desirable inundation or of one that was high but did not cause much damage. Only one pharaoh mentioned Hapy in his official titulary: Siptah, whose Horus name proclaimed him "beloved of Hapy."

Pharaonic ideology was solar, as well as Horian (that is, political), but not hydraulic.

Nineteenth Dynasty

Conventionally counted as the last king of the Eighteenth Dynasty, the general Haremhab, who restored the traditional order after the Amarna heresy, designated his colleague Ramesses as his successor. This Ramesses I (1293–1291 B.C.E.) established the family line of the first Ramesside dynasty, whose history was divided into two contrasting phases: a "golden age" and a period of internal conflicts. The former is attested by a huge number of temples, tombs, and inscriptions; the latter is revealed especially by the mutilation of cartouches and by scanty monumental production during a period of about twenty years.

FIRST PHASE

Sethos I (1291–1279) and Ramesses II (1279–1213) maintained an Egyptian hegemony in Asia. From the Fourth Cataract to the region of Damascus, their empire was filled with their religious foundations. Merneptah (1213–1204) beat back the Libyans and maintained his rule over Palestine. This period was characterized by a growing number of courtiers and soldiers of foreign origin; by the development of the delta; by an economic structure that was partly in the hands of the temples, whose clergies remained under royal control; by the exaltation of the "Ramesside triad" of Amun of Thebes, Re of Heliopolis, and Ptah of Memphis, along with the worship of Seth, the patron god of the royal family; and by the ostentatious cult of the sovereign incarnate in colossi. With his architectural gigantism and epigraphic prolixity, Ramesses the Great created a style of power and renewed literature and the arts.

SECOND PHASE

Sethos II (1204–1198 B.C.E.), son of Merneptah, was challenged by the usurper Amenmesse. Sethos' son, the infirm Siptah (1198–1192 B.C.E.), reigned under the tutelage of the dowager queen Twosre, who, like Hatshepsut before her, assumed the royal office (1192–1190 B.C.E.), and of the great treasurer Bay. "Many years without a chief," and then "empty years": thirty-three years later, a history writer would describe this brief intermediate period somewhat bombastically as one during which Egypt, lacking decisive authority, passed into the hands of dignitaries and local leaders. A "self-made" Syrian (Bay, or an imitator) managed to install himself as a potentate, governing the land while his minions engaged in plunder. The gods were treated no better than the people, and the temples were stripped of their revenues. Later king lists would mention no monarch between Sethos II and Sethnakhte, the founder of the Twentieth Dynasty.

All the kings of the Nineteenth Dynasty had rock-cut tombs prepared for themselves in the Valley of the Kings. Thebes remained the capital of the empire, but Memphis and Pi-Riamsese shared the functions of royal seat and administrative center.

C. Lalouette, *L'Empire des Ramsès* (Paris, 1985).

See Pi-Riamsese, Ramesses II, Ramessides, Sethos I, Twosre.

Ninth and Tenth Dynasties

The capital of these two dynasties was Herakleopolis Magna, a city in Middle Egypt, located south of the oasis of the Faiyum; it was otherwise capital of the twentieth nome of Upper Egypt. The Ninth Dynasty was founded by a pharaoh named Khety, the Achthoes of Greek tradition, which depicted him as a cruel tyrant who was devoured by a crocodile. Besides this king, there were three others, one whose name remains unknown, a Neferkare who is mentioned in the tomb of the nomarch Ankhtifi, and a third, Khety II. The dynasty seems to have extended over several generations, to judge by the genealogies of contemporary high officials (2130–2090 B.C.E.), and it appears to have claimed sovereignty, albeit a nominal one, over all of Egypt.

The reasons for the dynastic change from the Ninth to the Tenth Dynasty are obscure, all the more so in that the names of the kings suggest continuity, while the Egyptians used a single term, "the house of Khety," to designate them. We cannot exclude the possibility that Manetho's division of the pharaohs of Herakleopolis into two dynasties resulted from a reinterpretation of the list of Egyptian kings. Whatever the case, the Tenth Dynasty consisted of fourteen pharaohs, whose names are mostly unknown to us and whose reigns were mostly quite brief (2090–2022 B.C.E.). From this overall anonymity emerge a Neferkare, a Khety, and especially a Merykare, whose father addressed a famous instruction to him. Unlike the Ninth Dynasty, the Tenth Dynasty no longer pretended to control the entire land, and it recognized the existence of the rival dynasty of Thebes in Upper Egypt. The region of Abydos and Thinis, which was lost and reconquered by turns, was the frontier zone between the two kingdoms. The Tenth Dynasty drew inspiration from the tradition of the Old Kingdom, for it had control of Memphis, the home of that tradition. In fact, Merykare seems to have erected his pyramid at Saqqara. In the delta, the dynasty seems to have maintained its borders against the Asiatics. It preserved the cultural heritage of the Old Kingdom reasonably well, to the point that after their victory, the Theban pharaohs called on artists and bureaucrats from the defeated kingdom.

See Ankhtifi, Eleventh Dynasty, First Intermediate Period, Merykare.

Nitocris

Nitocris, the Greek form of Neithiqerty, is the name of a queen who became pharaoh at the end of the Sixth Dynasty, as was later also the case with Nefrusobk, Hatshepsut, and Twosre. She supposedly reigned either six or twelve years. Manetho credits her with building the third pyramid (that of Mycerinus), undoubtedly because she did significant repair work on it. In fact, we have no monument bearing the name of Nitocris. She was known for having an especially clear complexion and for avenging the assassination of her brother by drowning his murderers in the room where they were feasting. The latter anecdote probably reflects the struggles over the succession that ruined the monarchy during the troubled times at the end of the Sixth Dynasty.

A. de Sélincourt, *Herodotus: The Histories,* rev. ed. (Harmondsworth, Middlesex, 1972), p. 166.

See Sixth Dynasty.

Nubia

The term Nubia is applied to the territory stretching south from the First Cataract of the Nile, at Aswan, to the region of Dongola, or even beyond the Fourth Cataract; in our own day, this territory is divided between the Arab Republic of Egypt and the Republic of the Sudan. In Nubia, the Nile made its way through a narrow valley with little cultivable area, except in Dongola; navigation was difficult because of the cataracts, and it was sometimes necessary to avoid these obstacles by transporting boats overland using slides. On each side of the narrow valley were desert plateaus, but in the western desert, there were oases (Dunqul, Selima) that were linked to the oases of Egypt by caravan trails.

Throughout the pharaonic period, Nubia was a constant preoccupation for Egypt. This was true, first, for reasons of security: protection was needed against potential incursions by various Nubian peoples. There were economic reasons as well; in itself, or as an access route to the interior of Africa, Nubia offered many resources: cattle (goats and cows), ostrich plumes, mercenaries (the term Medjoi, which originally designated a Nubian people, became the name of a profession, "policeman"), amethyst, diorite, and above all, gold (the name Nubia comes from Egyptian *nub,* "gold"). Nubian imports also included ivory, ebony, incense, panther skins, giraffes, and pygmies.

The predynastic cultures of Egypt had already spread into Nubia. From the Archaic Period to the end of the Old Kingdom, relations took the form of military expeditions intended to assure the exploitation of the resources of Lower Nubia. Beyond the Second Cataract, the Egyptians contented themselves with expeditions for the sake of trade, or with exploration (e.g., Harkhuf) aimed at establishing ties with Nubian principalities.

The disorder of the First Intermediate Period evidently diverted Egyptian attention from Nubia. But many Nubians flocked to Egypt to enroll as mercenaries in the service of the potentates who were vying for power.

With the Middle Kingdom and the restoration of national unity, the pharaohs began a policy of retaking Nubia that was completed under Senwosret III. A system of eight massive fortresses sealed the border, which was at that time fixed at Semna, south of the Second Cataract; the fortresses prevented incursions by desert nomads and controlled traffic on the river. At the foot of one of these fortresses, that of Mirgissa, a trading post saw intense exchanges with the part of Nubia that remained independent: farther to the south, Kerma was the capital of a Nubian principality that had achieved an original synthesis of the local cultures and Egyptian influence. Profiting from (or provoking) the Egyptian retreat in the Seventeenth Dynasty, this principality expanded into Lower Nubia and allied itself with the Hyksos kingdom against the nationalistic dynasts of Thebes, though the Nubian rulers themselves employed many Egyptians.

The pharaohs of the Eighteenth Dynasty, the victorious successors of those dynasts, remembered, and they endeavored to establish a definitive supremacy over Nubia. The campaigns of Ahmose, Amenophis I, Tuthmosis I, Tuthmosis III, Amenophis II, and Tuthmosis IV ultimately extended the southern border of the empire south of the Fourth Cataract. Nubia was annexed and placed under a special administration headed by the "king's son (i.e., viceroy) of Kush," who was assisted by two deputies. Throughout the New Kingdom, all the local resources were systematically exploited, especially the gold mines, while African products continued to flow into Egypt. A number of temples were built in Nubia, including that of Abu Simbel, which is the most famous of the series erected by Ramesses II.

Wracked by internecine warfare, Egypt was unable to maintain its domination over Nubia during the Third Intermediate Period. At Napata, a city downstream from the Fourth Cataract that was undoubtedly founded by Tuthmosis III, a native but highly Egyptianized dynasty undertook the conquest of Nubia, and then of Egypt, which was weakened by its political divisions. Piankhy (Piye) established a new dynasty, the Twenty-fifth, also called the Kushite dynasty, for Kush was one of the Egyptian names for Nubia. Driven from Egypt by the Twenty-sixth (Saite) Dynasty, the Kushites retreated to Napata, and then, after 270 B.C.E., to Meroe, slightly downstream of the Sixth Cataract. There, an original civilization developed, the Meroitic culture, which used a writing system with signs borrowed from those of Egypt (hieroglyphic and Demotic), but which were used to write a native language that remains poorly understood.

F. Hintze and U. Hintze, *Les Civilisations du Soudan antique* (Leipzig, 1967); W.Y. Adams, *Nubia: Corridor to Africa* (London, 1977).

See Ahmose, Amenophis I, Harkhuf, Heqaib, Kamose, Kush, Kushite (Dynasty), Meroe, Ramesses II, Senwosret III, Sethos I, Tuthmosis I, Tuthmosis III, Tuthmosis IV.

Obelisks

With its rigorous geometry, an obelisk is a quintessentially Egyptian variant on a pillar of stone. Universal symbol of theophany, the obelisk leaves no doubt that it derived from the *benben,* a sacred stone that lent material expression to the emergence of the sun at the moment of creation, according to a myth of Heliopolis. Imitating the appearance of the *benben,* a single obelisk of bricks, perched on a raised platform, was the idol that was worshiped in the royal sun temples of the Fifth Dynasty. The earliest pairs of obelisks known, which date to the beginning of the Sixth Dynasty, were intended especially for the temple of Re at Heliopolis. The many surviving obelisks, now dispersed throughout the world, along with what the classical and Arab historians have to say, remind us of the enormous quantity of obelisks that once stood in the City of the Sun, where we can still gaze upon one of the two obelisks erected by Senwosret I when he rebuilt the temple there. The pharaohs of the New Kingdom erected many of these stone "needles" at Thebes, at Pi-Riamsese, and at the temples of various gods who were identified with the sun. Some obelisks were objects of worship, set up on the axis of a temple, such as the "unique obelisk" of Karnak, which is now on the square of St. John Lateran in Rome. Most obelisks were erected in pairs, one on each side of the entrance to a pylon. Such obelisks continued to be set up in front of temples into the Ptolemaic Period, as at Edfu and Philae.

The pointed top (called a pyramidion) of an obelisk was sheathed in gold or electrum. These monolithic pillars, which were generally made of hard, dense stones such as granite and quartzite, were of varying size, ranging from 6 to 130 feet in height, or even 190 feet, according to a literary text. Their extraction from the quarries, their removal with the help of the high waters of the inundation, their overland transport, and even more, the erection without breakage of these shafts weighing hundreds of tons are among the most astonishing accomplishments of pharaonic engineering. An obelisk was lifted onto its base with a rocking movement, using huge ramps and tall galleries filled with sand.

Dedicated in the name of the king, and elevating the radiant presence of the god skyward, these formidable monuments were called "Pharaoh's needles" by the Arabs, a term that suits them better than the ironic "skewer" (*obeliskos*) of the Greeks. The Romans appreciated the symbolic prestige and the monumental presence of obelisks. From Augustus to Constantius II, the ancient obelisks of Karnak, Heliopolis, and Sais were relocated to adorn their capitals (two at the Caesarium of Alexandria, nine in Rome, and one in Constantinople). Dedicated to the sun, the obelisk on the Campus Martius in Rome functioned as the gnomon of an immense sundial. Obelisks in Rome that lack hieroglyphic inscriptions, such as the one in the Vatican, were probably quarried in Egypt by command of Augustus. Domitian and Hadrian commissioned obelisks bearing hieroglyphic inscriptions that included their names. Popes of the Renaissance and later periods reerected these tall stones from Egypt in the four corners of the Eternal City. Napoleon, too, wanted the capital of his empire to have at least one of them; his wish came true only in the reign of Louis-Philippe (Place de la Concorde, 1832). Paris was imitated by London (1878), New York (1881), and ultimately Cairo (1962 and 1984). Whether a commemorative or a funerary monument, whether adorning a garden or a fireplace, the obelisk is the sole invention of pharaonic art to have entered into our own culture without being cheapened.

L. Habachi, *The Obelisks of Egypt: Skyscrapers of the Past* (New York, 1977).

Old Kingdom

We give the name Old Kingdom to the period that followed the Archaic Period and comprised the Third, Fourth, Fifth, and Sixth Dynasties (2635–2140 B.C.E.). It was characterized by a refined state organization that was capable of systematically controlling the goods and the workforce of the land, as well as of assuring the security of the borders and the obtaining of exotic imports. The efficient apparatus that was put in place siphoned off enough resources and mobilized enough energy to enable the pharaohs to erect immense pyramids and their associated complexes. Resident in Memphis, the capital, the king ruled over a united Egypt, the center of the universe. Certain foreign regions were to various degrees in the Egyptian sphere of influence: el-Dakhla oasis was integrated into the economic and social fabric of the land; the Sinai peninsula was regularly exploited by expeditions that focused on mining; Lower Nubia was kept under strict surveillance; contacts with the south reached farther and farther, to Punt and even to the principalities of Dongola; and Byblos and the Lebanese coast became indispensable trade partners. There was no policy of expansion into Asia, but rather only police operations to subdue troublemaking bedouins, as was also the case with Libyans in the west. It was not yet time for pharaonic conquest in the lands of Syria-Palestine.

In fact, the pharaoh was essentially occupied with the administration of domestic affairs, in which he relied on a class of high officials: the vizier, upper-level bureaucrats, and local managers whom he dispatched to the provinces. The officials were compensated by grants of land, prebends (often attached to a priestly office in the royal funerary cult), and gifts of goods or services, in particular the services of royal artisans who saw to the preparation of their funerary monuments. These high officials supervised large staffs of literate bureaucrats who administered the labor force and assessed, registered, calculated, and archived everything that was produced. This socioeconomic organization was justified by an ideological system that was centered, obviously, on the pharaoh, who in principle owned all the land and its resources. The various areas of economic activity corresponded to aspects of his person: personal property of the crown, funerary foundations, funerary temples and "pyramid cities," palace, personnel charged with his day-to-day care, and so forth. Even the administration of temples did not escape the attention of agents of the crown.

In the Old Kingdom, the pharaoh's power thus seems to have reached as high as the pyramid of Cheops. Nevertheless, a double contradiction developed. One was in the area of ideology. In the Archaic Period, when the world was limited to the experience of the senses, the pharaoh's position in the hierarchy was supreme; but later, when a more universalistic conception prevailed, the solar creator god became the supreme being. The pharaoh was thus relegated to the obviously prestigious, but nevertheless subaltern, role of earthly vicar of this god: metaphorically and mythologically, his "son." The creator god chose this vicar as he pleased, even if that sometimes meant a change of dynasty. Thus, in a myth that was downgraded into a popular tale, the origin of the Fifth Dynasty was ascribed to the sun god's union with the wife of a humble priest from Sakhebu to impregnate her with the first three kings of that dynasty.

The second contradiction was in the exercise of power. In the Archaic Period, a prevalent concept required high dignitaries to belong to the royal family, to the extent that the exercise of their offices entailed their being invested with part of the power incarnate in the pharaoh. This requirement gradually disappeared, and beginning with the Fifth Dynasty, high offices could be awarded to private persons with no blood relationship to the king. Moreover, in line with the custom of hereditary transmission of office, these offices tended to be treated as if they were the property of lines of descent. The same tendency occurred at the level of local institutions (funerary temples of former kings, temples of gods and goddesses) and local administrators (nomarchs), to the point that in the Sixth Dynasty, the king had to come to terms with regional powers, if only by means of matrimonial alliances. Thus, despite the precariousness of the sources, we glimpse the birth and development of a process that resulted in autonomy vis-à-vis the king, a process that ended by bringing about the collapse of the Old Kingdom at the end of the Sixth Dynasty.

The ancients themselves were aware that the Old Kingdom was the classical epoch of Egyptian civilization, for afterward, they accepted it as a model that they imitated either well or badly, more often the latter. In that period all the basic elements of the culture were either invented or systematically codified and elaborated (some of these elements had appeared in the Archaic Period). Above all, these cultural elements were brought into fruition in works of a perfection that would never be equaled: what funerary complex would ever compare with that of Djoser or those of the Great Pyramids? The monarchs of the Middle Kingdom also built pyramids, but they were smaller and less carefully conceived. Old Kingdom sculpture in the round and bas-reliefs also reflect an unsurpassable mastery. To be sure, later pieces are sometimes also affecting—the bust of Nefertiti provokes a gut-level reaction—but the reflective appreciation of the connoisseur will turn to the statue of Rehotpe. Works of gold, jewelry, products of the minor arts that good luck has preserved from the ravages of the millennia, all proclaim a know-how that no other epoch was able to equal. Some technologies, such as the manufacture of stone vases, disappeared after the Old Kingdom.

Otherwise, despite the gaps in our documentation, we can see that this period produced works of literature (wisdom texts) and religious and scientific (medical) treatises that enriched pharaonic culture until its extinction. But the genre of fiction would have to await the Middle Kingdom for its classics.

C. Aldred, *Egypt to the End of the Old Kingdom* (New York, 1965); A. Roccati, *La Littérature historique sous l'Ancien Empire égyptien* (Paris, 1982).

See Fifth Dynasty, Fourth Dynasty, Pyramids, Sixth Dynasty, Third Dynasty.

Oracles

The practice of oracles is not attested prior to the New Kingdom; is this due purely to the hazards of documentation? In any event, in oracles the god expressed himself through the movements of his processional barque, which was carried by priests on the occasion of major festivals. He signaled his approval by a forward movement or inclination of the barque, and his disapproval by making it move backward or keeping it still. In this way, he decided cases that were presented to him orally, or even in writing, on two tablets, one with the positive version of the question and the other with the negative version. Spoken oracles—for instance, via a conduit passing through a divine statue—are not attested until the Late Period.

Many oracles, generally given by particular forms (statue, image) of major deities, or even deified men (such as King Amenophis I at Thebes) and sacred animals, punctuated the life of private persons. Their inquiries involved such matters as the appropriateness of a trip, the validity of the purchase of a donkey, or the chances that a newly born child would escape death (hence personal names like "The god X says that he will live"). Oracles also served as a judicial authority to resolve many disputes or to establish the culpability of a criminal; in fact, they were cumulative, so that if someone was not satisfied with the response of one oracle, he could have recourse to one or more others.

The political role of oracles changed over time. During the Eighteenth Dynasty, it intervened only exceptionally, without being consulted, to choose the future king, as in the cases of Hatshepsut and Tuthmosis III. But if pharaohs consulted the god regarding an important project—such as an expedition to Punt under Hatshepsut, a campaign in Nubia under Tuthmosis IV—it was in the intimacy of the sanctuary and via direct inspiration. From the Ramesside Period on, as the domain of the temple of Amun grew, so did the importance of his oracle; Ramesses II consulted it to name the high priest of Amun, Nebwenenef. With the Twenty-first Dynasty and the beginning of the Third Intermediate Period, the advent of the Theban theocracy entailed a qualitative leap in the status of oracles. In the areas that were under the jurisdiction of the domain of Amun—that is, in Upper and Middle Egypt and at Tanis—Amun was believed to govern directly through his oracle, which was consulted by the high priest or by the king. This oracle intervened regularly, not only in judicial matters, but also as guarantor of private transactions and of funerary rituals and objects. It settled political matters, such as the question of the amnesty granted to those who had been banished to the oases, and it even controlled the power of the pharaoh. That is why Osorkon II, Taharqa, and undoubtedly many other pharaohs submitted their program of governance to the oracle of Amun for approval. Suffice it to say that the real power was thus in the hands of those who manipulated the oracle—the high clergy.

J. Leclant, in A. Caquot and M. Leibovici (eds.), *La Divination* (Paris, 1968), pp. 1–23; S. Sauneron, *The Priests of Ancient Egypt* (Ithaca, 2000), pp. 96–103.

Origins (Prehistory, Predynastic)

The first traces of human beings—mainly stone tools—appeared in what would be Egypt during the final phases of the transition from the Pliocene epoch to the Pleistocene, when the Nile dug its bed deeper through the accumulations that had previously filled it. There is nothing regionally specific about these tools, and prehistorians easily recognize the well-known types of the European Paleolithic period, the names of which often derive from sites in France, including the Paris area (Chellean, Acheulean, Levalloisian). But with the last phases of the Paleolithic, we find more highly differentiated cultures that are clearly related to those of the nomadic hunters of the Maghreb, the Sahara, and Sudan. And with them developed rock engravings in which typically African fauna (giraffes, elephants, ostriches, etc.) try in vain to frustrate the efforts of hunters wearing penis sheaths, who were as skilled at shooting arrows as they were at setting ingenious traps. Certain symbolic themes, such as the disk between the horns of a bovine, enriched the cultural patrimony of pharaonic Egypt. The Paleolithic cultures lasted for a long time in Egypt, for they are still attested around 6000 B.C.E., at the edge of the Nile.

In fact, the Neolithic had barely emerged in the fifth millennium B.C.E.: on high plateaus overlooking the Faiyum and the valley, and where desiccation was incomplete, populations had somewhat crude pottery, along with basket making, textiles, the ability to cultivate grains (wheat, barley), and the technology needed to do so (sickles, flails, silos). Nonetheless, agriculture appeared in Egypt much later than in western Asia. Contrasting with this somewhat crude Neolithic culture of the Faiyum and Merimda (in Lower Egypt, near present-day Cairo), and also during the fifth millennium but in Upper Egypt, there were cultures called Eneolithic or Chalcolithic because of their use of copper, which was apparently restricted to prestigious objects. These cultures, which had attained a remarkable mastery of pottery making and ivory working, are designated Badarian.

The period covering more or less the fourth millennium B.C.E. is called the Predynastic. It is characterized by a civilization attested in Upper Egypt and known chiefly through abundant and highly elaborate grave goods: vessels of stone (granite, basalt, alabaster), artistically decorated pottery, toilette objects and ivory figurines, copper amulets and needles, cosmetic palettes of schist, and votive weapons. This Naqada civilization developed in two distinct phases, Naqada I, or Amratian, and Naqada II, or Gerzean, which are distinguished in particular by stylistic trends. In the beginning, a taste for geometric simplification, and even abstraction, dominated the Amratian, while the Gerzean demonstrated a propensity for a certain realism. Moreover, we see clear influence from the Mesopotamian world, not only in the form of imported cylinder seals—which could be merely isolated objects—but also in style and iconographic themes (a man attacked from both sides by two lions, two monsters face to face). From this period, we also have wall paintings (tomb at Hierakonpolis) and objects decorated in relief (Gebel el-Araq knife, Bull Palette, Gazelle Palette).

The final phase of the Gerzean (sometimes called Naqada III) merits the name Protodynastic, for pharaonic elements (nome emblems, royal crown and attributes) appeared in it. In addition, artistic conventions reflected a vision of the world quite close to that which would prevail in the dynastic era: division of scenes into registers and half-registers, symbiosis of text and image (the first steps toward writing are perceptible), and "ideological realism" (the proportions of persons reflect their hierarchical status). It is thus difficult to tell whether the Narmer Palette belongs to the extreme end of the Protodynastic Period, or whether it is one of the first monuments of the dynastic era. In any event, it is obvious that at the end of the Predynastic Period, societies had already developed on a scale larger than that of a village or region, endowed with institutions controlling the production of certain consumable goods and affirming, both materially and symbolically, the unification of Upper Egypt, or a part of it, into a single kingdom.

Clearly, Egyptian civilization was the product of various population groups and influences. Certain anthropological indications reveal the subsistence of a strong ethnic element (dolichocephalic Mediterranean) from the Paleolithic to the Predynastic Periods, an element with which other populations were mingled. Thus, in the fourth millennium B.C.E., there was an irruption into the valley of a brachycephalic people of Armenoid type (perhaps in connection with the Mesopotamian influence). From a linguistic point of view, Egyptian is one of the branches of Afroasiatic, along with Semitic, Libyco-Berber, Cushitic, and Chadic; but its closest affinities are with the Semitic (i.e., Asiatic) languages.

E. I. Baumgartel, *The Cultures of Predynastic Egypt,* 2 vols. (Oxford, 1955–1960); *L'Égypte avant les pyramides: IVe millénaire* (Paris, 1973); K. W. Butzer, *Early Hydraulic Civilization in Egypt: A Study in Cultural Ecology* (Chicago, 1976); M. A. Hoffmann, *Egypt before the Pharaohs: The Prehistoric Foundations of Egyptian Civilization* (New York, 1979).

See Narmer, Scorpion.

Osorkon Twenty-second and Twenty-third Dynasties

Around 1080 B.C.E., the typically Libyan name Osorkon was already borne by a son of Herihor, the creator of the theocratic state of Thebes. Around 980 B.C.E., Osorkon the Elder, who is presumed to be the uncle of Shoshenq I, ruled as king during the Twenty-first Dynasty. Osorkon I (924–889 B.C.E.) maintained the order established by this Shoshenq, who was his father; he founded a residence near el-Lahun. Surviving reliefs and capitals at Bubastis illustrate his architectural activity in the city that had given birth to the Twenty-second Dynasty. Osorkon also richly endowed the temples of Heliopolis. His statue at Byblos bears witness to relations with the Lebanon.

Thanks to chance discovery, it is the reign of his grandson, Osorkon II (874–850 B.C.E.), that best illustrates the apogee of the Shoshenqides. At Bubastis, a monumental granite gate commemorates the celebration of the royal jubilee. At Tanis and Bubastis, fine palmiform columns removed from Pi-Riamsese, with Osorkon's names taking the place of those of the original owners, attest the proscription of the god Seth. Beautiful reliefs were sculpted in the tomb he appropriated for his own use at Tanis and in the vault constructed at Memphis by his eldest son, Shoshenq, who was high priest of Ptah. The mementos of his private secretary, Harmes, along with the funerary equipment of prince Harnakhte, the first prophet of Amun, who was buried at Tanis, and that of the Memphite pontiff Shoshenq represent a fine collection of the applied arts. Osorkon II dedicated a chapel at Thebes, which was governed by another of his sons, Nimlot, who was first prophet of Amun. Osorkon II had the main temple at Elephantine restored by the viceroy of Kush, who was his grandson. The king presented the god Amun with a political testament requesting that his progeny remain in the lucrative offices he had conferred upon them and expressing the wish that "brother not envy brother." In the following generation and thereafter, the heirs to these offices and the sons of new kings would find themselves in conflict. From the lengthy inscriptions carved at Karnak by a grandson of Osorkon II, we learn that this system failed: this eldest son of Takelot II, the "prince Osorkon," who was promoted to first prophet of Amun, and who used royal phraseology and covered his political actions and pious works under oracular decisions of Amun and Herishef, was obliged on a number of occasions to reconquer his seat against competitors from collateral branches of the royal family.

Osorkon III (787–757 B.C.E.), who was both first prophet of Amun and pharaoh, governed only Upper Egypt south of Herakleopolis. Monuments at Thebes bear witness to the ability of his sculptors and display the first manifestations of the archaizing renaissance that was just beginning.

Ensconced in the eastern delta, Osorkon IV (730–715 B.C.E.) was one of the last Shoshenqide pharaohs. He was an impotent bystander during the rise of Sais, the Kushite expansion into Egypt, and the advance of the Assyrians to the borders of Egypt.

Tanis: L'Or des pharaons (Paris, 1987).

See Bubastis, Third Intermediate Period.

Palace

Because of the needs of the major local cults and the constraints of domestic and foreign policy, the king and his entourage were often on the move. Palaces were therefore numerous: Memphis, which was the principal residence; Lisht, which replaced it during the Twelfth and Thirteenth Dynasties; Thebes; and Amarna, the latter's ephemeral rival. Palaces also existed in Heliopolis, Tanis, Sais, Pi-Riamsese, and Gurob (from which the court would go for recreation in the Faiyum). It is likely that in the Old Kingdom, each new pyramid city included, in principle, a royal dwelling. Each major divine sanctuary was supposed to include a palace from which the king would emerge when he went to officiate in the temple. Small palaces were adjacent to the royal funerary temples of Thebes. Texts inform us that from the Eighteenth through the Twentieth Dynasty, nearly all the kings founded a personal "house," with fields for their own provisioning, at Memphis, Heliopolis, Thebes, or elsewhere.

These buildings were made of mud brick and wood; only certain features, such as door frames, were of stone. Well preserved remains of palaces are therefore rare. The niched façades of Archaic Period funerary monuments are generally considered as reproducing the appearance of the earliest palatial dwellings. We know little about the palaces of the earliest periods, though some Middle Kingdom remnants at Bubastis and Avaris have been identified as palaces. The Seventeenth and Eighteenth Dynasty palaces at Ballas were spacious buildings on a terrace made of caissons, a type also attested from the Late Period in the palace of Apries at Memphis. At el-Malqata, where Amenophis III constructed his "House of the Radiant Disk," and at Amarna under Amenophis IV, we find vast royal cities that included official buildings, production annexes, temples, gardens, and the king's principal residence. The latter included apartments with bedchambers, dressing rooms, showers, a throne room, and a hypostyle reception room. The same structure survived, naturally, in the Ramesside Period, from which we have the remains of the walls of a palace of Merneptah at Memphis, and the palace of Ramesses III at Medinet Habu. A beautiful series of faience tiles employed as wall decoration remind us of the luxury of the palaces of Sethos I, Ramesses II at Pi-Riamsese, and Ramesses III.

In New Kingdom palaces, the decoration of the private chambers was rustic and prophylactic (depictions of the god Bes figures), while that of the official areas, like the decoration of temples, symbolized the triumphant might of the king. This type of decoration was particularly expressive on the dais that supported the throne and below the huge "windows of appearance" from which the king presided over parades.

Pedubaste Third Intermediate Period

This name, which means "gift of Bastet," refers to the lion and cat goddess of Bubastis. Patroness of the Libyan pharaohs, she enjoyed a growing popularity from the tenth century on.

Manetho makes a Pedubaste the first king of a dynasty of four "Tanite" monarchs, but as transmitted by the writers who cited excerpts from Manetho's history, the list of this dynasty seems corrupt; it is in no way confirmed by contemporary sources. The latter enable us to ascertain that at a time when the land was suffering from internecine warfare, a certain Pedubaste, "son of Bastet" (c. 818–793 B.C.E.), ruled contemporaneously with Shoshenq III, and that Pedubaste was recognized at Bubastis, Herakleopolis, Memphis, and Thebes. There is no mention of him, however, at Tanis. Later, a Pedubaste II, "king of Tanis," was one of the petty kings who ruled at the time of the Assyrian invasions (c. 680–665 B.C.E.). Some monuments of his have been found at Tanis and Memphis.

We cannot exclude the possibility that Manetho's Pedubaste is derived from these two personalities, as is undoubtedly the case with the "Pharaoh Pedubaste" of Tanis in whose time the epic adventures of a number of heroic warriors were believed to have occurred. These adventures are recounted in several romances that Egyptians of the Greek and Roman eras read in Demotic. In this "Pedubaste Cycle," we encounter a mélange of recollections of the princely battles and court customs of the Libyan Period, marginal allusions to the Assyrians (who were held at bay, according to the texts), and a proclamation of imperialist pretensions in a world as large as that of Alexander the Great. These texts reflect an obvious influence from Homer and from the events of the Hellenistic era. Pedubaste's vassals range beyond Babylon to fight and ally themselves with the queen of the Amazons, and they penetrate into India. Warriors from Tanis, Mendes, Sebennytos, and Leontopolis quarrel and joust with contingents from other provinces. A priest of Buto leads herdsmen from the marshes all the way to Thebes and takes the processional barque of Amun hostage, with a priestly benefice the ransom. In an Egypt brought to heel and dominated by foreigners, the men of letters who transmitted these glorious creations discovered, in the reign of this "Pharaoh Pedubaste," a dream of manly deeds and restive independence.

G. Maspero, *Les Contes populaires de l'Égypte ancienne*, 2d ed. (Paris, 1889).
See Third Intermediate Period.

Pepy I 2289–2247 B.C.E., Sixth Dynasty

Pepy I was the son of Teti and Queen Iput I. For a time, the usurper Userkare prevented him from succeeding his father. When he finally ascended the throne, he had a long reign, during the course of which he changed his throne name from Nefersahor to Meryre. He had to suppress a conspiracy fomented in the harem. He married two daughters of a family of Abydos, each named Akhnesmeryre; a certain Djau, who bore the title of vizier, might have been their brother.

Many traces remain of Pepy I's monumental activity: at Elephantine (naos), Abydos, Bubastis (*ka*-chapel), as well as a famous copper statue found at Hierakonpolis.

In promulgating a decree of immunity in favor of the pyramid city of Snofru, Pepy I made a concession to the autonomist pressure of provinces and institutions; that pressure increased during the dynasty. Expeditions to Byblos, Sinai, and Nubia, as well as military operations against Asiatics, punctuated his foreign policy. Pepy I built a pyramid at Saqqara; it was rather modest in size, but its name was the origin of the word "Memphis."

See Memphis, Nekhebu, Old Kingdom, Sixth Dynasty, Weni.

Pepy II 2241–2148 B.C.E., Sixth Dynasty

Fifth king of the Sixth Dynasty, Pepy II was the son of Pepy I and a half brother of Merenre. Since he came to the throne when he was still a child, his mother, Ankhnesmeryre, acted as regent, while the vizier Djau was an éminence grise. He had a long reign—ninety-four years, which was too long, undoubtedly. In studying how the reign progressed, we feel we can perceive the progressive weakening of the central power in the face of affirmations of local particularism. Thus, Pepy II promulgated two decrees of immunity, exempting the persons and goods of the temple of Min at Koptos from any imposition or requisition by the central administration. Moreover, the nomarchs tended to assume titles such as "overseer of Upper Egypt" or "vizier," which are clear proclamations of their pretensions to autonomy. Foreign policy also reveals the progressive crumbling of pharaonic power. To be sure, the expeditions to the mines and quarries of Sinai and Lower Nubia continued, as did the quest for exotic products from Byblos and Punt; the search for trading partners was even taken as far as the principalities of the Dongola region. Still, the inscriptions reveal the vulnerability of Egyptian caravans and the impotence of their armed escorts; the prestige of one official lay in his having recovered the body of a colleague massacred by bedouins during an expedition.

Pepy II erected his pyramid in the southern part of the plateau of

Saqqara; of middling size (barely more than 170 feet tall), it had the peculiarity of having had its base enclosed in a girdle wall, no doubt secondarily. Three small pyramids, each with its own enclosure, were dedicated to three of the queens of Pepy II: Wedjebten, Iput II, and Neit.

See Harkhuf, Heqaib, Old Kingdom, Sixth Dynasty.

Peribsen c. 2700 B.C.E., Second Dynasty

This pharaoh of the Second Dynasty reigned during the first half of the twenty-seventh century B.C.E. He is especially distinctive in that his Horus name, which is inscribed in the palace façade, is not surmounted by the usual image of Horus, but by that of Seth; one of his successors, Khasekhemwy, would have both deities represented there, face to face. During the Second Dynasty, there was thus a dialectical movement in the ideological structure—Horus, Seth, then Horus and Seth—that probably conceals a political process. But what process? Antagonism between an aristocracy brought up in the tradition of nomadic hunters and peasant commoners, followed by a reconciliation? It is also possible that Peribsen ruled over the south, while the north was controlled by a Memphite line that was concurrent, but not necessarily hostile. A chapel dedicated to Peribsen was erected in the funerary temple of King Senedj—a beautiful example of cohabitation, if only in the hereafter!

See Archaic (Period), Khasekhemwy, Pharaoh.

Persians

On two occasions, Egypt was integrated into the Persian empire. The first Persian domination lasted for 120 years (525–404 B.C.E.). The Great Kings were represented at Memphis by a satrap and a treasurer, but on the ideological level, these emperors were the successors of the Saite kings and composed Manetho's Twenty-seventh Dynasty. Liberated and valiantly defended from 404 to 342 B.C.E., the land would experience a second Persian domination that would last for only nine years.

Since the Saites had enabled the economy and the culture of Egypt to flourish brilliantly, Cambyses and Darius I acquired an especially lucrative province. These same Saites had opened Egypt to the outside world and introduced immigrants (Greeks, Carians, Phoenicians, Jews) into their kingdom, though they restricted them and confined them to their settlements. While the Persians recruited native officials who were highly qualified to administer the land, they also settled or reinforced the foreign garrisons (the Judeo-Aramaeans of Elephantine) and gave Greek and Phoenician merchants a freer hand. It was around 445 B.C.E., under Artaxerxes I, that Herodotus visited Egypt, asking Greeks and priests about the past and present marvels of the land. In the opposite direction, Egyptian physicians went to the court of the Great King, Egyptian workmen participated in the decoration of his palaces, and Egyptian sailors and soldiers participated in his wars with the Medes. During this time Egypt also acquired some Asiatic features: the camel, the white lotus, and astrology.

With the first Persian pharaohs, the dominator and the dominated seem to have accepted one another entirely: Cambyses (525–522 B.C.E.), though he was later maligned, and especially Darius I (522–485 B.C.E.), were depicted as genuine pharaohs on both public and private monuments. Things took a turn for the worse, however, under the kings who followed. The satrap's exploitation of the land and the restrictions he imposed on the temples grew more burdensome as the Median wars exposed the weaknesses of the empire. There was a revolt on the eve of Marathon, quickly put down by Xerxes (486 B.C.E.); a more serious revolt, supported by Athens, under Artaxerxes I (460 B.C.E.); and finally, the decisive revolt under Darius II, in the final years of the fifth century B.C.E. Quantitatively and qualitatively, there is a telling contrast between the canonical monuments and ritual objects bearing the cartouche of Darius I and the *alabastra,* the humble gifts of tributaries, inscribed with the cartouche and the cuneiform titulary of Xerxes and Artaxerxes. In their inscriptions, the elite no longer cited the name of the Achaemenid king, who was named only in legal documents. A sort of theological nationalism would come to identify the Asiatic invader with Seth, the murderer of Osiris and disrupter of temples. Persian reprisals extended even to the removal of cult statues from the land, while the Egyptians went so far as to degrade the person of Artaxerxes III into the figure of a donkey, the animal of Seth.

The Great King who succeeded (not without difficulty) in once again reducing Egypt to a satrapy (342 B.C.E.) struck coins depicting him dressed as a Persian but crowned with the *pshent.* Notaries writing in Demotic were obliged to date their legal documents to "Pharaoh Artaxerxes," but the people would recount that this emperor had made a banquet of the Apis bull and the ram of Mendes. After his death (338 B.C.E.), a native king, Khababash, was recognized for a time. In 330 B.C.E., after vanquishing Darius III Codomanus, Alexander substituted a new domination, that of the Greeks.

E. Bresciani, "Egypt in the Persian Empire," in H. Bengston, ed., *The Greeks and the Persians* (London, 1968), pp. 333–53; K. Myśliwiec, *The Twilight of Ancient Egypt: First Millennium B.C.E.* (Ithaca, 2000), pp. 135–58.

See Cambyses, Darius I, Saite (Dynasties), Udjahorresnet.

Pharaoh

The term "pharaoh" derives from Egyptian *per-aa,* "great house," which originally designated the palace (as an institution), and which from the New Kingdom on was applied to the person of the king. The king was otherwise called *nesu,* as well as "his/my majesty," often followed by the formula "life, prosperity, health." His titulary consisted of five names, each preceded by a title: Horus, Two Ladies, Horus of Gold, King of Upper and Lower Egypt (the name that followed this title is referred to as the "prenomen" or "throne name"), and Son of Re (this title preceded the name the king received at birth). The last two of these names were written in a "cartouche," originally a magic circle that was elongated into an oval to make it suitable for writing the names.

The appearance, the attributes, the activities—indeed, every aspect of the pharaoh's person—were highly codified and ritualized. He disposed of a complex set of insignia, including a false beard, scepters, crowns (especially the white crown of Upper Egypt, the red crown of Lower Egypt, and a combination of the two, the *pshent*), a uraeus (a diadem in the form of a cobra), and an animal tail. The storage and maintenance of the royal insignia, vestments, and jewels, as well as the personal care of the king, were conceived of as priestly tasks that were entrusted to high officials, who at first were exclusively members of the royal family. In fact, everyone who could come into physical contact with the king was impregnated with a sort of *mana* that demanded veneration and precaution: among the furnishings from the tomb of Tutankhamun is a sack to contain the kohl sticks used in his infancy!

Pharaoh's reign was punctuated by complex ceremonies, including his coronation, confirmation of his power each New Year, and a jubilee (*sed*-festival), originally intended to affirm and renew his capacities. Likewise, his funerary appurtenances—tomb, funerary temples, furnishings, mortuary cult—set an enormous ritual machinery into motion. All these ceremonies, along with the fact that the pharaoh was represented on the same scale as the gods and goddesses, suffice to show that the Egyptian monarchy was a "divine kingship."

FUNCTIONS AND ROLES OF THE EGYPTIAN KINGSHIP

The kingship originated with the creator god, who transmitted it to the gods who succeeded him, and then to demigods, the "followers of Horus," who immediately precede the historical pharaohs in the king lists. As rule by one man alone, the kingship reflected its very origin, for the principle quality of the creator god was to be "one." The pharaoh's essential function was to prolong the work of the creator by maintaining the order he had instituted, called *maat,* and by subjecting the flow of history to this order. That is, the pharaoh was to reduce history to the repetition of archetypes established at the moment of creation. All of Pharaoh's roles lead back to that function.

Pharaoh's Person

Events were dated by reference to the years of a reign, and by adding up the succession of reigns, to creation itself. Like the creator god, who named because he created, the pharaoh lent his own name to the territories conquered from neighboring peoples or reclaimed in Egypt itself from marshes, watercourses, or uncultivated areas. These new foundations—agricultural domains, units of production created to respond to the needs of the moment—were organized into institutions defined by an aspect of the personality of the king and could therefore be embodied in a temple, a pyramid, or a statue. Such embodiments were the object of a cult: thus, we see Ramesses II officiating before a statue of himself, which is the hypostasis of an institution called "Ramesses-meryamun-ruler-of-rulers"!

Divine Cult

Maintaining the order of the cosmos was to "satisfy" the deities who governed its major principles. It was thus the pharaoh's duty to build, restore, and enlarge their temples, and to see to their cults. He was the agent par excellence of the rites carried out on their behalf, and in the representations carved on the walls, it is he alone who officiates. In practice, he delegated this duty to the clergy, whose membership he officially controlled. The pharaoh's duties to the gods and goddesses were those of a son to his ancestors. They were just as much his ancestors as were his predecessors on the throne; thus, care for the divine temples and maintenance of the funerary cult of the royal ancestors were equally incumbent on him.

Foreign Relations

Just as the creator god made being arise from nonbeing and ceaselessly repelled the latter's return, so the pharaoh was obliged to create being by "extending the boundaries" and defending Egypt from the assaults of neighboring peoples in whom the threat of chaos was made manifest. He was thus in charge of the army and of diplomacy.

The Government of the Land

As representative of the creator god, the pharaoh was master of all the lands, goods, and people. In principle, he administered all the workforce and all the means of production via a labyrinth of institutions and the people assigned to them: crown lands, the central administration and its bureaus, temple domains, private funerary foundations. These all had varying degrees of autonomy, but they were all subject to the pharaoh, who had the power to impose taxes or compulsory labor on them, except when they had been granted immunity. He arbitrated conflicts over jurisdiction, saw to it that statutes that had been violated were respected, settled disputes over landholdings, reestablished or reorganized what had fallen into obsolescence, took social or economic initiatives as circumstances required, named or confirmed officeholders, and so forth.

EXERCISE OF POWER

In his exercise of power, the pharaoh depended on his vizier, a sort of prime minister who saw to it that the king's decisions were carried out. These decisions were made after consulting a council of courtiers and high officials; in the official genre called the "royal novel," their indecision and timidity serve as a foil to the pharaoh's spirit of initiative. But the pharaoh had the great advantage of being inspired by divine speech (*Hu*) and perception (*Sia*), which permeated him. Every word he spoke under the force of this inspiration was set down in writing and was issued with the formal pomp that authenticated it as a "royal decree" (*udj nesu*). These decrees were addressed to individuals and groups, and their content ranged from greetings to decisions of general interest. There was no independent legislation to which the king was obliged to refer, but only an aggregate of "laws" that represented the normative content of all the "royal decrees" and "ancient writings." He consulted these ancient writings because his exercise of power was dominated by the need to maintain the original order that constituted both its justification and its limit.

THE LEGITIMACY OF THE KING

In the dogma, the basis of Pharaoh's legitimacy lay in his divine descent: the solar creator god had engendered him by uniting with a human woman in the guise of her husband. In practice, this belief was subject to various interpretations.

Since kingship was an office, the customary principles that regulated the inheritance of offices applied to it: male primogeniture, or, by default, inheritance by the oldest brother. In fact, succession from father to son or from brother to brother occurred often in Egyptian history.

If there was no male heir, the office could fall to a female member of the royal family. But women rarely held the office as pharaohs in their own right (as in the cases of Nitocris, Nefrusobk, Hatshepsut, and Twosre); most often, a female pharaoh was simply the person who held the power until she transferred it to her husband. This fact, however, in no way means that royal legitimacy in general was based on marriage with a female relative; incest has too often been asserted, either for lack of critical sense or for love of the spectacular.

The creator god could even choose a pharaoh whom neither the customary principles of succession nor even his own social or geographical origin seemed to predispose for this office. In such cases, he signaled his choice by some sign: by a prodigious birth (the first three kings of the Fifth Dynasty), by a dream granted to the lucky choice (Tuthmosis IV was promised the throne while sleeping at the foot of the Sphinx), or by an oracle or unexpected event (Hatshepsut, Haremhab). We can easily imagine the ideological manipulations carried out by factions or individuals desirous of sanctioning their coups d'état by means of fabricated miracles. In a pinch, any pharaoh could legitimate his assumption of the kingship by emphasizing that the circumstances that brought him to office were a manifestation of divine will, relying on an ancient belief that the royal office found its justification in the very ability to exercise it. This belief explains the archaic rituals of the *sed*-festival, which affirmed the abilities of the king, as well as the theme of the "sporting" king, which made its appearance in the New Kingdom.

There was thus no objective rule defining the legitimacy of a king. And we can easily see how every succession to the throne aroused its share of ambitions, cabals, and rivalries. That is why a pharaoh did his utmost to consolidate the pretensions of his eldest son or his chosen successor by naming him *erpa* (hereditary prince) and head of the army, or even associating him on the throne as coregent. Conversely, that is why a newly crowned pharaoh had to endeavor to solidify his position through intense propaganda—for example, by publishing an apologetic assessment of the reign of his predecessor, as in the case of the Instruction of Amenemhet I, written in the reign of his son Senwosret I, and Papyrus Harris, a summary of the reign of Ramesses III, which was composed under his son Ramesses IV.

PHARAOH: HUMAN DIVINITY OR DIVINE HUMAN?

In contrast to the official texts that heap laudatory epithets on pharaohs—to the point of assimilating them to the gods—some literary sources depict historical pharaohs in terms that are scarcely flattering. The examples range from Cheops, rebuked for his lack of respect for human life, to Pepy II, scrambling nightly via a ladder to satisfy his passion for his general. Close examination of the official texts reveals their rhetorical character. What was divine was the royal office. He who held it was chosen by the creator god as the vehicle of his will; although divine inspiration flowed through the king, divine power in no way inhabited him. The pharaoh sometimes benefited from miracles, but never did he perform any himself; far from acting as a god, he was acted on by the divine. In short, he was only an intercessor through whose mediation the plans of the gods descended to invest the world; or conversely, thanks to him, human activities were organized so as to consummate the order established by the gods.

H. Frankfort, *Kingship and the Gods: A Study of Ancient Near Eastern Religion as the Integration of Society and Nature* (Chicago, 1948); G. Posener, *De la divinité du pharaon*, Cahiers de la Société Asiatique 15 (Paris, 1960); P. Vernus, in E. Le Roy Ladurie, ed., *Les Monarchies* (Paris, 1986), pp. 29–42; D. O'Connor and D. P. Silverman, *Ancient Egyptian Kingship* (Leiden, 1995).

See Amenemhet I, Conspiracy, Coregency, Loyalism, Merykare, Ramesses III, Sources for History, Third Intermediate Period.

Pinudjem 1070–1032 B.C.E., Twenty-first Dynasty

Piankh, a soldier of obscure origin, had succeeded Herihor as head of Upper Egypt during the final years of Ramesses XI. After him, his son Pinudjem became first prophet of Amun and generalissimo. His monumental policy was comparable to Herihor's: embellishments and restorations at Karnak and Medinet Habu, care of the mummies of former kings (cachette in the tomb of Amenophis II). His career was also comparable to that of the founder of the Theban theocracy in the south, though he carried matters further. After about fifteen years of rule, Pinudjem assumed the canonical attributes of a pharaoh, thus becoming the colleague of Smendes, the founder of the Twenty-first Dynasty. With his wife Henuttawy, who was descended from the Ramesside family, he formed a sort of pivot in the redistribution of power. One of his sons, Psusennes I, who was married to his own sister Mutnodjmet, went to Tanis as the successor of Smendes. Pinudjem's daughter Maatkare was the first virgin bride of Amun. Two of his sons, Masaharta and Menkheperre, would each inherit the pontificate, which would then pass through the generations of the latter's descendants. The bodies of King Pinudjem and his family—with the exception of those of the pontiffs Menkheperre and Smendes, which are still being sought—were found in the royal cachette of Deir el-Bahari. They had been regrouped, just like the bodies of former kings, with the burials of the high priest Pinudjem II, grandson of Pinudjem I, and his wives and daughters.

See Cachettes, Herihor, High Priest of Amun, Third Intermediate Period.

Pi-Riamsese

The name Pi-Riamsese means "house of Ramesses," or, in its complete form, "house of Ramesses-beloved-of-Amun, great of victories"; during the reign of Ramesses, it was renamed "house of Ramesses-beloved-of-Amun, the great *ka* of Re-Harakhty." The two names summarize the program of Ramesses II: political offensives and exaltation of the solar aura of the monarch. The city was the most important of the many foundations of this great king, a new capital city whose core was the former Avaris.

Located on the easternmost branch of the Nile between the river and the eastern desert, the former Hyksos capital of Avaris and its old temple of Seth had experienced new activity at the end of the Eighteenth Dynasty. Under Sethos I, the godson of Seth and a military man who was born in the region, a royal residence was installed there, and Ramesses II developed it into a vast city when he ascended the throne. As at Amarna, there was a prestigious ensemble of palaces, temples, government buildings, villas, and quarters inhabited by common people. The city included Avaris in the south and stretched far beyond it to the north. The "store city" named "Ramses," on which the Children of Israel were forced to labor, was none other than Pi-Riamsese. The promotion of the ancestral home of the Nineteenth Dynasty was an act of strategic importance in the face of the recurrent restlessness of the bedouins of the Isthmus of Suez and the thrust of the Hittites toward Palestine. At Avaris, the king's residence, the quarters of his armed forces, and the shipyards of his fleet would be better placed to control the eastern borders of the delta and to intervene more quickly in Canaan and Phoenicia. The city functioned fully as a capital again under Ramesses III. Like everything else, it declined under the following Ramessides. Doomed by a reduction in the flow of the eastern branch of the Nile, and exposed to Libyan and Asiatic incursions, it was replaced by Tanis as seat of government and port around the year 1100 B.C.E.

Pi-Riamsese is located slightly north of Faqus, between Tell el-Daba, Khatana, and Qantir, and it lies deep below the level of the cultivation. Three categories of sources permit us a picture of its ancient functions and splendor, a fine corpus of texts and two sets of archaeological data:

1. Carved in stone, many accounts give us a glimpse of this city. These accounts include details of the deeds of Ramesses II, along with administrative and technical documents, the titularies of high officials, and literary texts written in praise of the city. It was a parade ground and a naval base at the frontier between Egyptian and Asiatic territory; it was also a pleasant place to visit or to settle in. It was the

sumptuous residence where the pharaoh received his tributaries and celebrated his jubilees, and where offerings were made to the three major gods of the state, Amun, Re, and Ptah, to the dynastic god Seth, to other "gods of Ramesses," and to various hypostases of the royal person manifested in mighty colossi.

2. After the metropolis declined, it became a quarry and a warehouse for the kings of the Twenty-first and Twenty-second Dynasties, who carried off a striking series of monuments that were reused at Tanis, along with pieces that have been found at Bubastis and Leontopolis. The remnants of these monuments reveal the proportions and the excellent workmanship of Ramesside statuary, as well as the pantheon worshiped in Ramesses' temples. The remains include colossi (among them a fragment of the largest one known), original statues and older statues to which the Ramessides added their own names, tall columns and monolithic chapels, obelisks large and small, fragments of immense walls, and stelae lauding the piety and the victories of Ramesses II, all of it fashioned in all sorts of stones that the founder of the city commanded to be brought from the deserts and the cataract. A unique inscription, the 400-Year Stela, commemorates Ramesses' god Seth-Baal and the ancestors of the king.
3. The soil of Qantir and its environs contains scarcely more than sparse remains of temples, but it has yielded many noteworthy finds: the brilliantly decorated ceramic wall coverings of a palace, molds used in issuing scarabs glorifying the kingship and colossi that were worshiped, vestiges of workshops where arms were manufactured, door and window frames of villas in which princes and ministers lived, and many stelae on which soldiers and hirelings had themselves represented adoring colossal effigies of Ramesses II.

M. Bietak, "Avaris and Piramesse: Archaeological Exploration in the Eastern Nile Delta," *Proceedings of the British Academy* 65 (1979): 225–90.

See Avaris, Ramesses II.

Pithom

The city of Pithom was otherwise called "House of the god Atum in the territory of Tjeku." Along with Ramses (i.e., Pi-Riamsese), Pithom was one of the two store cities whose bricks the Children of Israel were obliged to make, according to the biblical book of Exodus. Located at Tell el-Rataba, an earlier Pithom was a small Ramesside foundation, a secondary base with a fortress that controlled access from the Isthmus of Suez. Its temple to Atum was still functioning in the time of Osorkon II. In the Saite Period, the base and its temple of Atum, along with some of the statues that adorned it, were moved several miles east to Tell el-Maskhuta, which later served as a stop along the canal between the Nile and the Red Sea that was dug under Necho II and Darius I.

Piye (*or* Piankhy) 747–716 B.C.E., Kushite Dynasty

Piye is the first Sudanese pharaoh from Napata who is well-known to us, thanks to his tomb at el-Kurru, his temple at Gebel Barkal, and especially to two stelae discovered at the latter site. His name is written Piankhy in hieroglyphs, literally "Living One," but it seems that this writing conceals a Sudanese word, *piye,* with the same meaning, which was written phonetically as *py* in hieratic. One of the stelae evokes the creation of an Egypto-Sudanese empire, proclaiming that by the will of Amun of Napata, the sovereign of Kush made and unmade, as he pleased, kings and leaders in both Egypt and Nubia. The other stela, often called the Triumphal Stela, contains a detailed account of how Piye, beating back a northern coalition led by Tefnakhte, extended Kushite sovereignty over the delta.

The Triumphal Stela is an exceptional document that represents an initial adaptation of Egyptian literary conventions and pharaonic ideological standards to the interests of the dynasty that emerged from the south. This original work stresses Piye's strict devotion, his respect for traditional taboos, and his solicitude toward the royal stables. With a sort of naive objectivity, it reflects the give and take between the universalistic concepts of an outsider who incarnated the theocracy of Amun and a recognition of the pretensions to royalty that the final successors of Shoshenq I displayed. Thanks to the new school of scribes who worked at Napata, we catch a glimpse, for once, of the personality of a general and diplomat, and at the same time, of the complex political situation at the end of the eighth century B.C.E.

K. Myśliwiec, *The Twilight of Ancient Egypt: First Millennium B.C.E.* (Ithaca, 2000), pp. 73–85.

See Kush, Kushite (Dynasty), Napata.

Princes, Princesses

The boys and girls born to the king bore the titles "king's son" and "king's daughter." In various periods, this title was extended to nonroyal individuals. At the beginning of the Fourth Dynasty, true "king's sons" were among the highest officials.

Under later dynasties, some of their descendants, now less influential, bore the titles of princes and princesses. Delegation of power could entail

FIGURE 6. *Ramesside prince with "sidelock of youth" wrapped in a band of cloth. From J.-F. Champollion,* Monuments de l'Égypte et de la Nubie, *vol. 3 (Paris, 1845), pl. 215.*

the assigning of such titles, and we find hypothetical "king's sons" among the local governors of the Second Intermediate Period. This usage was retained in the New Kingdom to designate those who conducted divine processions in place of the king ("king's sons" of Amun and of Nekhbet) and the viceroy of Nubia, the "King's Son of Kush."

Certain actual daughters of the king were closely associated with their father on monuments and in the cults; their names were enclosed in cartouches, which was not at all the case with royal sons. Even adult princes and princesses were depicted wearing a false sidelock, a sign of youth. Until the Eighteenth Dynasty, the lock was braided; afterward, it hung down and was wrapped in a band of cloth (see figure 6).

During the well-attested reign of Ramesses II, who commissioned representations of endless processions of both his sons and his daughters, a number of princes were invested with military and priestly offices, a practice that seems to have been infrequent in Egyptian history. At the end of the Eighteenth Dynasty, an old title, *erpa* (originally *iry-pat,* which meant something like "member of the landed nobility"), was used to designate the highest-ranking individual in the kingdom. In the Ramesside Period, this title, which is conveniently translated as "prince," distinguished the son whom the reigning monarch had chosen to be his deputy and his heir presumptive.

Psammetichus Twenty-sixth Dynasty

This name, perhaps of Libyan origin, was borne by three kings who reigned at critical moments in the Saite dynasty: its rise, its apogee, and its sudden fall. Herodotus tells a number of stories about Psammetichus I (664–610 B.C.E.): how he eliminated approximately twelve other kings, how he recruited Greek and Carian pirates, how his Egyptian soldiers, deprived of their privileges, migrated to the Sudan, and how he created a corps of interpreters to forge fruitful and permanent links with the Greek world. Egyptian sources are in accord with these traditions.

In 664 B.C.E., the Kushites, who had just reconquered the principalities of the delta, were driven back to the Sudan by the Assyrians. Psammetichus prevented a return of the Kushites and eliminated the Meshwesh chieftainships of the north. In 656 B.C.E., he annexed the Thebais, where his daughter Nitocris became "adoratrice of Amun." In Upper and Middle Egypt, his administrators were new supporters or notables from the delta, where autonomous "great chiefs" now disappeared.

Militarily and diplomatically, the state once again became strong. A general mobilization put an end to Libyan incursions, the Scythian hordes were turned back from Egypt, a raid penetrated into Lower Nubia, and Psammatichus was even able to send troops to the Euphrates in an attempt to aid the dying Assyrian empire.

The reign of the first Psammetichus was remarkably long. That of his grandson, Psammetichus II (595–589 B.C.E.), was quite brief. Nonetheless, the great number and the sculptural quality of the monuments that have come down to us from the latter and his ministers are significant. The major event of his reign was his war against the Kushite kingdom of Napata; his Egyptian soldiers and foreign auxiliaries penetrated beyond the Third Cataract and undoubtedly went as far as the city of Napata itself. In a final manifestation of the old enmity between the Saites and the Kushites, the names of the Twenty-fifth Dynasty kings were erased, retrospectively annulling their pretensions to rule over Egypt.

Down to the Ptolemaic Period, many Egyptians were baptized with the glorious name of Psammetichus. One of them, the son of the usurper Amasis, had the misfortune of coming to the throne just when the Persians attacked Egypt. His reign lasted only six months (526–525 B.C.E.). The Great King Cambyses dethroned him and then forced him to commit suicide.

A. de Sélincourt, *Herodotus: The Histories,* rev. ed. (Harmondsworth, Middlesex, 1972), pp. 129, 139–40, and 190–94.

See Adoratrice, Amasis, Erasures, Kushite (Dynasty), Saite (Dynasties).

Psusennes 1040–993 B.C.E., Twenty-first Dynasty

This son of the Theban pontiff Pinudjem went to Tanis and succeeded Smendes. His reign was especially long. On occasion, he took the name "Ramesses Psusennes," styling himself a successor of the Twentieth Dynasty, but the deeds of this personage, who proclaimed himself both king and first prophet of Amun, characterize him as one who established a Lower Egyptian regime dominated by Theban theology. On eleven acres of the flat, sandy hilltop of Tanis, he founded a temenos dedicated to Amun. Beautiful old statues, the famous so-called Hyksos monuments, embellished its temple. In building his tomb at Tanis, Psusennes broke with the tradition of preparing the pharaoh's final resting place in the Valley of the Kings. The subterranean areas of this tomb, miraculously unravaged, were excavated and explored by Pierre Montet between 1939 and 1946. This pharaoh, whose reign spanned the turn of the first millennium, thus owes his fame today to his gold mask, his silver coffin, his precious vessels, and his abundant collection of jewelry, which are complemented by the treasures of his minister Undebaunded and his successor Amenemope. The quantity of precious metals shows that the royal treasury was relatively full at this time, though Egyptian expansion was on the wane. It was in the reign of Psusennes that Saul, and then the young David, laid the foundations of Judah and Israel with no intervention from Egypt.

P. Montet, *La Nécropole royale de Tanis,* vol. 2: *Les Constructions et le tombeau de Psousennès* (Paris, 1951).

See Pinudjem, Tanis, Third Intermediate Period.

Ptahhotpe

Tradition credited Ptahhotpe, who was supposedly the vizier of Djedkare Izezi, with authoring a wisdom text (the Instruction of Ptahhotpe) so famous that it even influenced the monastic ideal of the Copts. The historical reality of Ptahhotpe is far from certain, but the spirit that animates the work seems indeed to be that of the Old Kingdom; the world is ruled by an immanent order (*maat*), which punishes transgressors more or less automatically, while the creator god who established this order remains somewhat aloof.

M. Lichtheim, *Ancient Egyptian Literature: A Book of Readings,* vol. 1: *The Old and Middle Kingdoms* (Berkeley, 1973), pp. 61–80.

Ptahwash (*or* Washptah)

Ptahwash was overseer of works and vizier during the reigns of Sahure and Neferirkare. He had an experience so prodigious that the latter king commanded that an account of it be carved in Ptahwash's tomb. Unfortunately, the inscription has come down to us in a highly damaged condition. We can see, however, that this adventure brought him both glory and death. In fact, he was struck by an illness that had such unusual symptoms that ancient writings had to be consulted—in vain, though, for he could not be saved. The king made a point of assuring him a sumptuous funeral.

A. Roccati, *La Littérature historique sous l'ancient empire égyptien* (Paris, 1982), p. 108.

Ptolemy

Satrap of Egypt when the empire of Alexander the Great was divided up, the Macedonian general Ptolemy, son of Lagos, became its king—"Pharaoh Ptolemy" to the native inhabitants—after the disappearance of his very nominal sovereign, Alexander Aigos (309 B.C.E.). His name would be borne by his fourteen successors on the throne of Alexandria, and this Ptolemaic (or Lagide) dynasty would rule nearly three centuries (323–30 B.C.E.). The dynasty was part of the political and cultural history of both the young Hellenistic world and the ancient world of Egypt. It thus had two aspects, one Alexandrian and the other pharaonic. The Ptolemies, who practiced consanguineous marriage, endowed themselves with Greek epithets characterizing their family relationships, which were presumed to be affectionate, or attributing to them certain virtues that the Greek morality of the times conferred on an ideal sovereign. The epithets included Philadelphos (brother loving), Philopator (father loving), Philometor (mother loving), Soter (savior), Euergetes (beneficent), Epiphanes (revealed), and Eucharistos (endowed with divine grace). Translated into Egyptian, these epithets took their place in the kings' hieroglyphic titularies, along with native epithets that related or associated them with the deities of the land: Re, Amun, Ptah, Isis, and the Apis bull. The Ptolemies also were distinguished by the major political role played by the sister-queens, from Arsinoe Philadelphos, the divine companion of Ptolemy II, to the marvelous Cleopatra VII.

Though Hecataeus of Abdera had written a philosophical treatment of the merits of the ancient monarchy for the information of Ptolemy I, and though Manetho, a priest from Sebennytos, had written works in Greek about the history and beliefs of his native land, there is nothing pharaonic in what history has to say about the bloody quarrels that eventually tore apart the royal family and threw Alexandria into turmoil. Egyptian priests were rarely caught up in these quarrels. In Alexandria, politics involved the royal circle, the soldiery, and the people; legislation, customs, dress, architecture, sculpture, language, science, and culture were essentially Greek, except in the mixed quarter where the Serapeum was located. Foreign policy was conducted on the scale of the Hellenized world; as geopolitics obliged, the first three Lagides conquered Palestine and southern Syria, as the Ramessides had done long ago, but their Greek and seafaring horizon also led them to dominate the Aegean, Cyrenaica, Cilicia, Caria, and Cyprus. Their military force consisted of Greeks and others, who were settled en masse and were granted the benefit of hereditary land tenure. It was Ptolemy IV who rearmed the Egyptian military caste, who played a decisive role in the defensive victory over the Syrian adversary Antiochus III at Raphia in 217 B.C.E. This reawakened native population would turn against the regime on more than one occasion. A number of nationalist revolts broke out, and under Ptolemy V, the native pharaohs Harwennofre and Ankhwennofre even liberated the Thebais.

During the second and first centuries B.C.E., resistance in the provinces and the weakness of the government in Alexandria increased the autonomy of the clergies, economic powers well placed to influence the psychology of the people. These hereditary priests, who controlled the sacred revenues and preserved the ancestral writings and arts, thoroughly integrated the Greco-Macedonian kings and queens into their ritual system. A typical product of the times was the drafting of honorific decrees by priestly synods to exalt the victories and the pious deeds of the Ptolemies; the texts were issued in hieroglyphs, Demotic, and Greek. In the course of journeys in the delta, or even as far as Upper Egypt, certain Lagides donned the clothing and performed the immemorial ritual acts of a pharaoh: coronations at Memphis, visits to sacred animals, foundation or consecration of temples. The high priests of Memphis frequented the Alexandrian court, and the latter even received communications from a minor priest and visionary who lived at Saqqara. Along with Sarapis, who was identified with Osiris-Apis, Isis became a Greek deity, and the Hellenic rulers borrowed her insignia.

Under the Lagide dynasty, the temples in many cities were enlarged or entirely rebuilt in pure Egyptian style. Philae, Ombos (Kom Ombo), Edfu, Esna, Dendara, and el-Madamud are the best preserved of the great constructions that were begun in the names of the Ptolemies. The learned scribes who composed the inscriptions covering the walls of these temples used a complex writing system that radically expanded the expressive potential of written characters that were also images; at the same time, they refined the architectural semantics and the ornamental grammar of the language. To a greater extent than ever, they used representations and texts to make explicit records of the rituals necessary for the security of the cosmos, as well as of the myths that determined its configuration. As had always been the case, in the reliefs and in the texts that accompanied them, the king was the sole mediator, performing the rituals that maintained the gods and goddesses and receiving their blessings on the kingdom and its inhabitants. It is thus the vast, intact Ptolemaic temples, with their superabundance of inscriptions, that have preserved the most extensive sources for reconstructing the pharaonic ideological system and understanding its symbols. And yet, under these Ptolemies, another aesthetic, another description of power and of man, and other interpretations of the universe were winning over the elites of the land.

M. Chauveau, *Egypt in the Age of Cleopatra* (Ithaca, 2000), chapters 1 and 2.
See Alexandria, Cleopatra.

Punt

When the sun rose, it appeared "to the southeast, behind the land of Punt." This distant land is sometimes mentioned in royal inscriptions and private autobiographies as the destination of peaceful expeditions dispatched by the king, principally to obtain incense, myrrh, and olibanum, products that were indispensable to the cults of the gods and to human luxury (censings, unguents). This land of aromatic substances was sometimes accessed by ship. Prefabricated boats were carried along the trails of the eastern desert and were launched on the Red Sea at Quseir or Wadi Gawasis, and the journey to Punt was sometimes combined with an expedition to the Sinai. The Puntites also sailed small boats of their own to the shores of Egypt. Egyptologists have long since given up on locating Punt in Arabia Felix (Yemen), or on equating it with the biblical land of Ophir and its "mines of King Solomon." In fact, there was also a land route that brought the products of Punt to Egypt; the "mountain of Punt" and its auriferous pools clearly lay on the borders of Kush, in the Nile valley of Nubia. Scholars no longer feel a need to go as far as Zanzibar or Socotra, or even to Somalia in search of Punt.

Punt was home to various incense-bearing trees (*Boswellia* and *Commiphera,* which thrive on low rainfall), *dom*-palms, and species of hard, black trees called *heben* in Egyptian, the origin of our own word "ebony." Visitors to Punt encountered panthers and cheetahs, monkeys and baboons (the latter on dry hills), as well as giraffes and rhinoceroses, animals that dwelled in the plains. Gold also came from Punt. In the middle of summer, rain fell on the mountain of Punt only in the miraculous form of veritable deluges. These details gleaned from texts enable us to locate the famous shores of Punt and their vast hinterland. The land called Punt included a desert region and a Sahelian region between the 22nd and the 18th parallel N. The south of Punt might have included the present-day province of Kassala and the north of Eritrea. To the west and the northwest, an undefinable border separated it from Kush and the land of the Medjoi (roughly Etbaya).

Egyptian explorers could get to Punt by land, though they had to cross vast stretches of mountains and desert. Punt could also be reached by sea, but at the cost of huge logistical efforts and a lengthy, coast-hugging journey. Even so, the land was both divine and familiar. Min of Koptos, the patron god of the trails in the eastern desert, was the prototype of the Medjoi from Punt and of the wanderers who explored that land. The sky goddess Hathor, patroness of major voyages to foreign lands, was "mistress of Punt."

The importing of precious incense "from hand to hand and at the price of numerous exchanges" was unpredictable and irregular. Sending a naval expedition meant exposure to the perils of the sea and to the mysteries of the ends of the earth. (It was on a voyage to those regions that the hero of the Tale of the Shipwrecked Sailor found himself on the ephemeral island of a divine serpent.) For a king of Egypt, to send a large fleet to this distant land of incense, gold, and exotic African products was an act of considerable economic and religious significance. Such an act, inspired by the god Amun, was the sole major foreign exploit during the reign of Queen Hatshepsut, who had the happy circumstances recorded in beautiful texts and picturesque images.

The first known mentions of relations with Punt date to the Fifth Dynasty, and thus to the twenty-fifth century B.C.E. (in the reign of Sahure, and then that of Izezi, to whom a pygmy was brought). The latest attested expeditions to that land date to the Twenty-sixth Dynasty. We may wonder whether, when he planned a canal linking the two seas and when he launched Phoenician triremes on the Red Sea, Necho I intended to compete with southern Arabia by introducing aromatics and other products from Punt into the Mediterranean market.

C. Lalouette, *Thèbes ou la naissance d'un empire* (Paris, 1986), pp. 246–56.
See Hatshepsut, Henenu, Inyotefoqer, Ramesses III, Sahure.

Pyramids

As mediator between the people and the universe ruled by the divine, the royal office conferred a divine nature on the one who exercised it, and this higher destiny continued after death. As early as the Archaic Period, rituals and buildings intended for the burial of the pharaoh were different from those that benefited his subjects. The Old Kingdom was an inordinate example of the difference. Large brick structures (called mastabas) were erected above the burial vaults of the Archaic kings. Under Djoser, a series of stone mastabas placed one atop the other yielded the Step Pyramid, which was surrounded by a vast imitation jubilee palace. Under Snofru, the "true" pyramid was achieved in stages: the step pyramid of Maidum, the "rhomboidal" southern pyramid of Dahshur, and the true northern pyramid of Dahshur. Cheops created the largest of the pyramids, while that of Chephren is nearly as tall. At Giza, Saqqara, and Abusir, the pharaohs who succeeded them contented themselves with far less ambitious mountains of stone, but there is still a marked difference between these monuments and the surrounding mastabas of their officials. Constructed on the western plateau above the plain of Memphis, each pyramid had a funerary temple at its foot; this temple was connected by a roofed causeway to a valley temple and a "pyramid city" whose residents farmed the countryside. Smaller pyramids were built next to that of the king to receive the burials of his queens.

Beginning with Wenis, the Pyramid Texts were copied in the king's (and later the queens') burial chamber; these were formulas whose recitation enabled the king, identified with Osiris, to regain his corporal integrity, to ascend to the sky, to share in the eternity of the sun, to escape the dangers of the netherworld, and to take nourishment. The Step Pyramid surely represented the idea of ascension, while the shape of the true pyramid can only be the object of conjecture (projecting sunbeams, primordial mound). Specialists in ancient architecture continue to debate certain details of how the pyramids were constructed, principally the method of constructing the ramps used to lift the stones. The specialists recognize the increasing know-how of those who built them and the undeniable process of trial and error they went through. Despite earlier speculation, scholars now know that the Memphite pyramids were not conceived to ward off plunderers, who would have been unimaginable at that time, or to transmit some message to our own day. The volume of the fills is enormous relative to that of the access corridors and the chambers, which is not practical. But a pyramid was not just a funerary locale; it was the pinnacle of the monument that each reign represented.

With the exception of Mentuhotpe II, at least, who had a sort of stepped mastaba with porticos at Deir el-Bahari, the pharaohs of the Middle Kingdom endowed their tombs with a pyramidal form. These include the cemeteries of el-Tarif (Eleventh Dynasty); of Lisht, el-Lahun,

Dahshur, and Hawara (Twelfth Dynasty); of Mazghuna and Saqqara South (Thirteenth Dynasty); and of Dra Abu el-Naga (Seventeenth Dynasty). From the Eleventh Dynasty on, the Pyramid Texts became accessible to private persons, and—though in reduced size—the pyramid form became common atop the funerary chapels of the nobles in the New Kingdom. The monarchs of the Eighteenth through the Twentieth Dynasties prepared rock-cut tombs in the Valley of the Kings, and later pharaohs located their funerary monuments in the temples of cities. But the Kushite kings of the Twenty-fifth Dynasty returned to the ancient custom, erecting royal pyramids in Nubia, as did their Napatan and Meroitic successors.

J.-P. Lauer, *Le Problème des pyramides d'Égypte* (Paris, 1952); G. Goyon, *Le Secret des bâtisseurs des grandes pyramides* (Paris, 1977); I. E. S. Edwards, *The Pyramids of Egypt*, rev. ed. (Harmondsworth, Middlesex, 1985); M. Lehner, *The Complete Pyramids* (New York, 1997).

Queens

Egyptian couples were singularly modern. Men had only one official wife at a time. Women had their own property and enjoyed full legal rights, and in the iconography, they were depicted on the same scale as their husbands. Exogamy was the rule; consanguineous marriage did not become widespread until the Hellenistic era. The king, however, was superhuman; this was reflected in his matrimonial arrangements and in the status of his wives. He had a number of wives, one of whom, from the Twelfth Dynasty on, was titled "great king's wife." He could even marry his sister. In the first half of the Eighteenth Dynasty, the "great wife" was regularly the king's half sister, and this practice was almost a rule in the Macedonian family of the Ptolemies. Sometimes, a "king's daughter" assumed the rank of "great wife." Princes generally took wives from among the subjects, while the king sometimes welcomed the daughter of an allied sovereign as his bride.

Pharaonic matriarchy, along with a principle of a necessary solar consanguinity, is a speculative model in which we can no longer believe. The role of the womb in transmitting legitimacy was passive and doctrinally limited to a mythic "theogamy": the mother of the king was believed to have been impregnated with a predestined child by the supreme deity, who was incarnated in the body of the physical father. Nor did a private person who managed to ascend the throne have to legitimize himself by marrying an heiress of the preceding dynasty; verified cases of such unions, whose importance was more political than juridical, are quite rare.

From as early as the Archaic Period, as demonstrated by their titles and their tombs, queens enjoyed a status that distinguished them from ordinary women. In the Old Kingdom, their burial place was not a simple mastaba, but rather a small pyramid. In the New Kingdom, they would be buried in the Valley of the Queens. The headdress in the form of a vulture (symbolic of the goddess Nekhbet) is first attested in the Fifth Dynasty; the frontal uraeus (symbolic of the goddess Wadjit) is first attested in the Sixth Dynasty. The custom of enclosing the names of certain wives and daughters of the king in a cartouche made its appearance in the Middle Kingdom. The many titles employed in the course of the centuries summarize what it meant to be a royal wife: daughter of a god, united with the crowns, mistress of the Two Lands, divine mistress of the world. The titles also praise her gracious beauty and identify her as the fragrant source of joy in the palace, model of ritual purity, and sovereign among all women.

The queens had priestly functions; it was they who shook the sistra (rattles) and the rustling collars (called *menat*) as they stood before the gods and goddesses. Queens were the only human beings who shared the headdresses of pharaohs (the uraeus) and goddesses (Hathor horns, plumes, vulture). In monumental statues and representations of rituals, the mother and wives of the king are frequently present, as well as certain of his daughters, who are distinguished by the same insignia. This participation of two generations of women in representations of royal theophany is easily explained by reference to the double function—wife and daughter—of the divine consort of the sun, who was the companion, the creatrix, and the generative organ of the creator god. The informal representations of Nefertiti and her little daughters in the Atenist imagery is a somewhat extravagant example of this sacral function. But the religious interpretation of these themes cannot erase our visceral impression of monarchs nursing a genuine affection for their wives (Amenophis III and Teye, Ramesses II and Nofretari), given that conjugal love was a virtue in Egyptian wisdom literature. Both in sculpture in the round and in reliefs, Egyptian art affirmed the perfect beauty and the eternal freshness of every woman represented. The charming images of queens adorned as goddesses clearly conform to this principle. Of course, queens had their own households (residence, landed property, personnel) and shared in the administration and the income of large "harems."

These lovely persons who ritually incarnated the female component of divine kingship were well placed to participate occasionally in the exercise of earthly sovereignty. At the beginning of the Eighteenth Dynasty, the dowager queens Ahhotpe and Ahmose-Nofretari were clearly political personalities, and their regencies undoubtedly paved the way for the astonishing career of Hatshepsut, the queen who became a king. Apparently in the reign of Ninetjer, the third king of the distant Second Dynasty, it was decided that a woman could exercise the office of king, and the name Uadjenes, which tradition preserved as that of the fourth ruler of that dynasty, is indeed a feminine name. In fact, the precedent was followed on only four occasions, widely dispersed in time, each of which present problems for scholars today:

Nitocris, at the end of the Sixth Dynasty; according to legend, she committed suicide.

Nefrusobk, reportedly feeble-minded, but who marked the end of the Twelfth Dynasty.

Hatshepsut, whose memory was obliterated both by her coregent, Tuthmosis III, and by tradition.

Twosre, the last sovereign of the Nineteenth Dynasty, who also suffered postmortem condemnation.

We might have imagined that the religious prestige of royal wives and daughters, along with the high moral and legal standing of Egyptian women, would have entailed equal opportunity and success for both genders in the matter of kingship. Such, however, was not the case. As we have seen, the cases in which circumstances enabled a woman to become a king in her own right were exceptional and short-lived, and in the two cases best known to us, they were condemned after the fact. Theology integrated femininity into myth and ritual, to be sure, but wisdom literature and custom restricted the role of women to that of mistress of the household and of honored companion and mother. We know little of female scribes and physicians, and queens usually had no administrative responsibilities in areas other than religion. Control over warriors and administrators remained a man's affair.

L. Troy, *Patterns of Queenship in Ancient Egyptian Myth and History,* Boreas 14 (Uppsala, 1986); G. Robins, *Women in Ancient Egypt* (Cambridge, Mass., 1993), chapters 1–2.

See Adoratrice; Ahmose-Nofretari; Erasures; Harem; Hatshepsut; Nefertiti; Nitocris; Princes, Princesses; Teye; Twosre.

Ramesses II 1279–1213 B.C.E., Nineteenth Dynasty

Ramesses II was the son of Sethos I and Muttuya (or Tuya). His father had familiarized him at an early age with the royal profession, and, to consolidate the young dynasty, he conferred the crowns and a complete titulary on Ramesses while he himself was still alive. During this coregency, Ramesses founded temples of his own (Abydos, Beit el-Wali). He began his sole reign with an increase in activity in the gold mines, the quarries, and the construction sites (including development of Pi-Riamsese). After that, foreign policy long occupied this haughty warrior; the policy is well attested by the monumental texts of Ramesses himself as well as by the Hittite archives.

In year 4, a military excursion penetrated as far as Phoenicia, and the land of Amurru (the Lebanon) removed itself from the Hittite sphere of influence. In year 5, open warfare occurred. The Hittite king Muwatallis concentrated an enormous coalition of his Anatolian and Syrian vassals in the vicinity of Qadesh. Ramesses, who was leading the first division of the Egyptian army, was deceived by enemy agents and found himself attacked in his camp, while his three remaining divisions were still on the march far behind him. The desperate resistance of the king and his Sherden guard threw the attacking Hittite chariotry into confusion, and disaster was avoided by the arrival of Egyptian reinforcements. The respite that followed was scarcely a success for Egypt, which again lost Amurru. But the heroism of Ramesses (with the moral support of Amun) revealed him exemplifying the ideal of a king as sole agent of his victories. The Qadesh Poem, along with immense temple reliefs commemorating the Battle of Qadesh, turned the event into personal propaganda for the sovereign.

In the wake of the battle, however, Ramesses was obliged to pacify his restive possessions in Canaan and Transjordan. After that, he launched raids into Syria and found himself in a position to intervene diplomatically in the internal quarrels of the Hittites (Urkhi-Teshub against Hattusilis). The threat posed by Assyria finally led the two adversaries to put an end to sixteen years of conflict with a treaty in Ramesses' year 21, and then to a cooperation that entailed two successive marriages of Ramesses II to daughters of Hattusilis.

The Egyptian frontier included the south of the Lebanon and the plain of Damascus, a Syrian capital where a stela carved in local rock, depicting Ramesses II paying homage to Baal-Seth, was discovered in 1993. The land of Kush remained quiet and was well administered by devoted viceroys who made displays of their luxury. Great courtiers, whose loyalty to the ruler and whose personal wealth are attested by their magnificent votive and funerary monuments, clearly knew how to make peace and prosperity reign in Egypt. Ramesses the warrior repulsed marginal peoples who disturbed the delta: the Shasu, bedouin troublemakers in the east; the Sherden, pirates held in check by Egyptian warships; and the Libyan hordes of Marmarica, who were kept under surveillance by a string of fortresses.

Adding his own name to them, Ramesses II completed the decoration of temples built by his father (e.g., Abydos, Gurna, Hypostyle Hall of Karnak) or by still earlier kings (rear exterior wall of Karnak). He also restored images that had been effaced under Akhenaten. But above all, he inaugurated scores of new foundations and buildings. From Napata to Palestine, there are few sites where some stone bearing his name has not been found. The projects he initiated reflect new styles of carving in stone: massive geometrical forms (including monostyle columns, group statues in raised relief, and statues backing onto walls). We also witness the spread of sunk relief (from "solar" symbolism), the apogee of the historical genre of texts, and epigraphic prolixity. The works include the two temples of Abu Simbel (see figure 7), his Theban temple (called the Ramesseum), his obelisks, and his colossi. Though it has long been disliked by historians of art, the reign of Ramesses created a new style, harmonious in its enormousness, and not corrupt or slapdash. He usurped far fewer old works than has been claimed (and rather late in his life).

Between his year 30 and his death at the age of ninety, Ramesses II celebrated at least thirteen jubilees. He was buried in an especially vast tomb in the Valley of the Kings. His mummy was found in the cachette of Deir el-Bahari; he had been a redhead, like the god Seth, the patron of his family. His various "great wives" (Nefertari was the first of them, and one of the last was Maathor-Nefrure, a Hittite princess) and his other wives bore him many sons and daughters (about one hundred princes and princesses have been counted). He honored Canaanite deities, and his eldest daughter and one of his dogs were named after the goddess Anat. To mark his direct and intimate relations with all the deities, he even set up special idols called "gods of Ramesses" for adoration; he also multiplied the theological aspects of his own person, which were incorporated in colossi. At Karnak and elsewhere, he justified his epithet Meryamun, "beloved of Amun," yet his foundations and pious acts favored the Heliopolitan cult of the sun and the cult of the fearsome god Seth, patron of his family.

Unlike that of Amenophis IV, the case of Ramesses II, who completed the work of Haremhab and Sethos I, demonstrates how a strong personality could find fulfillment and assert itself in the traditional role of a pharaoh. The monumental and epigraphic style of his reign served as a reference point down to the end of the Libyan Period. Though overshadowed by that of the legendary Sesostris, the glory of Ramesses, as estab-

FIGURE 7. *Temple of Ramesses II at Abu Simbel. Photo by Nancy J. Corbin.*

lished by his formidable constructions and his victory bulletins, was still remembered in the Roman era (Diodorus' Osymandias, Tacitus' Ramses). Two of his foundations preserved the name of Ramesses in cultural memory (the store city of Ramses in the Bible) and on the soil of Egypt (*Ramsîs* of Beherah). He is the only pharaoh to have a major street in Cairo named after him.

K. A. Kitchen, *Pharaoh Triumphant: The Life and Times of Ramesses II* (Warminster, 1982); *Ramsès le Grand* (Paris, 1976).

See Diplomacy, Khaemwese, Merneptah, Nineteenth Dynasty, Ramessides, Sethos I.

Ramesses III 1187–1156 B.C.E., Twentieth Dynasty

The funerary temple of Ramesses III at Medinet Habu, which is almost entirely preserved, is the most expressive example of the "mansions of millions of years" erected by the Ramessides on the west bank of Thebes. Its general plan, its decorative program, the phraseology of its inscriptions, and the composition of its reliefs imitate the Ramesseum, the homologous (though more spacious) monument of Ramesses II. With great panache, Ramesses III, who was the second member of a new dynasty, emulated the royal "look" that had embodied the grandeur of the preceding dynasty. But the situation of the kingdom was no longer the same. Ramesses II had fought on the Orontes, while Ramesses III fought for the security of the delta. On land, he was obliged to clear the entire western delta of Libyan hordes, and to conduct two wars to confine them to Marmarica. The second Libyan war is one of the epics recorded at Medinet Habu in dramatic reliefs and verbose poems. Another epic in that temple is dedicated to the battles that saved Egypt from the Sea Peoples: the Philistines, the Tjeker, and the Danaeans. Their fleet was defeated by land and sea forces at the entry of a branch of the Nile; families of immigrants arriving from Asia in ox-drawn chariots were massacred or captured. Ramesses III was able to maintain some bases in Canaan (e.g., Beth Shan) to pacify the bedouins of Idumaea and exploit the copper of Timna on the Gulf of Aqaba, and to dispatch a fleet to Punt.

Three dossiers on papyrus illustrate what was happening on the domestic front. The Great Papyrus Harris, written under Ramesses IV, enumerates the foundations and calculates the donations that his father had made to the gods. In this papyrus, Amun of Thebes appears as by far the preponderant economic power. This document, and other texts as well, convey a sense of an increasing subordination of royal to divine power. The Strike Papyrus testifies to difficulties in provisioning: the workmen of Deir el-Medina demanded the payment of their in-kind salary from a financially strapped administration. Four transcripts drawn up after the king's death list top servants of the palace, including a physician and military leaders, who, in collusion with the women of the harem, plotted to foment uprisings and to make an attempt on the life of the king with the help of magic. An ostracon informs us that the actions of an "enemy" troubled the peace of Thebes toward the end of the reign. We do not know whether Ramesses III died as a result of the plot or of the evil spells, but his mummy, which was buried in the Valley of the Kings (KV 11) and was found in the royal cachette of Deir el-Bahari, bears no trace of violence. Beautiful rock-cut tombs prepared for four of his daughters and two of his queens (Isis and Tity) are located in the Valley of the Queens. We have lovely faience plaques from his two palaces at Medinet Habu and Tell el-Yahudiya.

C. Lalouette, *L'Empire des Ramsès* (Paris, 1985), pp. 298–344.

See Libyans, Ramessides, Strikes, Twentieth Dynasty.

Ramesses IV 1156–1150 B.C.E., Twentieth Dynasty

Ramesses IV was the son of Ramesses III and his designated successor. We do not know why he changed his throne name in the second year of his reign. His building activity in the temples amounted to little: the decoration of the rear of the temple of Khons at Karnak and the widespread reconsecration or restoration of existing edifices, marked by bands of hieroglyphic texts in the margins of bas-reliefs or by the insertion of his cartouches. Although he laid the foundations for an immense funerary temple, ultimately he contented himself with a building of rather modest size.

Aside from inscriptions left in the Wadi Hammamat by large expeditions sent to quarry *bekhen* (graywacke) intended for statues, the most vivid mementos of this king are the two stelae on which he prays in personal terms to the deities of Abydos. In particular, when he reached the age of forty, he prayed to Amun and Osiris for a reign as long as that of Ramesses II (67 years!), or in other words, for the longest lifetime that Egyptians considered possible (110 years). In support of his request, he asserted that in four years, he had enriched the gods more than his formidable predecessor had done in all his reign. To accelerate the preparation of his tomb, he radically increased the workforce in the Valley of the Kings; perhaps he was in fear for his health. He died in his year 6. Ramesses IV, who was the first of the obscure Ramessides, gives the impression of having had a spirit that was more religious than political. Except for mining expeditions to the Sinai, we have no attestation of activity in Asia during his reign. His mummy was found in the cachette in the tomb of Amenophis II.

See Ramessides, Twentieth Dynasty.

Ramessides

The term "Ramesside" is an adequate designation of both the period of a little more than two centuries that constituted the second part of the New Kingdom (1293–1069 B.C.E.) and the kings of that period, who composed our Nineteenth and Twentieth Dynasties. The adjective comes from the name Ramesses, variant Ramses, two Greek transcriptions of the Egyptian *Re-mes-su,* "Re has created him."

With the possible exception of Amenmesse, all the kings of the Nineteenth Dynasty, the best-known of whom was Ramesses II, were descended from the vizier Ramesses, son of Sethos, who became Ramesses I. Sethnakhte, the founder of the Twentieth Dynasty, was succeeded by his son and grandson, Ramesses III and Ramesses IV. All the kings descended from Ramesses III placed the name Ramesses in front of the names they had been given at birth (e.g., Ramesses VI and Ramesses IX both called themselves Ramesses-Amenhirkhopshef).

It is apposite to extend the qualification "Ramesside" to the institutions, the art, and the culture. The entire period displays a style that took shape, for the most part, during the lengthy reign of Ramesses II.

While continuing to hand down classic works of the Old and Middle Kingdoms, the scribes of the period produced a teeming wealth of literature written in Late Egyptian. Miscellanies (collections of satirical essays, well-turned model administrative letters, brief hymns, poems in praise of the king, etc.) were used in the training of students. In the same genre, the lengthy Letter of Hori furnishes a lively picture of the tasks and the competencies of scribes during the reign of Ramesses II. Stories of various sorts were also penned: moralizing (Truth and Falsehood), mythological (Contendings of Horus and Seth), and fantastic (The Doomed Prince, The Two Brothers). New wisdom texts were written, in particular the famous Instruction of Any and Instruction of Amenemope.

C. Lalouette, *L'Empire des Ramsès* (Paris, 1985); G. Steindorff and K. C. Seele, *When Egypt Ruled the East,* 2d ed. (Chicago, 1957), chapter 16.

See Nineteenth Dynasty, Ramesses II, Twentieth Dynasty.

Rekhmire

Rekhmire was a vizier from the second part of the reign of Tuthmosis III to the beginning of the reign of Amenophis II. He was a descendant of a family of viziers (his grandfather Amtju and his uncle User(amun) had also exercised that office) but also the last member of the family to hold the office. Among other tasks, it fell to him to supervise the erection of the temple of Tuthmosis III at Deir el-Bahari. But Rekhmire owes his fame above all to his tomb in the Theban necropolis, in which two basic texts dealing with the office of vizier were copied: the Installation of the Vizier and the Duties of the Vizier. Additionally, many scenes in the tomb depict Rekhmire at work, overseeing the efficiency of the workshops of the temple of Amun and receiving tribute from a number of foreign lands, in particular those of the Aegean world.

T. G. H. James, *Pharaoh's People: Scenes from Imperial Egypt* (London, 1984), pp. 56–71; G. P. F. van den Boorn, *The Duties of the Vizier: Civil Administration in the Early New Kingdom* (London, 1988).

See Amenophis II, Tuthmosis III.

Romans

Octavian conquered Egypt in the year 30 B.C.E. The last Lagide descendant, Ptolemy Caesarion, the son whom Cleopatra had borne to Julius Caesar, was liquidated. The kingdom became a province of the Roman republic, but a province with imperial status: it was the *princeps* alone who appointed a prefect and equestrian procurators at Alexandria. Only rarely would the Roman army in Egypt play a role in the designation of emperors. The Hellenized gentry and the masses in the countryside had no political weight in their overly exploited land. The Romans secularized the temple lands and turned the priests into functionaries. Nevertheless, the clergy maintained the pharaonic concept, and traces of it can be found even in Hermetic philosophy. The Roman principate was not a kingship, but for the sacred scribes, who were little inclined to revise their lore, the absence of the immutable Lord of the Two Lands was existentially inconceivable. On the temple walls, and in the documents drawn up by notaries writing in Demotic, Augustus Caesar and the Caesars who followed him became "Pharaoh." Two cartouches surrounded their names and titles, and like the pharaohs of old, a Tiberius, a Marcus Aurelius, and a Caracalla were depicted officiating before the gods wearing a kilt and crowned with a *nemes,* a *pshent,* or some other crown adorned with a uraeus. For Augustus and his successors, the priests composed lengthy synthetic titularies that not only recalled the domination they exerted over the universe from Rome, but also affirmed their ties to the primordial deities and the sacred animals that Roman authors often mocked. Still, there was innovation: Caesar no longer received a prenomen that included the name of the sun god Re, or the canonical, fivefold royal titulary.

The imperial cult was organized in the Roman fashion, but sometimes, as under Caracalla, an Egyptian-style colossus was erected to honor the lord of the world. Even emperors who sympathized with the religion of Isis, which was practiced by Roman men and women, seem never to have donned the costume of a pharaoh. Few of the Caesars visited Alexandria, much less made a tour of Upper Egypt, as did Hadrian and the Severans. The priests, whose activities were strictly supervised under the watchful eye of an official called the Idios Logos, continued to include the name of the distant god-king in their hymns. Temples continued to be constructed and decorated in the distinctive Ptolemaic style, and the Antonine period even marked a singular renaissance of sacred arts and writing. The formidable hypostyle hall of Esna was begun under Claudius and was decorated principally under Domitian, Trajan, and Hadrian; the cartouches of various emperors, from Augustus to Marcus Aurelius, can be read on a large number of monuments in Upper Egypt. A sacred scribe from Egypt went to Rome to write the text carved on an obelisk that Hadrian intended for the tomb of his favorite, Antinous.

With the crises of the third century C.E., construction work and inscriptions (Egyptian as well as Greek) became rare, and the remaining carvers of hieroglyphs became less and less competent; after the name of Decius was written at Esna, all work ceased there. The last known official hieroglyphic stela known to us is the epitaph of a Buchis bull, the sacred animal of Hermonthis, who died in 340 C.E. At that date, under Constantius II, son of Constantine the Great, Christianity prevailed in the empire. The priests posthumously dated the stela to the era of Diocletian, rallying to the cartouche of the last great emperor who stoutly defended polytheism, and to whom Egypt could still attach the cosmic role of the pharaoh.

P. Derchain, *Le dernier obélisque* (Brussels, 1987); H. I. Bell, *Cults and Creeds in Graeco-Roman Egypt* (Liverpool, 1953).

See Pharaoh.

Sahure 2444–2433 B.C.E., Fifth Dynasty

Sahure was the second pharaoh of the Fifth Dynasty. He built a sun temple, the exact location of which remains unknown, and a funerary complex with a pyramid (height: 161 feet) at Abusir. The bas-reliefs of the pyramid's funerary temple and valley temple depict, among other things, different types of relations with foreign peoples: war against Libyans, but the dispatching of a peaceful expedition to Asia (probably Byblos). The reliefs also include picturesque details of foreign climes (e.g., representations of bears). Official chronicles credited Sahure not only with expeditions to the Sinai and the diorite quarries of Nubia, but also to Punt (probably on the Sudanese coast).

See Fifth Dynasty, Khentkaus, Punt.

Sais

This city in the western delta was situated on the present-day Rosetta branch of the Nile. The site, which still bears its ancient name, Sa (el-Hagar), is deplorably destroyed. Its goddess Neith, whose red crown of Lower Egypt and whose bow were her emblems, was widely depicted in religious representations from the Archaic Period on. She was identified with the cow goddess Mehet-weret, the image of the primordial ocean. The city's political promotion, however, was late. After becoming the capital of a vast kingdom put together in the eighth century B.C.E. by the great chiefs of the Libu, the city was home to the Twenty-fourth and the Twenty-sixth Dynasties, which fought from 730 to 650 B.C.E to reunify a dismembered Egypt. During the Saite renaissance (664–525 B.C.E.), and then under the Persians (525–404 B.C.E.), Neith, mother of Re, supplanted Amun as premier patron of the kingship. Magnificently embellished by Psammetichus I, Psammetichus II, and Amasis, Sais became a prestigious center of sacred lore, as noted by Plato and other Greek writers. Its rulers were well positioned to mount an effective resistance to the Persians, thanks to the city's strategic position: in contact with Libya, with two branches of the Nile that flowed into the Mediterranean, and with the nearby marshes, which were the refuge and habitat of a fierce population (the herdsmen, or *boukoloi*). Amyrtaios of Sais founded the Twenty-eighth Dynasty.

See Amasis, Bocchoris, Persians, Psammetichus, Saite (Dynasties), Tefnakhte, Udjahorresnet.

Saite (Dynasties)

At the time of the "Libyan anarchy" of the eighth century B.C.E., the chiefs of the Libu and the Meshwesh unified the nomes of the western delta around Sais, while the rest of the land remained divided. This territory, adjacent to Libya and the Mediterranean, was able to recruit foreign reinforcements (Libyans, then Greeks) and constituted a stronghold in the face of the assaults of conquerors from afar, both Kushites and Assyrians. Between 730 and 665 B.C.E., under Tefnakhte and Bocchoris of the Twenty-fourth Dynasty and then under the first, obscure kings of the Twenty-sixth Dynasty, this kingdom impeded the undertakings of the Kushites and rivaled them for control of Memphis. Posterity would remember the wise Bocchoris, as well as Nechepso, reputed to be an expert in astrology, and Necho I, who died in battle. Psammetichus I, son of this Necho and whose realm was hemmed in between Kushites, Assyrians, and petty rulers, would reunify Egypt in 656 B.C.E. From the regional dynasty it had been, the Twenty-sixth Dynasty became the sole national dynasty.

Loyal to their native city, its members located their tombs at Sais, while Neith, their patron goddess, became a dominant figure in the royal pantheon. The real capital was at Memphis, but we speak of a "Saite Period" to characterize the regime and the culture of the era ruled by kings named Psammetichus, Necho, Apries, and Amasis (664–625 B.C.E.). It was a period of peace and economic prosperity, and of artistic accomplishments in which innovation was slipped into an archaizing mold. This "Saite renaissance" saw Egypt take its place in a new international alliance, which included not only recruitment of Greek and Carian hoplites, Jewish auxiliaries, and Phoenician shipowners but also maritime activity and exchanges with Greek cities. Confrontation with the Kushites and the Babylonians led to a lengthy combat in which the kings were unable to establish a lasting dominion in Asia or to save Judah, but managed at least to keep Egyptian territory inviolate and prestigious. Thanks to their incommensurably superior military force, the Persians would defeat this house of Sais, but the first of these pharaohs from Iran, who were proclaimed sons of Neith, would maintain religious forms and resources inherited from the Saites.

In the fifth century B.C.E., a man from Sais named Amyrtaios led a revolt against the Persians. A second Amyrtaios (404–398 B.C.E.) was the sole ruler of the Twenty-eighth Dynasty.

K. Myśliwiec, *The Twilight of Ancient Egypt: First Millennium B.C.E.* (Ithaca, 2000), pp. 110–34.

See Amasis, Apries, Bocchoris, Libyans, Necho II, Psammetichus, Sais, Tefnakhte.

Scorpion Protodynastic Period

SCORPION I

Scorpion I was probably the first king of Dynasty Zero (c. 3150 B.C.E.). His tomb, which was discovered in 1988 in the Archaic Period cemetery at Abydos, had rich tomb furnishings, including many inscribed objects, such as jars with painted inscriptions and ivory labels.

SCORPION II

Scorpion II was a king of the Protodynastic Period. His name is written with the scorpion sign, but its reading is uncertain. The name is known especially from the fragments of a historiated limestone mace head found at Hierakonpolis. On this mace head, the king is represented wearing the crown that would be the Upper Egyptian crown of pharaonic Egypt; with a hoe in his hand, he solemnly inaugurates irrigation works. The decoration already exhibits an organization and themes that would be customary during the historical period, in particular, nome emblems with lapwings hanging from them. These birds represented the commoners in the population of Egypt; thus, not only the symbol, but also its semiotic use, belong to the properly pharaonic cultural repertoire. Scorpion is thus unanimously considered one of the immediate predecessors of Narmer; he would have reigned shortly before the historical period.

See Narmer, Origins (Prehistory, Predynastic), Zero (Dynasty).

Sebekhotpe Thirteenth Dynasty

The name Sebekhotpe, which means "the god Sobek is satisfied," was borne by eight pharaohs whose reigns spanned nearly all of the Thirteenth Dynasty.

Sebekhotpe I, Sebekhotpe V, Sebekhotpe VI, and Sebekhotpe VII are known only from a few uninformative monuments. Sebekhotpe VIII reigned when Hyksos pressure was probably already making itself felt. He also is known for erecting a stela at Karnak relating the measures he took to preserve the temple from an exceptionally high Nile inundation. Three other kings of this name emerge, however vaguely, from the shadows surrounding those just mentioned:

Sebekhotpe II (throne name Sekhemre-khutawy), fifteenth king of the Thirteenth Dynasty. He carried out a somewhat active building policy in the south of Upper Egypt (Madamud), and also in Nubia, where he conducted a military campaign. He also warrants attention because it is from his reign that we have an account book from his court at Thebes (Papyrus Boulaq 18).

Sebekhotpe III (throne name Sekhemre-swadjtawy), twentieth king of the Thirteenth Dynasty. He ruled three years and some months. He merits the same comment as the preceding for his activity in Upper Egypt, and for also having escaped the humdrum, thanks to the chance preservation of a document: from his reign, we have the verso of a roster of prisoners that is of exceptional interest for our knowledge of the organization of the work force in this period.

Sebekhotpe IV (throne name Khaneferre). He ruled at least eight years (1730–1723), succeeding his brothers Neferhotep I and Sihathor, with whom he constituted one of the most powerful—or least insignificant—lines of the dynasty. He worked on a great number of temples in Upper Egypt, obtaining materials through expeditions conducted to the mines and quarries, while many of his predecessors and successors contented themselves with usurping older monuments. He marked his attachment to Thebes, his native city, by increasing the offerings to Amun with provisions for which administrative offices were responsible. He overcame hostilities that broke out in Nubia. But though he still held Lisht and Memphis, it seems that an independent kingdom had already formed around Xois in the delta.

See Ankhu, Neferhotep I, Thirteenth Dynasty.

Sebennytic (Dynasty)

The Thirtieth Dynasty took up the torch of the Twenty-ninth (Mendesian) Dynasty when Nectanebo, a general from Sebennytos, dethroned Nepherites II by force. In thirty-seven years (378–341 B.C.E.), three pharaohs—Nectanebo I, Teos, and Nectanebo II—wrote the fearsome epic of the "last native dynasty," succeeding, despite palace crises, in dotting the land with splendid monuments of stone and maintaining a prosperous, independent status for Egypt, which remained alone in the face of the enormous Persian empire. Technically, the national defense was assured by mercenaries led by great commanders, such as the fearsome Agesilaus of Sparta and Chabrias of Athens: in military matters, the Egyptian nation would no longer be master of its own fate. In the religious realm, the priests who represented Egypt watched over its safety with their rituals. Brilliantly assuming the security role of the divine king, the two Nectanebos scrupulously provided for the maintenance of the gods and the burial of sacred animals. In the temples, they undertook vast programs of architectural embellishment (including enclosure walls, propylons, processional roads, shrines, and monoliths), thus assuring a rejuvenation of

Saite art. Eight years after the disappearance of the last native Egyptian king, the Greeks, under Alexander, took possession of an Egypt whose national culture would long continue to flourish.

See Nectanebo, Sebennytos, Teos.

Sebennytos

The name, which survives as Arabic Samannud, is the Greek transcription of Egyptian Tjebenuti. The city is located in the delta, on the central branch of the Nile, slightly south of el-Mansura. Its early history is practically unknown. In the present state of our sources, Sebennytos makes its historical appearance in the Libyan Period. Its pantheon, the warrior god Onuris and his companion, the lion goddess Tefnut (otherwise called Mehyt), made it a religious branch of Thinis. Seat of a principality around 730 B.C.E., Sebennytos was one of the ambitious cities of the northern delta, and it would be the home of the last native dynasty, the Thirtieth Dynasty, two of whose rulers would call themselves "chosen by Onuris." The few archaeological traces found at the site date to this dynasty and to the first Greco-Macedonian kings.

Known from texts beginning with the New Kingdom and the center of a cult of Isis, Hebyt (present-day Behbeit el-Hagar) was part of the Sebennytic nome. The city was already honored by the Saites, and Nectanebo II (who called himself "beloved of Isis") and Ptolemy II endowed it with a large and magnificent temple made of granite.

See Nectanebo, Sebennytic (Dynasty), Teos.

Second Dynasty

See Archaic (Period).

Second Intermediate Period

Some scholars begin the Second Intermediate Period with the advent of the Thirteenth Dynasty, ignoring its obvious social, ideological, and artistic continuity with the second half of the Twelfth Dynasty. A more logical starting point is the Hyksos capture of Memphis (1650 B.C.E.) and the patent decline in the style of monuments and inscriptions that resulted from it. The Thirteenth Dynasty seems to have lasted for a short while after that date, before being supplanted at Thebes by the Seventeenth Dynasty. At the same time, the Hyksos pharaohs of Avaris (Fifteenth Dynasty) ruled in the northeast of the land, while the rest of Egypt was divided into Asiatic chiefdoms and principalities that were in the hands of Egyptian collaborators of the occupying power. The fortresses controlling the Nile valley of Lower Nubia were eventually evacuated under pressure from Nubians who seized Buhen (near Wadi Halfa) and founded an independent principality, even going so far as to hire Egyptian administrators.

Though we have no war account other than that of Kamose, the titles and epithets of private persons and pharaohs, along with archaeological discoveries (e.g., Inyotef V buried with bows and arrows), clearly indicate that this was a time of armed conflict. The Hyksos had prevailed because of their military technology, and advances continued in that domain. In addition, the Egyptians recruited excellent warriors from among a Nubian group called the Medjoi, who had ties to the so-called pan-grave culture. The militarization of society entailed in the reform of the state apparatus during the Middle Kingdom reawakened "feudal" tendencies when unity collapsed. Protected by the ramparts and garrisons of their cities, the nomarchs, especially at Edfu and el-Kab, acted like potentates, even though the Theban pharaohs used periodically renewed matrimonial alliances to confine them to their spheres of influence. In any case, expressions of loyalism began to disappear from autobiographies, while individualism and the exaltation of personal success reemerged; the inscriptions employed phraseology borrowed from the repertoire of the First Intermediate Period. Famines also recurred, and again the problems were dealt with on a purely local basis.

The loss of centers of tradition like Memphis and Lisht led to a decline in culture. Knowledge of the hieratic script and of administrative techniques was maintained, but without education on a national scale, hieroglyphic writing and monumental art degenerated. Scribes blundered when transcribing their cursive drafts, confusing some signs and deforming others with outlandish strokes. Knowledge of the canons was lost, and both two- and three-dimensional sculpture became clumsy and heavy. The beginning of the Eighteenth Dynasty would continue to reflect this decline in quality.

Although the times continued to be troubled, they were undoubtedly less barbarous than those of the Second Intermediate Period. We define the latter's end as the coronation of Ahmose and the beginning of the Eighteenth Dynasty (1539 B.C.E.), though the Hyksos occupation was eliminated only during Ahmose's reign.

See Apophis, Avaris, Hyksos, Inyotef, Kamose, Seqenenre Tao, Seventeenth Dynasty, Sixteenth Dynasty, Thirteenth Dynasty.

Senenmut

Son of a middle-class family of Hermonthis, Senenmut owed his eminent position to his staunch devotion to Queen Hatshepsut; he was her favorite, and perhaps her lover. He accumulated administrative offices in the domain of Amun (steward, overseer of the two granaries, overseer of fields) and in the personal domains of members of the royal family. As "overseer of works" of the king and of Amun, he supervised the great undertakings of the reign, such as the carving, transportation, and erection of a pair of obelisks in the temple of Karnak, and the construction of Hatshepsut's funerary temple at Deir el-Bahari. He bore other titles that associated him directly with the royal family itself: thus, he was the tutor of Nefrure, the daughter of Tuthmosis II and Hatshepsut, and he was in charge of the queen-pharaoh's adornments and insignia on the occasion of her jubilee. Far from being an uncouth upstart, Senenmut pretended to erudition: he invented sophisticated cryptograms by exploiting the resources peculiar to the hieroglyphic writing system.

His social success can be measured by the number and the quality of his monuments. He placed more than twenty statues of himself in the temples of Thebes and Upper Egypt, he constructed a cenotaph at Gebel el-Silsila, and he had two tombs excavated for himself. One of them, concealed in a corner of the court of the funerary temple of Hatshepsut, contained a sarcophagus of a type otherwise reserved for pharaohs. What is more, he was even depicted in this temple, a rare privilege for an ordinary private person, even if these representations were rendered unobtrusive by their clever placement.

Senenmut illustrated what often happens to this sort of favorite, however: the higher they rise, the harder they fall. He fell into disgrace even before the death of Hatshepsut, and he was subjected to a relentless *damnatio memoriae:* his name and his images were mutilated, and his monuments were smashed.

T. G. H. James, *Pharaoh's People: Scenes from Life in Imperial Egypt* (London, 1984), pp. 31–37.
See Erasures, Hatshepsut.

Senwosret (*or* Sesostris) Twelfth and Thirteenth Dynasties

This name, which means "man of the goddess Usret," was borne by pharaohs of the Twelfth and Thirteenth Dynasties.

Two kings of the Thirteenth Dynasty had the name Senwosret, and they can thus be counted as Senwosret IV and Senwosret V. This is about as much as can be said about them, given the very small number and the uninformative nature of their monuments.

Senwosret I 1971–1926 B.C.E., Twelfth Dynasty

Senwosret I was the second king of the Twelfth Dynasty. He was returning from an expedition against the Libyans when he was informed of the assassination of his father, Amenemhet I, with whom he had served as coregent for ten years. He thus had to overcome a serious political crisis. He not only succeeded; he also solidly established the legitimacy of the Twelfth Dynasty, which had been contested. He did so by inspiring hired intellectuals to write works whose literary quality made their apologetic content easily acceptable. The works were: the Instruction of Amenemhet I, a political testament in the form of a posthumous speech by the assassinated king to his son and successor; the Story of Sinuhe, the masterpiece of Egyptian literature, illustrating the theme of Sesostris I's famed clemency; and the Loyalist Instruction, a plea for allegiance to the king in the form of a traditional instruction text.

This propaganda, which was obviously addressed to the literate elite, was reinforced by practical measures, including the continuation of the practice of coregency with the chosen successor, in this case Amenemhet II, Senwosret's son. With stability thus established at home, and external security assured by operations in Nubia, Senwosret I could complete the task that his father had undertaken but not completed: restoring an order like that of old—that of the creator god—while taking account of contemporary realities. This policy accounts not only for the commemoration of Snofru and Sahure, prestigious pharaohs of the Old Kingdom, but also that of the ancestor of the Theban dynasties, the "prince" Inyotef. While drawing on the spirit of the Old Kingdom, Senwosret also demonstrated his attachment to the city where the Middle Kingdom originated; it was at this time that the theme of "victorious Thebes" was elaborated.

In practical terms, the order of the creator god was foremost the smooth functioning of the temples, many of which had suffered from the earlier disorders and civil wars. A systematic program of construction and restoration was begun, to the point that, from Bubastis to Elephantine, there were scarcely any cities whose sanctuaries were not the object of the king's attention. Such work included construction of a new temple, additions, setting up of obelisks and statues, and increases in the offerings. The needed materials were furnished through intensive exploitation of the mines and quarries; an expedition to the Wadi Hammamat in year 38 of Senwosret I consisted of 17,000 men, and it brought back no fewer than 60 sphinxes and 150 statues.

But this impressive balance sheet had a debit column. The new dynasty still had to deal with a strong "feudal" tradition, especially in Middle Egypt, where the nomarchs kept their offices in their families, even if the king's assent was required for each transmission. Generally speaking, the organization of institutions and of the administrative apparatus conformed, mutatis mutandis, to the old model.

Senwosret I built his pyramid complex at Lisht, where his funerary cult was long perpetuated. The major accomplishments of his reign, along with those of certain other kings, were the source of the Greek legend of Sesostris.

Senwosret II 1897–1878 B.C.E., Twelfth Dynasty

Senwosret II was the son and successor of Amenemhet II, with whom he shared the throne as coregent for three years. His reign, whose length has not been precisely established, constituted a transition between the two parts of the Twelfth Dynasty. On the one hand, he continued the previous policy of drawing inspiration from the traditional order without disowning the Theban roots of his dynasty. On the other hand, his reign planted the seeds of the major innovations of the second half of the dynasty: the establishment of a system of fortifications in the Nile valley of Lower Nubia and, especially, the beginning of the reclamation of the marshes of the Faiyum. In fact, Senwosret II built his pyramid complex, with its town of workmen, at el-Lahun, where the Bahr Yusuf, a branch of the Nile, enters the depression of the Faiyum to flow into its lake.

Senwosret III 1878–1843 B.C.E., Twelfth Dynasty

This son of Senwosret II is noted for two salient accomplishments in his reign, aside from the usual construction activity in the temples and the capture of Shechem in Palestine.

One of these was the integration of Lower Nubia into Egyptian territory. A canal was dug at Sehel to facilitate passage through the rapids of the First Cataract. There were four campaigns (in years 8, 10, 16, and 19) to bring hostile populations to heel. A system of eight massive fortresses was set in place to keep watch over the Nile valley as far as the Second Cataract; from that time on, no Nubian was to enter Lower Nubia except to go on a mission or to conduct business in the trading post established at the foot of the fortress of Mirgissa. This policy led to the deification of Senwosret III in Nubia, and he was one of the pharaohs who inspired the Greek legend of Sesostris.

The other achievement was a reorganization of the administration. Under Senwosret III, the last family lines of old-style nomarchs came to an end. At the same time, titles appeared that reflected a reorganization of the administrative apparatus and of the central institutions. The men who held these titles constituted a lower rank of the ruling class, but they shared the elite's ability to erect inscribed funerary monuments, even if they were of middling, even mediocre quality.

Senwosret III built his pyramid complex at Dahshur. Archaeologists discovered important cachettes there, which included jewelry and ceremonial finery.

Seqenenre Tao 1550 B.C.E., Seventeenth Dynasty

Seqenenre Tao was the next to the last pharaoh of the Seventeenth Dynasty. A story that we know of from a Ramesside copy, the Quarrel of Apophis and Seqenenre, narrates how the Hyksos pharaoh Apophis provoked Seqenenre by demanding that he "do away with his hippopotamus pool," because the noise displeased him. This allegorical formulation cloaks a humiliating demand, undoubtedly that the Thebans cease practicing the ritual killing of hippopotami, which were animals of Seth, the god adopted by the Hyksos. Since the manuscript of the story is incomplete, we do not know how the story ended. Scholars postulate that Seqenenre was caught up in a war in which he died; the numerous wounds visible on his mummy seem to have been made by weapons of Hyksos type.

J. A. Wilson, in J. B. Pritchard, ed., *Ancient Near Eastern Texts Relating to the Old Testament,* 2d ed. (Princeton, 1955), pp. 231–32.

See Apophis, Hyksos, Seventeenth Dynasty.

Sethnakhte 1190–1189 B.C.E., Twentieth Dynasty

A number of the rare surviving mentions of the founder of the Twentieth Dynasty consist of his name replacing erasures on usurped monuments from the condemned sovereigns of the end of the Nineteenth Dynasty, or of homages rendered to him by his successors. We do not know where this man, who was probably a soldier, came from when he ended the civil war and the moral anarchy that were weakening Egypt only decades after Ramesses II. His grandson Ramesses IV characterized him as the one whom the neglected gods had designated to eliminate dissidents, rehabilitate the royal office, and restore the economy of the temples. A stela from Elephantine preserves a beautiful proclamation by Sethnakhte himself that confirms this picture: assuming the sun's role as creator god, deploying the energy of Seth, his patron, and mandated by divine oracles, he expelled the bad leaders and their Asiatic auxiliaries. Certain high officials (a vizier, the viceroy of Kush) remained in place.

Sethnakhte was buried in the enlarged rock-cut tomb of Twosre, the female pharaoh who had preceded him. The reign of this restorer did not last more than two years. His son and designated successor, Ramesses III, then assumed the throne.

C. Lalouette, *L'Empire des Ramsès* (Paris, 1985), pp. 295–98.

See Erasures, Ramesses III, Twosre.

Sethos I 1291–1279 B.C.E., Nineteenth Dynasty

Ramesses I, the founder of the Nineteenth Dynasty, ruled for no more than two years. As his designated successor, his son Sethos conducted affairs and was perhaps even invested as coregent. Continuing the policies of Haremhab, he solidified the reestablishment of Egypt as an international power, and he carried out a vigorous building program on behalf of the gods. Though his reign was relatively brief, we have many beautiful inscriptions and a number of intact buildings from it. At Abydos, there is a "temple of millions of years," flanked by a subterranean cenotaph. This, along with his other funerary temple, located at Thebes, and his immense rock-cut tomb in the Valley of the Kings offer some of the finest surviving bas-reliefs. The gigantic hypostyle hall at Karnak was completed under Sethos I and was partially decorated in his name. The Flaminius obelisk now in the Piazza del Popolo at Rome is a souvenir of the major embellishments carried out at Heliopolis. Beautiful enameled tiles have survived from the palace he constructed at Avaris. In the Wadi Miya, on one of the trails in the eastern desert, a speos (rock-cut chapel) recounts the measures that were taken to resume exploitation of the gold mines.

Prosperous and tranquil from Napata to the Mediterranean, Egypt once again took the initiative beyond its borders. A campaign to the west was the first of a series of actions by means of which the Libyans, who had become a threat, were put in their place. In the east, Sethos first pacified the bedouins of the Isthmus of Sinai, whose activities were disturbing the eastern border and traffic to Gaza. Palestine and Transjordan were conquered once again. A stela from Beth Shan describes the tactics Sethos employed to break up rebel bands north of Mount Carmel. The advance toward the north provoked an open clash with the Hittites at Qadesh on the Orontes.

When Sethos died, he left the throne to Ramesses II, on whom he had conferred certain formal attributes of the kingship during his lifetime. By then, Egypt had recovered the southern portion of its former empire in Asia, the gods were well served, and the upper administration was solid and loyal (according to the dossier of the vizier Paser). The mummy of the king, who passed away in his fifties, was found in the royal cachette of Deir el-Bahari.

C. Lalouette, *L'Empire des Ramsès* (Paris, 1985), pp. 88–104; K. A. Kitchen, *Pharaoh Triumphant: The Life and Times of Ramesses II* (Warminster, 1982).

See Nineteenth Dynasty, Ramessides.

Seventeenth Dynasty

The Seventeenth Dynasty was the direct successor of the Thirteenth Dynasty, under conditions that remain obscure. The Seventeenth Dynasty undoubtedly came to power slightly after Hyskos supremacy was established in 1650 B.C.E. The dynasty controlled only Upper Egypt and a part of Middle Egypt, as far as Cusae, the remainder belonging to Asiatic chiefdoms that were vassals of the Hyksos, to Egyptian collaborators, or to the Hyksos themselves. The pharaohs of the Seventeenth Dynasty were obliged to pay tribute to these Hyksos and to tolerate their garrisons, which were installed in strategic places, such as Gebelein. Moreover, the fortresses in Lower Nubia had been abandoned, and the southern boundary was now at Elephantine. The Theban dynasts thus had to cope with a difficult situation. They relied on an alliance with other provinces, such as those of Edfu and el-Kab, whose temple domains were closely associated with that of Amun. The spirit of reconquest animated the Seventeenth Dynasty, but it was hampered by an unfavorable balance of power due to the superiority of Hyksos military technology. Phases of hostility, with victories and defeats on both sides alternated with phases of peaceful coexistence. The actual war of liberation, which was conducted using large contingents of Nubian mercenaries (Medjoi), began with Kamose and ended during the reign of his successor Ahmose. Neither the order nor all the names of the pharaohs of the Seventeenth Dynasty are certain: Inyotef V (Nubkheperre), undoubtedly the founder; Rehotpe; Sebekemzaf I (Wadjkhau), an active king who reigned for 16 years; Djehuty; Sewadjen [. . .]; Nebireyeraw I; Nebireyeraw II; Semenneferre; Seuserenre; Sebekemzaf II (Sekhemre-shedwaset); Inyotef VI and Inyotef VII; Senakhtenre; Seqenenre Tao; Kamose.

These pharaohs had a residence at Ballas (Ombos, not far from Koptos), but they evidently reigned at Thebes, where they were buried in tombs surmounted by brick pyramids. These tombs, which were at Dra Abu el-Naga, next to the cemetery of the Eleventh Dynasty (a symbolic location), were pillaged under the Ramessides.

See Apophis, Hyksos, Inyotef, Kamose, Second Intermediate Period, Seqenenre Tao, Sixteenth Dynasty.

Seventh Dynasty

According to Manetho, the Seventh Dynasty consisted of seventy pharaohs who each reigned seventy days. This obviously legendary formulation reveals the disarray of Egyptian annalistic tradition confronted with a period during which multiple pretenders disputed the throne without any of them succeeding in imposing himself, probably after the death of Nitocris (2140 B.C.E.).

See First Intermediate Period, Nitocris.

Shoshenq Twenty-second Dynasty

This Libyan name illustrates the fortunes, which would last for nearly five centuries, of the pharaohs of Libyan descent, who are otherwise called "Shoshenqides." In the obscure beginnings of the tenth century, under the Twenty-first (Tanite) Dynasty, parts of the Meshwesh, an ethnic group that had long inhabited the delta and had settled as far as the borders of the Faiyum, dominated the armed forces. The supreme commander, Shoshenq the Elder, was strong enough for one of his sons to impose himself as pharaoh. Forty years later, his grandson Shoshenq, "great chief of the Meshwesh and chief of chiefs," whose residence was at Bubastis, dominated the state; he was master of an army and a treasury of his own. The royal puppet of Tanis asked Amun to guarantee that Shoshenq would transmit his power to his heirs, but the latter achieved even more: he succeeded Psusennes II, founding the Twenty-second Dynasty. His reign (945–924 B.C.E.) saw a great deal of restoration: a renewal of building activity at places such as Karnak, el-Hiba, and Tanis, reorganization of the territory divided among the privileged Libyan princes, and the successful resumption of activities in Asia. Around 925 B.C.E., the king (the Shishak of the Bible) led his Egyptian, Libyan, and Nubian contingents through Philistia, the kingdoms of Israel and Judah, and the Negeb, imposing a heavy war tribute on Jerusalem. Traditional relations between Egypt and the Lebanese port of Byblos were reestablished. This Shoshenq, who was sometimes confused with Sesostris (the Greek form of the name Senwosret), would be cited by tradition as one of the great Egyptian conquerors.

Shoshenq III (825–773 B.C.E.) and Shoshenq V (767–730 B.C.E.) both had especially long reigns, so they are frequently mentioned in the dates of private stelae. Under Shoshenq III, a rival arose in the person of Petubastis, and violent struggles occurred over the pontificate of Amun and the governorship of Herakleopolis, while the cities of the delta passed into the hands of autonomous "great chiefs." Shoshenq III completed the great temple of Tanis, where his burial vault was discovered. Shoshenq V ruled only a north that was divided into principalities. A large and beautiful temple to the god Khons was constructed in his name at Tanis.

Tanis: L'Or des Pharaons (Paris, 1987).

See Bubastis, Libyans, Third Intermediate Period.

Sinuhe

Scholars today agree that the Story of Sinuhe is the masterpiece of pharaonic literature. Even the Egyptians counted it as one of the classics that they chose for the purpose of training apprentice scribes or delighting those enamored of fine writing.

In the form of an autobiography, Sinuhe narrates the tribulations he experienced abroad. Traveling in the following of Senwosret I when the latter was returning from an expedition to Libya, Sinuhe overheard the announcement of the death of Amenemhet I. Fearing he would be implicated in the plot that led to this death, he deserted. After traversing the delta, he arrived in Palestine, dying of thirst; a sheikh saved him, and he continued his journey in Asia, passing through Byblos. Eventually, the prince of Upper Retjenu took him in sympathetically, presenting Sinuhe with his daughter and a fief. Sinuhe prospered in the service of the prince, to the point that he aroused envy. An arrogant Asiatic challenged him, with the intent of despoiling him, but Sinuhe triumphed. With age, his nostalgia for Egypt grew. Happily, Senwosret I authorized his return, and in a formal audience, he granted him a pardon and heaped honors on him.

The story is an extremely rich work that incorporates various text genres: hymn, royal decree, narration, folklore. Its historical background is precisely documented: succession crisis, realistic description of Asiatic customs, foreign names, historical personages. It draws considerable inspiration from the loyalist propaganda that the new dynasty spread with the help of excellent paid writers. (This propaganda also included apologies of Amenemhet I and Senwosret I, the theme of royal clemency, and a call for an active foreign policy.)

M. Lichtheim, *Ancient Egyptian Literature: A Book of Readings*, vol. 1: *The Old and Middle Kingdoms* (Berkeley, 1973), pp. 222–35.

See Autobiography, Senwosret I, Twelfth Dynasty.

Sixteenth Dynasty

This dynasty comprises Asiatic chieftains, vassals of the Hyksos, who divided Lower Egypt (outside the eastern delta) among themselves, and small kingdoms in Middle Egypt ruled by Egyptians who collaborated with the occupiers. These rulers held power concurrently with the Fifteenth and Seventeenth Dynasties.

See Hyksos, Second Intermediate Period, Seventeenth Dynasty.

Sixth Dynasty

The reasons for the change from the Fifth to the Sixth Dynasty remain unknown, but the transition does not seem to have occurred in a context of political turbulence. The list of the pharaohs of the Sixth Dynasty is as follows:

Teti (2321–2289 B.C.E.), founder of the dynasty
Userkare (2289–? B.C.E.), a usurper who apparently had a short reign
Pepy I (2289–2247 B.C.E.); son of Teti, he reestablished the legitimate succession
Merenre (2247–2241 B.C.E.), who succeeded Pepy I at a very young age; his mother might have acted as regent at the beginning of his reign
Pepy II (2241–2148 B.C.E.), half brother of Merenre, had an extremely long reign during which he progressively lost control of the country
Merenre-Nemtyemzaf, son of Pepy II, came to the throne at a time of trouble and unrest and could not have maintained his rule for long (perhaps a year and a month)
Nitocris (Neithiqerty), a woman who, like Hatshepsut and Twosre, became pharaoh; she ruled for six or twelve years in the context of plots and disorder that marked the end of the Sixth Dynasty and the beginning of the First Intermediate Period

The Sixth Dynasty saw the continuation of a process that had begun during the Fifth Dynasty of diminishment of the pharaoh's control over the country:

Certain institutions—"pyramid cities" and regional temples—obtained a status of immunity, exempting them from subjection to the imposts and requisitions of the central administration.
High officials increasingly imposed the principle of the hereditary transmission of office to the detriment of the free choice of the king, thereby forming family lines of office holders.
This tendency was especially strong at the regional level; the nomarchs set themselves up as local potentates, arrogating to themselves titles of the central administration (vizier, overseer of the south) and sometimes becoming so powerful that the king had to come to terms with them (thus, Pepy I married two daughters of an influential family of Abydos).

It is clear that the collapse of the Old Kingdom at the end of the Sixth Dynasty proceeded essentially, even if not exclusively, from the exacerbation of these tendencies toward autonomy.

The process was gradual, however, and on the whole, the Sixth Dynasty maintained the high cultural level of the period that preceded it. The supplies of exotic commodities and products from the Sinai, Byblos, and Punt continued; in fact, Egyptian penetration into Nubia extended into the principalities of the Dongola region, through which Egypt entered into contact with the African interior (e.g., the pygmy brought back by Harkhuf). In the same vein, we cannot really speak of a decadence in craftsmanship during the Sixth Dynasty; its bas-reliefs and statues are not lacking in finesse, though the powerful massiveness of the Fourth and Fifth dynastics was on thc wanc. Thc pharaohs still built pyramids with complexes consisting of a funerary temple and a valley temple, more or less in accordance with the pattern established by Wenis. These pyramids were built of blocks bonded with a mortar of Nile silt and covered with a limestone casing, though they were smaller (a little over 160 feet in height) than those of the Fourth Dynasty. Considerable architectural skill continued to manifest itself in the funerary temples, but the use of "expensive" materials (granite, quartzite) diminished over time.

I. E. S. Edwards, *The Pyramids of Egypt,* rev. ed. (Harmondsworth, Middlesex, 1985), pp. 176–90.

See Harkhuf, Heqaib, Izi, Kagemni, Nekhebu, Pepy I, Pepy II, Teti, Wenis.

Smendes 1069–1043 B.C.E., Twenty-first Dynasty

This king's name refers to the cult of the ram god of Mendes. Smendes was undoubtedly a native of this ancient city of the eastern delta. The account of Wenamun (c. 1080 B.C.E.) depicts him residing farther to the east, at Tanis, from which he administered Lower Egypt and traded with Asia. When Ramesses XI died, he became king, founding the Twenty-first (Tanite) Dynasty; he reestablished internal peace, if we believe the high-flown titulary he gave himself. His reign evidently lasted about a quarter of a century, but his monuments are regrettably rare. Two of his canopic jars were secretly spirited away from the royal necropolis of Tanis, where he was probably the first occupant.

M. Lichtheim, *Ancient Egyptian Literature: A Book of Readings,* vol. 2: *The New Kingdom* (Berkeley, 1976), pp. 224–30.

See Mendes, Tanis, Third Intermediate Period.

Smenkhkare 1337–1335 B.C.E., Eighteenth Dynasty

This little-attested personal name is once associated with the prenomen "Ankhkheprure, beloved of Neferkheprure (= Akhenaten)," and this prenomen sometimes also occurs with the personal name "Neferneferuaten, beloved of the Unique One of Re (= Akhenaten)." This phantom-like figure is known only from rare mentions of his name in inscriptions, from small objects, and from items of burial equipment that, either in pristine condition or usurped, ended up as part of the tomb furnishings of Tutankhamun. Smenkhkare was married to Merytaten, the eldest daughter of Akhenaten, and he ruled for two years. Scholars debate all other matters regarding this sovereign. Some items from Tutankhamun's tomb might depict him, but reliefs from Amarna in which some have believed they have seen him associated with Akhenaten could very well represent a queen. No argument enables us to state with certainty whether he was the coregent or simply the successor of the heretic king. It has even been suggested that Smenkhkare was a woman, and even more, that he was Nefertiti become pharaoh, a thesis that many specialists in Amarna view as unsound. It goes without saying that his genealogy is also debated. His successor, Tutankhamun, might have been his brother (according to cranial measurements). He has been identified with a male body found in the rear of Tomb 55 of the Valley of the Kings, lying in a gilded coffin that supposedly belonged to a queen, but which profaners rendered anonymous by obliterating the names and the faces. The coffin was found surrounded by disparate and incomplete tomb furnishings, items that had once belonged to the queen mother Teye, to Queen Kiya, and to Akhenaten: none bear the names of Smenkhkare. Some Egyptologists and medical authorities have concluded that this body is Akhenaten's.

Fortunately, one definite trace of his reign lends him some substance: our pharaoh had a funerary temple at Thebes, "in the domain of Amun," thus reviving a basic pre-Atenist practice. An obscure priest attested to the existence of the temple in a pious graffito that expresses his profound desire to see, with his eyes and in his heart, the consoling presence of the returned Amun. The restoration that took place under Tutankhamun was thus begun during the reign of his ephemeral predecessor.

See Amenophis IV, alias Akhenaten; Tutankhamun.

Snofru 2561–2538 B.C.E., Fourth Dynasty

First pharaoh of the Fourth Dynasty, Snofru reigned at least twenty-four years, and perhaps longer. No fewer than four pyramids are associated with his name:

The pyramid of Maidum (south of the plain of Memphis), conceived as a step pyramid, was perhaps originally intended for Snofru's predecessor; it remained uncompleted.

Two pyramids at Dahshur. The southern pyramid is called "rhomboidal," because its slope exhibits a sudden change of angle at mid height. The northern, true pyramid has an angle (about 45°) which is consistently that of the upper part of the "rhomboidal" pyramid. The two pyramids comprised a huge ensemble onto which a socioeconomic complex was grafted (a pyramid city, conceived as a government-controlled institution).

Recent excavations have shown that we must also credit Snofru with the small pyramid of Seila in the Faiyum, not far from Maidum.

That Snofru could have undertaken such vast enterprises indicates his strict control over the means of production and their effective deployment; in fact, in his reign, cattle counts were added to the already-known inventories of other consumables. Resources from abroad did not escape this pharaoh. An expedition consisting of forty ships was sent to the Lebanon in search of wood (pine, cedar). The Sinai was so effectively exploited during the reign of Snofru that he became a local deity, though he was not the first to have dispatched troops of soldiers and workmen there. Operations carried out in Nubia and on the Libyan frontier assured the security of the marches and a huge booty of cattle.

The famous statues of Rehotpe and Nofret bear clear testimony to the technical mastery attained by artists in the reign of Snofru. This reign was so fondly remembered that posterity viewed him as the most popular of all the pharaohs of Egypt. Not only were his local cults maintained for a long time at Dahshur and in the Sinai, but literature, both stories and works of propaganda, depicted him as a good-natured and sympathetic sovereign whose patronage continued to reward those kings who laid claim to it.

See Fourth Dynasty, Kagemni.

Sources for History

What sources, and for what history? Such are the questions that torment modern scholars. In attempting to deal with pharaonic Egypt, they are overwhelmed by the quantity and the difficulty of the documentation, and at the same time, frustrated by the poverty of its informative content. On the whole, the sources can be divided into four categories that are quantitatively and qualitatively disparate.

EGYPTIAN HISTORIOGRAPHY

There was indeed an Egyptian historiography, though we suspect that it worked with a concept of history far different from the modern one. It responded to two necessities. One of these was practical: juridical and administrative activities—in particular, those having to do with taxation—obviously required a chronology. Since the year count was set back to zero at the outset of each reign, it was necessary to keep lists of pharaohs in order to have precise chronological reference points.

There was also an ideological necessity: since history was conceived of as the prolonging or repetition of creation, it was necessary to make a record of events, or what were considered events, to reduce them to basic stereotypes and to set them as such into a sacral framework. Thus, scribes made chronicles of Pharaoh's activities; when he was engaged in an important undertaking, such as a war, it was their task to create journals of the campaign. Sometimes, these documents served as sources for triumphal compositions, such as the Annals of Tuthmosis III. In the case of the Battle of Qadesh, which was fought by Ramesses II, we have a double account, a literary and a pictographic one, carved in several temples, as well as a parallel account that was circulated in the form of a poem. These reign chronicles were food for a genuine annalistic tradition: thus, the Palermo Stone enumerates the memorable deed of each reign of the first five dynasties, examples being the celebration of festivals, the construction of temples, the setting up of statues, and military expeditions.

The Royal Canon of Turin lists all the pharaohs and the lengths of their reigns; this list has a modicum of organization, in that it distinguishes groups of kings who are characterized, for example, by the city they chose as their capital or by their city of origin. This attempt at periodization reveals the beginning of historical reflection, and the Royal Canon of Turin thus contrasts with other lists, compiled in temples, which seek only to commemorate pharaohs who had worked in those temples and whose construction activity must have been recorded as the temples were being enlarged.

Finally, during the reigns of the first two Ptolemies, Manetho, an Egyptian priest writing in Greek, composed a history of Egypt using historiographic documentation from the pharaonic period. Unfortunately, it has been preserved only in the form of extracts cited by summarizers and by writers who used his history for purposes of their own.

We thus have only vestiges of the products of Egyptian historiography, and they are quite incomplete. This situation is all the more regrettable in that recent criticism has recognized a certain value in them, mutatis mutandis; they are in no way tissues of poppycock and legends, as they had once been called, when Egyptology was still young and scholars were dissatisfied with the early decipherments.

ANCIENT SOURCES FROM OUTSIDE EGYPT

As one of the great powers of the Near East for nearly three millennia, pharaonic Egypt could not fail to enter into the preoccupations of other civilizations, and thus to appear in the documentation they left to us. The Hittite archives, and later, the chronicles of the kings of Assyria, grant ample space to their relations and their wrangles with Egypt. Furthermore, the Bible turns more than once to this land so closely linked to the most ancient history of the Hebrew people and whose culture was an important source of inspiration to them.

But it is the Greek and Latin authors who furnish the most important of our ancient sources, for Hellenism was fascinated by pharaonic Egypt. Contacts were established as early as the Minoan era. These contacts intensified with the Twenty-sixth Dynasty, with its concession of the port of Naukratis to the Greeks, and even more with the Ptolemaic Period and with Egypt's annexation into the Roman empire. The accounts of curious visitors, the recollections of traders, soldiers, and administrators who went to Egypt for professional reasons, and even the hearsay passed along from port to port nourished a dense classical tradition regarding Egypt. This tradition was a mixture of complex strata of pure legend, jumbles of chronologically heterogeneous notations, distortions and reinterpretations of facts, and of authentic information. The particularly outstanding classical works are that by Plutarch (46–120 C.E.), which is especially oriented toward religion; the *Bibliotheca* of Diodorus Siculus (first century C.E.), much of which is devoted to pharaonic Egypt and takes earlier writings into account, as well as offering some personal observations; book 17 of the *Geography* of Strabo (first century C.E.), a curious spirit who knew how to enrich his travel notes from Egypt with information derived from earlier geographers and ethnographers; and, finally, the *Histories* of Herodotus (fifth century B.C.E.). Setting out to describe the Persian empire that the Greeks had just defeated, Herodotus dwells at length (in book 2 and part of book 3) on one of its provinces, Egypt, which he takes to be the most astonishing. His work is a veritable treatise on cultural history that draws on various sources, including earlier writers and the tales of dragomen who he says guided him during his visit (which certain scholars have claimed never occurred). It is not all nonsense, especially when he reports on events that occurred close in time to his own century, and an excellent Egyptologist has even devoted a learned thesis to the value of the information he supplies regarding the Twenty-sixth Dynasty.

On the whole, the classical sources offer rather uneven material for the history of pharaonic Egypt. The systematic distortion of the information by *interpretatio graeca* (or *romana*) requires such critical acumen that it is far more often the case that Egyptology sheds light on a classical account than the other way around.

ARCHAEOLOGY

Inspired by research on the prehistoric period, archaeology has shown how much it can bring to history, thanks to the techniques and methods it has forged for itself. At the same time, the heroic era of pharaonic archaeology appears, with the advantage of hindsight, to be an age of obscurantism: obsessed with their quest for inscriptions and beautiful objects, the experts were little concerned with stratigraphy, and they quickly eradicated everything that was not built of stone. Since these excavators were working at major sites, the amount of information thus lost was considerable.

Somewhat later than neighboring disciplines such as Assyriology, Egyptology opened itself to archaeology, justly (though sometimes with some indulgence) denouncing the methods and customs of the past. Ceramic typologies were elaborated, stratigraphy held no more secrets, and researchers deployed the arsenal of modern techniques, such as aerial photography, proton magnetometers, and thermoluminescence. Some results were spectacular: the model excavations of Manfred Bietak at the site of Avaris facilitated the determination of the various phases of Asiatic settlement there, upsetting the traditional picture of a Hyksos invasion. Additionally, these excavations shed light on the historical geography of the eastern delta and explained the choice of the site of Pi-Riamsese as capital, as well as its later abandonment in favor of Tanis.

With good reason, we expect fresh information regarding the history of Egypt from modern excavations. Still, we should not entertain too much hope. Although it is easy to besmirch the earliest excavators, the conditions peculiar to archaeology in Egypt must be taken into account. Over the millennia, the great majority of sites suffered extensive damage from pillagers, treasure hunters, and the removal of earth for brick making or *sebakh*—that is, when the remains of ancient sites did not disappear under modern settlements. Thus, even when they are well conducted, excavations cannot always yield the results that are theoretically anticipated. In particular, urban archaeology, one of the most informative areas for historians, is irremediably handicapped, for rare are the settlements that offer some hope, such as the Old Kingdom town of Balat in el-Dakhla Oasis.

The reevaluation of archaeology has entailed a renewal of interest in uninscribed material: tools and objects of daily life, as well as nonmonumental architecture. Inventories, descriptions, classifications, and typologies demand laborious, unspectacular work, but in the last analysis, such work can contribute to our knowledge of the chronology and the ethnology of the historical period.

Still, one point remains incontrovertible. As precious as archaeology has proven to be, when it comes to the history of pharaonic Egypt, it can never be more than an indispensable complement to the written sources.

WRITTEN SOURCES

At first sight, the written sources are disconcerting in the variety of their type and their content. Still, it is pertinent to divide them into two major groups that correspond to the status assigned to them by the ancient Egyptians themselves. One group consists of purely mundane texts, most often written in cursive (hieratic) script on perishable materials: papyri, wooden tablets, and ostraca (splinters of stone or fragments of pottery with a surface smooth enough to be written on). The other group comprises religiously weighted inscriptions, most often in hieroglyphs on more durable materials (stone, metal, wood), precisely because they were made to last and thus to perpetuate the vision of the world invoked by the monuments on which they were written. The same document—a royal decree, for example—could be published in two versions: a secular version for the archives, preserving the entire text with the formal attributes that authenticated it, and a religiously weighted version, set up in an appropriate place and provided with an ideological apparatus (divine images, phraseology) that inserted it into a vision of the world. The impact of the latter version most often worked to the detriment of the literal content of the original, which could be abridged to the point of reducing it to the basics. Any critical work on the written sources must begin with a recognition of the dichotomy between these two types of documents.

Secular Sources

To one surveying what has survived to us of the immense production of secular texts in pharaonic Egypt, the number seems quite large: private letters, administrative correspondence, account books of institutions, registry office contracts, tax registers, contracts of sale or rental of goods or persons, minutes of trials, compendia of customs . . . the complete inventory would be rather lengthy. Unfortunately, a more attentive examination results in disenchantment. The number of documents, which is considerable on the scale of the scholar who must interpret them, is actually small for more than two and a half millennia of history. Moreover, many of the documents are filled with lacunae or are incomplete, or they survive only as scarcely informative *membra disjecta* of groups of texts in which they originally made sense.

And what are we to say of their distribution in time and space? For entire centuries, there is an absolute, or near absolute, silence. The third millennium has yielded only the archives from Gebelein and those of two funerary temples of the Fifth Dynasty. From the Middle Kingdom, we have only the archives of a private domain run by a certain Heqanakht, the archives of a construction site near Abydos, jumbles of paperwork from the pyramid cities of el-Lahun, some pages from an accounting book of the court of Thebes under Sebekhotpe II, and a roster of prisoners. In the New Kingdom, the situation improves, thanks to the abundant documentation from Deir el-Medina; we are finally able to follow, with some precision, the functioning of the institution of the royal tomb, the daily life of its members, both administrators and workmen. Figures accumulate with some consistency to the point that an eminent scholar, Jaroslav Černý, succeeded in making quantitative studies on the evolution of prices, which is unthinkable for other periods. The situation is none too good for the Third Intermediate Period, not only because the sources are scarce, but also because they still resist total decipherment. With the Late Period, a rather abundant documentation written in Demotic emerges, but the hour for its synthesis has not yet arrived.

Beyond the unevenness of the distribution of evidence for administrative and juridical practice, the historian constantly comes up against problems in interpreting them. Neither the functioning of institutions nor the status of institutions and persons can easily be discerned; in particular, taxation, so fertile a field for historians, remains highly obscure for Egyptologists, despite a fortunate gift of chance, Papyrus Wilbour. This papyrus, which is more than thirty-two feet long, is a tax register produced by a commission of surveyors working in a ninety-three-mile area of Middle Egypt under Ramesses V. That such a document—for once nearly complete—raises such difficulties demonstrates the scarcely enviable lot of economic and social historians (and perhaps all historians) of pharaonic Egypt.

Another type of secular source offers a meager consolation: literature. Many works that survive to us are rich in historical information, often because they are politically oriented. Pharaohs in fact paid authors to spread political or propaganda messages via attractive writings; typical cases are the Story of Sinuhe and the Instruction for Merykare. Even when they are free of such aims, many works are grist for the historian's mill, because they are rooted in an explicit social experience—most often, obviously, that of the ruling class. But literature itself cannot compensate for the insufficiency of other secular sources. Historians must therefore make maximum use of religiously weighted sources.

Religious Sources

If religious sources abound, it is because the prime characteristic of sacralization was recording on durable material. We shall distinguish between private sources and royal sources.

Private Sources Every Egyptian who had the means to do so sought to increase his chances of survival after death, not only by erecting a tomb that was provided with an abundance of inscribed tomb furnishings, but also by setting up stelae, statues, or offering tables in the temples. We thus have an enormous quantity of private documents, and while they most often contain only a religious formula, the names and titles of these persons constitute precious supplementary information for the historian. In fact, thanks to meticulous efforts of classification and inventorying, scholars have been able to elaborate prosopographic groupings by region, by type of activity, or by family, and their results are richly informative. Working out genealogies, they have followed the transmission or loss of offices, as well as the accumulation of offices, matrimonial strategies, and the gain or loss of the favor of the ruler. The quality of funerary monuments enables scholars to appreciate the relative wealth of their owners. Some of our knowledge—and the great bulk of it for some periods—rests on these methods. They sometimes give us a glimpse of the crest, at least, of the great waves that shook Egyptian society, and especially its ruling class: the transfer of high offices outside the royal family under the Fifth Dynasty, the rise of a middle class during the second part of the Middle Kingdom, the multiplication of parvenus in the New Kingdom, and so forth.

All these private monuments contain at least some information. Even when they consist only of a string of clichés, autobiographies can be precious, for at the very least these clichés reflect the spirit of an age. When they are lengthy and detailed, they constitute some of our basic sources, and their contents sometimes dovetail with those found in other documents, such as royal sources.

Royal Sources Obviously enough, the pharaohs placed their names on a great number of monuments. They did this first because like others, they wanted to assure their survival; to this end, they set in motion the enormous means that the eminence of their position put at their disposal. Secondly, and especially, they did this because the very exercise of Egyptian kingship implied the multiplication of inscribed monuments. In fact, as successor to the creator god, each pharaoh prolonged the act of creation by transforming history into a manifestation of the order that was instituted at the First Moment. This highly ideological activity demanded that each undertaking be authenticated by the name of the pharaoh who was responsible for it, and that this authentication be inscribed on durable material. A godsend for the historian? That would be saying too much; historians must content themselves with what they have, which most often means cartouches or brief inscriptions carved in various parts of temples. For one of the prime duties of a pharaoh was to construct and to restore temples. And for many kings, the bulk of our documentation indeed consists of an inventory of the religious edifices that they erected, enlarged, or rebuilt, or in which they dedicated statues or set up obelisks. Although such monumental activity reflects a king's power—and beyond that, the political and economic conditions of his era—this is a somewhat crude means of evaluation, all the more so in that the hazards of destruction or preservation contribute to inaccurate conclusions. Alas, historians must all too often resign themselves to these realities.

Fortunately, pharaohs sometimes made voluble use of the "creative utterance" with which they were endowed to inscribe their words for posterity. We thus have monumental versions of decrees, of lengthy enumerations of offerings or favors granted to the deities, detailed accounts of military campaigns and of conquests, with lists of subjected regions and peoples, commemorations of ceremonies conducted with great pomp, acts of familial and ancestral piety, and so forth. In such cases, the sources are expansive, and the doors stand ajar for the historian's eye. The glance thus obtained is often a fleeting one, for the rhetorical scope of these highly ideological inscriptions masks the poverty of their informative content. Nevertheless, newly discovered royal inscriptions sometimes contain veritable revelations, such as the stela of Kamose, which sheds light on the political situation in Egypt under the Hyksos.

This survey of the sources for pharaonic history must conclude with a somewhat disenchanted assertion: the lot of the historian is scarcely satisfying. The documentation is apparently abundant, but it is very unevenly distributed. The earliest periods are ill served, not only because time has had more opportunity to accomplish its work of destruction, but also because they produced fewer documents; as time went on, Egypt produced more texts of use to the historian. Unequal distribution, then, but also equal difficulty: few documents have survived to us intact, and when they are, their interpretation remains a delicate matter, for we do not have a perfect mastery of the writing system and the language, nor do we have the background information that the documents presuppose. Finally, the efforts required by interpretation often end in deception. The ancient Egyptians did not have the advantage of reading our treatises on the writing of history; for three millennia, they persisted in reporting their experience as they saw it, not as we would like them to have seen it. Egyptologists therefore cannot even stammer an answer to the most elementary questions that specialists in modern history begin by asking of their sources. Clio, the muse of history, does not deign to adorn herself with the gold of Tutankhamun.

S. Donadoni, ed., *Le Fonti indirette della storia egiziana,* Studi Semitici 7 (Rome, 1963); K. Weeks, ed., *Egyptology and the Social Sciences* (Cairo, 1979); D. B. Redford, *Pharaonic King-Lists, Annals and Day-Books: A Contribution to the Study of the Egyptian Sense of History,* SSEA Publication 4 (Mississauga, Ontario, 1986).

Sport

As war chief, the pharaoh had to train. The divine king had to demonstrate his vigor by combating animals that embodied evil forces. The master of the palace amused himself with the same diversions as the nobles of his court. He went to hunt waterfowl and to fish in the marshes of the Faiyum, and to shoot gazelles behind Giza or Heliopolis, wild oxen in the Wadi el-Natrun, and onagers in Syria. He hunted lions and hippopotami at close quarters. He thus knew how to use the bow and the spear. The ritual character of certain hunts reflected the traditional damning of animals incarnating chaos, just as the "run with the Apis bull" and other ritual runs had a religious aim. But these activities were also a means of recalling the infallible capability and the youthful vigor of the ruling sovereign. Tuthmosis III commemorated a rhinoceros hunt that occurred on the Sudanese steppes. Amenophis III dedicated an issue of commemorative scarabs to his killing of 102 lions in ten years. Ostrich feathers stuck in a fan belonging to Tutankhamun had been brought back by the boy king from a hunt east of Heliopolis.

One sovereign testified that physical training was part of the education of a prince: Amenophis II made media events of the feats of which he was capable from the age of eighteen on. Likewise, he exhibited his taste for violence by relating the blows he personally struck in Asia and his brutal reprisals against his enemies in battle. These were cases of egoistic justifications of his predisposition for kingship; his insistence on anecdotes shows that his exploits were in no way required by a supposed "initiation ritual" that conferred access to the throne. No one could catch up with the young Amenophis in a footrace. He tested a series of the stiffest bows. He maneuvered a parade vessel by himself, after its two hundred oarsmen had worn themselves out. He personally trained his horses, which he harnessed and took on long rides. Riding his chariot at full speed, he unfailingly shot his arrows through metal targets that were three inches thick.

See Pharaoh.

Strikes

Yes, there were strikes in the time of the pharaohs, or at least during the Twentieth Dynasty. The workmen who labored on the royal tombs were paid in the form of allotments of consumable goods furnished by the state; but these allotments were regular only when the granaries and storehouses were full. In year 29 of Ramesses III, a crisis struck that would darken the end of the New Kingdom: the rations ceased to be distributed in due course. Driven by necessity, the workmen left their village (the present-day Deir el-Medina) to occupy the funerary temples—first that of Tuthmosis III, then those of Ramesses II and Sethos I—at the margin of the cultivated fields. To do so, they passed by the five fortified posts that guarded access to these temples from the mountain, marking their breach with the normal; thus, in their day, "pass by the (five) fortified posts" was the equivalent of our expression "go on strike." These movements were spontaneous and unorganized, and the demands of the strikers were basic:

> If we went there, it was because of hunger, because of thirst; there are no clothes, no unguent, no fish, no vegetables. Write about it to Pharaoh, life, prosperity, health, our goodly lord, and write to the vizier, our superior, so that he might procure us a means of living.

When all was said and done, the allocations were delivered, and the strikers went back to work. But other strikes broke out shortly thereafter, and they would be repeated until the end of the Twentieth Dynasty. The authorities attempted to deal with the most urgent matters first, employing captious rhetoric and half measures, such as furnishing a portion of the rations owed, until eventually they came up with the means of satisfying the legitimate demands of the workmen. Conflict resolution was more complicated, however, when the motive of the strike was to denounce the corruption, the dishonesty, and the scandals that were rampant in the institution of the Tomb; in such cases, our sources become curiously reticent regarding the measures that were taken!

P. Vernus, *Affaires et scandales sous les Ramsès* (Paris, 1993), chapter 2.

Sun Temples

During the Fifth Dynasty, from Userkaf to Menkauhor, six successive kings erected sanctuaries to the sun god Re, in their own names and in the proximity of their funerary temples. These cult places, which were almost entirely open to the sky, were dominated by a monumental obelisk. The sun temple of Neuserre (Abu Ghurab) is the one that has been the best studied. It is famous for its remains of a small "chamber of the world" in which bas-reliefs representing the cycle of the year, undoubtedly the most ancient treatise on natural history, evoke the reproductive process of mammals, birds, and fish.

See Fifth Dynasty.

Taharqa 690–664 B.C.E., Twenty-fifth Dynasty

In 701 B.C.E., when Jerusalem was threatened by Assyria, it was aided by Taharqa, the brother and designated heir of the king of Egypt and Kush. In the book of Kings, the Jewish scribes credited this intervention to the memorable "Taharqa, king of Kush." This is a minor anachronism, but no error with regard to the person. From Gebel Barkal to Tanis, we have many remains of his buildings, and high quality statues depicting the sovereign wearing the tall plumes of the god Onuris. We also have an exceptional quantity of lengthy, diverse, and detailed inscriptions informing us that Taharqa, a ruler born in the Sudan but crowned king at Memphis, was the most opulent of all the kings of the Twenty-fifth, Kushite Dynasty. An immense column in the first court of Karnak reminds visitors of his enormous building activity.

From the originality of the form and the content of his proclamations, Taharqa seems to have been a highly personal author of both official and devout literature. In the political and ethical program that he submitted to Amun of Karnak and in many other texts, the king provides extraordinary details about his youth, his role as mediator, and his initiatives. One proclamation was disseminated everywhere to draw a lesson from a terrifying Nile inundation that occurred in his year 6, only to be followed by an especially successful agricultural season. One stela relates how the king organized a training course for his army in the desert outside Memphis. In the Sudan, written accounts and inventories detail the circumstances of the construction and endowment of the temples of Sanam and Kawa. For himself, Taharqa built an enormous pyramid on the virgin site of el-Kurru, near Napata, and a more modest one at Sedeinga. No doubt because of the many inscriptions that multiplied during the first sixteen years of his rule, tradition would count him as one of the warrior kings. But the thirteen years that followed were pitiful indeed: the Assyrians penetrated Egypt all the way to Thebes, dealing decisive blows to the Egypto-Sudanese empire that the name of Taharqa had come to symbolize.

See Kush, Kushite (Dynasty), Napata.

Takelot Twenty-second and Twenty-third Dynasties

Three kings of the Twenty-second and Twenty-third Dynasties bore the Libyan name Takelot, and every one of them was as obscure as the others. Takelot I (889–874 B.C.E.) is a mere name between the illustrious Osorkon I and Osorkon II; we do not have a single monument of his. The reign of Takelot II (886–840 B.C.E.), whose plundered coffin was discovered at Tanis, saw the outbreak of a civil war that marked the outset of the breakup of the Libyan regime. Episodes of the war are narrated in the inscription left at Karnak by his eldest son, the high priest Osorkon. Takelot III (764–757 B.C.E.) is the next to the last known king of the Twenty-third Dynasty; his control was confined to Upper Egypt.

See Third Intermediate Period.

Tanis

Situated near the northeast corner of the delta, the immense site of Tanis still bears its ancient name Djame, which is now pronounced San. A high hill of sand emerging from the midst of recent silt, with the young Tanitic branch of the Nile running alongside it, Tanis made a relatively late entrance onto the stage of history; earlier, the city had been frequented solely by poor population groups who buried their dead there. At the end of the Twentieth Dynasty, a man named Smendes took up residence at Tanis, from which he administered Lower Egypt as representative of the god Amun. Around 1069 B.C.E., he founded the Twenty-first, Tanite Dynasty. Psusennes, Siamun, and then the kings of the Twenty-second, Libyan Dynasty built great temples there to the Theban gods, using stones and portable monuments taken from Pi-Riamsese to construct and adorn them. After Smendes, and at least until the reign of Shoshenq III, the kings had themselves buried in the temple of Amun.

Bocchoris of Sais and the Kushite Taharqa secured recognition at Tanis during the period of conflict over the reunification of Egypt. Meanwhile, highly obscure kinglets whose power was confined to the eastern delta—the Horus Sankhtawy (alias Sekhemkare), Gemenefkhonsubak, and a king with the throne name Neferkare—were still active in the temple of Khons. Tanis, which had served as the northern counterpart of the city of Thebes, lost its status of royal city after Pedubaste II, but its temples were embellished by later pharaohs and were repaired in the Ptolemaic Period.

J. Yoyotte, in *Tanis: L'Or des pharaons* (Paris, 1987), pp. 25–48.

See Osorkon, Psusennes, Shoshenq, Smendes, Third Intermediate Period.

Tefnakhte

With Sais as his capital, this "great chief of the western provinces" of the delta formed a coalition of the principalities of Lower Egypt, and around 730 B.C.E., he attempted to reconquer the south from the Kushites. Piye repelled the northern army and forced the princes to accept his nominal sovereignty, but the account of his campaign testifies that the Saite kingdom remained inviolate. From Diodorus Siculus, we know that Tefnakhte was the father of the pharaoh Bocchoris.

Two donation stelae inform us of a man of royal status named Tefnakhte, who called himself "son of Neith," goddess of Sais. He might have been Piye's adversary, crowned pharaoh after the withdrawal of the Kushite forces, or he might have been the Stephinates (to be corrected into Tefinastes) whom Manetho places at the beginning of his Twenty-sixth, Saite Dynasty and who must have reigned around 700 B.C.E. In any event, according to the Kushite testimony, Tefnakhte symbolized the dynamism of the Egyptians of the western delta, who attempted for three quarters of a century to restore unity.

See Piye, Sais, Saite (Dynasties), Third Intermediate Period.

Tenth Dynasty

See Ninth and Tenth Dynasties.

Teos (*or* Tachos) 361–359 B.C.E., Thirtieth Dynasty

Teos was the second pharaoh of the Thirtieth (Sebennytic) Dynasty. From his ephemeral reign, we have only a few fragments of temple decoration. His personality is nonetheless famous because of what is related in the *Oikonomika* of Pseudo-Aristotle and the *Stratagemata* of Polyaenus. He was preoccupied by the offensive war against the Persian empire, and this activity had an enormous financial and social impact. At the advice of the Athenian leader Chabrias, the king requisitioned all the precious metal in the land and extorted nearly all the revenue of the temples. He led an army of 90,000 men to occupy Syria. His brother, the regent Tjahapimu, who governed Egypt in his absence, turned against this despoiler of gods and men, putting his own son, Nectanebo II, on the throne. Teos fled to the court of the king of Persia, whose strike force he had (luckily for his successor) broken. He died in Persia. Of this first pharaoh to strike coins, we have only the image of a cosmopolitan financier, contrasting with the traditional religious style of his father, Nectanebo I, and his nephew, Nectanebo II.

See Persians, Sebennytic (Dynasty).

Teti 2321–2289 B.C.E., Sixth Dynasty

Teti was the first king of the Sixth Dynasty. He might have been assassinated, perhaps to the profit of the usurper Userkare. During his reign, he maintained the traditional policy of trade relations with Byblos, and he began to extend Egyptian penetration deeper into Nubia. He built his pyramid northeast of the complex of Djoser, with two satellite pyramids for his queens, Iput and Khuit; like those of Wenis and the other pharaohs of the Sixth Dynasty, the walls of his subterranean chambers are inscribed with the Pyramid Texts.

See Kagemni, Sixth Dynasty, Wenis.

Teye

A native of Akhmim (Panopolis), Teye was the daughter of a prophet of Min named Yuya and a "chief of the harem of Min" named Tuya. Teye married Amenophis III at the beginning of his reign. She survived him and died at some point after year 8 of the reign of her son, Amenophis IV/Akhenaten. Since the beginning of the Eighteenth Dynasty, certain queens had played an important role, but Teye's position was more eminent still. Her husband associated her with all the events of his reign, making her an officiant in his jubilee ceremony and treating her as the hypostasis of personifications specific to ideology, such as the goddess Maat (who represented the order of the world), or even as a sphinx trampling enemies! Temples were dedicated to the royal couple, such as that of Sedeinga in Nubia; in addition, the name of Teye survives in the Nubian toponym Adeye (derived from Hut-Teye, "mansion of Teye"), and perhaps also in another toponym, Tahta, the name of a village in the region of Panopolis. Amenophis III had built a huge irrigation basin (*hod*) in the queen's name in her native province and had commemorated the event by issuing scarabs. Teye's importance was not purely ritual or eponymous; in fact, the letters that survive to us from Amarna reveal that she conducted Egyptian diplomacy while her husband was incapacitated by illness at the end of his reign: she exercised a de facto, if not a de jure, regency. Among the portraits of Teye, the most famous is probably the ebony head in the Berlin Museum that has been attributed to her. Some of her tomb furnishings have been found, but the identification of her mummy is still the subject of debate.

See Amenophis III.

Thebes

The Egyptian name of Thebes was *Waset,* "the scepter"; it was the capital of the fourth nome of Upper Egypt, which was called "The Throne." Later, Thebes was called Nut, or No, "the city" (par excellence). The name Thebes comes from a Greek interpretation of Djamet, the name of Medinet Habu.

Though the site had already been occupied during the Predynastic Period, Thebes remained an obscure town during the Old Kingdom, and few monuments from that period have been found there. Moreover, Hermonthis competed with it for preeminence in the nome. Thebes owed its prodigious fate to an accident of history. On two occasions, national unity was restored by Theban dynasts: the reunification of Egypt and the rise of the Middle Kingdom under Mentuhotpe II (2022 B.C.E.), and the expulsion of the Hyksos and the rise of the New Kingdom under Ahmose (1554 B.C.E.).

On each of these occasions, the pharaohs favored their native city, primarily by increasing the fields and the offerings of Amun, who had imposed himself as the chief god of the city at the end of the Eleventh Dynasty, at the expense of Montu, who was nevertheless worshiped throughout the region (at Thebes, Hermonthis, Tod, and el-Madamud).

What is more, the Middle Kingdom began to develop a doctrine of the supremacy of Thebes: the city, which was called "victorious, the regent of all the cities," was personified with the attributes of a warrior goddess, armed with a bow, a club, and later a scimitar. Myths also situated the creation of the world in this city. But although Thebes was the dynastic city of the Middle Kingdom and the Eighteenth Dynasty, and the city of the greatest national god during the remainder of the New Kingdom, its location in the deep south was scarcely favorable for the role of capital of the land. The city became even less suitable for that of capital of the Egyptian empire when the latter extended into Asia. Thus, while pharaohs built palaces and resided there on the occasion of major festivals, and even had themselves buried there (except in the Twelfth Dynasty), they preferred to govern from cities with a more central location: Lisht in the Middle Kingdom, Memphis in the New Kingdom, or Pi-Riamsese under the Ramessides, all of them closer to Asia. In the Third Intermediate Period, Thebes became the capital of the theocracy of Amun, whose territory comprised Upper Egypt and Middle Egypt as far as el-Hiba, and which was considered an autonomous principality in the Assyrian chronicles contemporary with the end of the Twenty-fifth Dynasty. In the Saite Period, when Thebes was administered by the bureaucracy of the "divine adoratress of Amun," the city lost its political importance. Under the Romans, a part of its territory was administratively attached to Hermonthis, its old rival.

The region of Thebes covered both banks of the Nile. On the east bank, the temple of Amun of Karnak and those of Montu, Khonsu, Mut, and other deities were located in the north, while to the south, linked to these temples by a processional way nearly two miles long, was the temple of the ithyphallic Amun of Luxor. On the west bank, at the border of the cultivated land, was a row of huge funerary temples, from that of Sethos I (Gurna) in the north to that of Ramesses III (Medinet Habu), and to the south of the latter, the palace of Amenophis III at el-Malqata. At the foot of the cliffs were the temples of Deir el-Bahari and the private cemeteries

(Dra Abu el-Naga, Asasif, el-Khokha, Sheikh Abd el-Qurna, Qurnet Murai). Finally, in the wadis of the mountain were the Valley of the Kings, the Valley of the Queens, and the workmen's village of Deir el-Medina. The unity of the region was symbolically affirmed on the occasion of major festivals, when the barque of Amun of Karnak would leave his sanctuary on solemn processions to visit Amun of Luxor, the temples of Deir el-Bahari, or those of the primordial deities at Medinet Habu. In the Middle Kingdom and in the Eighteenth Dynasty, the political and administrative centers were located on the east bank. Under the Ramessides, however, they were moved to the west bank, at Medinet Habu, where the massive enclosure walls of this funerary temple of Ramesses III, along with those of other temples (in particular the Ramesseum), assured protection against incursions of brigands or Libyans from the desert. From that time on, the east bank had its own mayor, and the bulk of the economic activity was concentrated there.

Despite millennia of destruction, beginning with that wreaked by Akhenaten and then against him, and of pillaging, beginning with the end of the Ramesside Period, Thebes still offers an astonishing quantity of ruins and standing monuments. Let us remember that the temple of Luxor was an Egyptian temple, and then the heart of a Roman military camp, and later a basilica, before becoming home to a mosque!

H. Kees, *Ancient Egypt: A Cultural Topography* (Chicago, 1961), chapter 10; C.F. Nims, *Thebes of the Pharaohs: Pattern for Every City* (New York, 1965); N. Strudwick and H. Strudwick, *Thebes in Egypt: A Guide to the Tombs and Temples of Ancient Luxor* (Ithaca, 1999).

See Adoratrice, Middle Kingdom, Third Intermediate Period.

Third Dynasty

The Old Kingdom begins with the Third Dynasty. But from the viewpoint only of events, the transition from the Second to the Third Dynasty seems to have occurred without a rupture. The first king of the Third Dynasty set up a statue to his predecessor, and what is more, a queen named Nimaathapi, who was called "mother of the royal children" under Khasekhemwy, the last king of the Second Dynasty, was called "king's mother" under Djoser, the second king of the Third Dynasty, suggesting that the two dynasties were united by family ties. The list of the pharaohs of the Third Dynasty is as follows:

Nebka (2635–2617 B.C.E.)

Djoser, Horus name Netjerykhet (2617–2599 B.C.E.), the builder of the Step Pyramid at Saqqara

Djoserty, Horus name Sekhemkhet (2599–2594 B.C.E.), whose uncompleted funerary monument was found south of that of Djoser

Nebkare (?), Horus name Zanakht (?) (2594–2589? B.C.E.), who also was able to take the construction of his funerary monument no further than its enclosure wall; he was apparently so insignificant that Egyptian annalistic tradition lost track of his name

Huni, Horus name Khaba (?) (2583–2561 B.C.E.), who constructed a fortress on the island of Elephantine, and a pyramid at Zawyet al-Aryan; the predecessor of Snofru

An enigmatic pharaoh with the Horus name Zahedjet, who awaits identification with one of the preceding kings

The pharaohs of the Third Dynasty, who reigned at Memphis, laid the foundations of classical Egyptian civilization. From that time on, the monumental use of stone was mastered, and the copper and turquoise resources of the Sinai were regularly exploited. The tradition of itinerant tax collection, which went back to the Predynastic Period, was given up in favor of a biennial inventory of wealth over which an improved bureaucracy attempted to maintain better control. (The first known vizier, Menka, appears in the Third Dynasty.) The high officials of the period were notable in particular for their ability to administer the organization of craftsmanship and the creation of manufactured products. The bas-reliefs of Akhetaa and the sculpted wooden panels of Hezyre illustrate the social stratum of the ruling elite.

N. M. A. Swelim, *Some Problems on the History of the Third Dynasty,* Publications of the Archaeological Society of Alexandria 7 (Alexandria, 1983).

See Djoser, Imhotep, Pyramids.

Third Intermediate Period 1069–664 B.C.E.

An eventful period of more than four centuries separated the faded era of the last Ramessides from the day when the reunification of the land by Psammetichus I inaugurated the magnificent Saite renaissance. Scholars long referred to the period as "pre-Saite," while more recently, the term "Late New Kingdom" has been advocated, though Egypt was not a united kingdom through much of the period. The multiplication of regional powers led to the coexistence of several pharaohs at a time and to the weakening of Egyptian imperial expansion; the land was even infiltrated and then invaded by foreigners. As in the case of the preceding two "intermediate periods," these circumstances justify the employment of a neutral term. The term refers to a known geopolitical model and signifies how these difficult times served as a transition between Ramesside culture and institutions and the renascent institutions and culture that took form under the Kushites and Saites.

The turbulence of the period included the predominance of Libyan warriors, lack of public safety and pillaging of tombs, promotion of Amun by his priests, and weakness of the royal government. This intermediate period began under the final Ramessides, but scholars find it convenient to begin it around 1080 B.C.E., when the general and pontiff Herihor assumed quasi-royal power at Thebes, while Smendes controlled the administration of Lower Egypt from Tanis. What followed this illusory, self-styled "renewal" (*uhem-mesut*) can be divided into four phases:

The period of Tanite kings and "priest-kings" (1069–945 B.C.E.) Smendes inaugurated the Twenty-first Dynasty, whose most illustrious ruler would be Psusennes I, the son of the Theban pontiff and king Pinudjem. The line of high priests of Amun would govern the south, while Libyans spread through Lower and Middle Egypt.

The apogee of the kings of Libyan descent (945–850 B.C.E.) Shoshenq I founded a Twenty-second, Bubastite dynasty. For a century, Egypt recovered some power beyond its borders, and monumental activity was begun anew (Osorkon II). Royal sons were appointed high priests of Amun and governors of Herakleopolis.

The "Libyan anarchy," a period of progressive dismemberment (850–730 B.C.E.) This period saw internecine warfare, competition among various lines of subordinate princes, the coexistence of two pharaohs, and finally, around 780 B.C.E., rupture between Lower and Upper Egypt. Ultimately, the land was divided among five persons pretending to the rank of king, while in the northern provinces, a good ten "great chiefs" recognized at best the religious suzerainty of one or another of these minor pharaohs.

The struggle for the unification (730–656 B.C.E.) The Kushite dynasty definitively annexed the south, where the "intermediate period" thus came to an end. The pacifier from Kush trampled his enemies in the north, though the Twenty-fourth and Twenty-sixth Dynasties from Sais hotly disputed with him over control of Memphis and the delta. Assyrian invasions caused the precipitous abandonment of Egypt by the Kushites. Thanks to the void created by their retreat and then by the sudden decline of Assyria, the Saite ruler rapidly restored the unity of the land, whose divisions had not prevented the beginning of a cultural renewal.

From inscriptions carved on stone, we can see that on a formal level, royal ideology was maintained throughout these uncertain times, even when there were five "Lords of the Two Lands." The palace—the "great house" (*per-aa*)—continued to be considered the seat of universal empire. It was under the Libyans that the custom (which has become our own) began of using *per-aa* as a title preceding the birth name of the king (thus, "Pharaoh Osorkon"). In reality, Pharaoh was assuredly less august than his inscriptions and images would make him seem: princes came to date their inscriptions to the years of one of the competing kings, although they left his cartouche blank. The devout pharaoh Piye refused to receive two of his petty Egyptian colleagues, who did not respect the rules of purity that were obligatory in the "house of the king." Despite the theocratic ideology cultivated by the "priest-kings" and the great Libyans and Kushites who subordinated their political affairs to the will of Amun, priestly ritualism continued to preserve the fundamental role of the royal name as mediator.

In the history of the kingship during this period, we note two salient, connected aspects: the supremacy accorded by propaganda to divine power over human powers, and the importance assumed by priestly families responsible for the temple cults and property. Under the Tanites and the Libyans, recourse to the sanction of Amun's oracle was generalized to regulate public affairs. The local chiefs, who were both commandants of troops and overseers of priests, were believed to have received their powers, and sometimes the royal office, from the deity of their city. It was also during the Third Intermediate Period that the traits of Saite Egypt appeared or developed: the primacy of the cities of the delta, the cults of sacred animals, recourse to ancient models, the solar spiritualization of funerary practices, the appearance of priestly titles reflecting local myths, the popularity of Osiris in everyday life, the demonization of Seth, and fervor for the child forms of gods.

Notwithstanding internal conflicts and invasions from without, the period assured the preservation and enrichment of Egypt's literary and artistic patrimony in forms whose study has only just begun. In the time of the "priest-kings," erudition in the matter of funerary theology and magic had increased in the priestly circles of Thebes (e.g., collection of "supplementary chapters" to the Book of the Dead, final compilation of Papyrus Greenfield, and popularization of the Amduat). Chance has preserved a few of the literary works that were appreciated or created by the scribes of the period: the Tale of Wenamun, an edifying adventure; a letter in which the Heliopolitan priest Wermai recounts his woes; the Onomasticon of Amenemope, a list of words for geographic, social, and economic realities of the Ramesside Period. The traditional genres of inscriptions experienced a rejuvenation (e.g., autobiographies of the Shoshenqide era).

K. A. Kitchen, *The Third Intermediate Period,* 2d ed. (Warminster, 1986); *Tanis: L'Or des pharaons* (Paris, 1987).

See Herihor, High Priest of Amun, Kushite (Dynasty), Libyans, Osorkon, Pedubaste, Pinudjem, Psusennes, Saite (Dynasties), Shoshenq, Smendes, Tefnakhte.

Thirteenth Dynasty

The Twelfth Dynasty came to an end with the reign of Nefrusobk, but the dynastic change entailed little rupture in the functioning of the state or in the style of monuments and inscriptions. But while the preceding dynasty had constituted a familial unity, this was not the case with the Thirteenth Dynasty. About sixty kings succeeded one another during a century and a half, most of them occupying the throne for only a brief period—a few months to a few years. Very few of them succeeded in founding a line, and when they did so, the lines were ephemeral. A number of these kings were commoners, soldiers, or foreigners (Asiatics), as shown by their original names, which they employed as their throne names or associated with the latter in their cartouches. The succession principle was obviously in crisis, with the legitimacy of the reigning pharaoh no longer conferring sufficient credibility for his son or another member of his family to impose himself as successor. The reasons for this crisis escape us: election of pharaohs on a temporary basis by a college of high officials? Decisive influence of certain army corps who made and unmade kings, after the fashion of the Praetorian Guard at Rome, thanks to their hold on the court of Thebes? These pharaohs claimed a Theban origin, and in fact, the Egyptian annalistic tradition characterized the Thirteenth Dynasty as Theban. Lisht, however, remained the administrative capital. And paradoxically, while the throne was agitated by incessant jolts, the state apparatus set in place during the second half of the Twelfth Dynasty remained in place. Moreover, high officials remained in office through successions of ephemeral reigns, sometimes marrying a princess of the moment and often succeeding in passing their office along to their sons, or at least to one of their other family members (thus, the vizier Ankhu). Thanks to this administrative stability, the pharaohs of the Thirteenth Dynasty carried out their duties like any other kings: they built or restored temples, maintained or increased the offerings of the gods, and erected statues and pyramids for themselves (thus, Auibre, Khendjer, Meremkha, and Aya). They could do this because they still had disposal, albeit limited, of the organization of property and people. The workforce remained strictly supervised, expeditions were sent to the mines and quarries (Wadi Hammamat, Wadi el-Hudi), and the system of fortresses protecting the Nile valley of Lower Nubia remained in place; in addition, the Egyptianized kinglets of Byblos continued to pledge their loyalty. Until at least the beginning of the Second Intermediate Period, the Thirteenth Dynasty so directly continued the latter half of the Twelfth that the attribution of specific monuments to one or the other dynasty is often a tricky matter.

Nevertheless, we must qualify this somewhat overly idyllic picture. The extent of the territory controlled by the administration of the Thirteenth Dynasty was progressively reduced. The dismantling began in Lower Egypt, with the appearance of an independent kingdom (Fourteenth Dynasty) at Xois, near the marshy fringe of the northwest delta, and the appearance, around 1720 B.C.E., of another dynasty at Avaris, the riverine port leading to Asia and Byblos. (The latter dynasty is also included under the label Fourteenth Dynasty.) By supplanting the rulers of Avaris, the Hyksos began their hold on Egypt, which was sanctioned by their capture of Memphis, beginning the Second Intermediate Period around 1650 B.C.E. This weakening of the pharaohs can be attributed not only to their ephemeral reigns, but also to an excessive multiplication of state offices, which tended to be awarded purely as benefices, draining the resources of the state.

We cannot present an exhaustive list of the pharaohs of the Thirteenth Dynasty, for too many of them are little known or unknown. Here are the salient points:

After Wegaf, the first pharaoh of the Thirteenth Dynasty, there were fifteen minor kings, including Auibre, Amehemhet V, Amenemhet VI, Amenemhet VII, and Sebekhotpe I.

The Thirteenth Dynasty culminated, if that is quite the right term for it, with a group of kings including Sebekhotpe II, Khendjer, Sebekhotpe III, Neferhotep I, Sebekhotpe IV, Ibyau, and Aya (1750–1685).

With a final group of pharaohs, we glimpse a serious deterioration in the situation: Neferhotep-Iykhernofret boasted of having saved Thebes from famine in the course of struggles that put him in opposition to Asiatics and their Egyptian collaborators; it is clear that the Hyksos were making their presence felt. Around 1650 B.C.E., the fall of Memphis, the center of cultural and artistic traditions, led to a striking decline in the quality of monuments and inscriptions during the reigns of the last kings of the Thirteenth

Dynasty, beginning with that of Dedumose. Drained, the Thirteenth Dynasty huddled in Upper Egypt, from Asyut to Aswan.

See Amenemhet, Ankhu, Mentuhotpe, Neferhotep I, Sebekhotpe.

Thirtieth Dynasty

See Sebennytic (Dynasty).

Tutankhamun 1335–1326 B.C.E., Eighteenth Dynasty

The "king's son Tutankhaten" makes his appearance toward the end of the reign of Amenophis IV/Akhenaten on a fragment from an Amarna temple found at Hermopolis. The debate concerning his parentage has subsided somewhat. Viewing him as a child of Amenophis III and Teye seems impossible; the arguments for doing so, which entail postulating a lengthy coregency of Amenophis III and Amenophis IV, are quite weak in the face of a mass of contrary evidence. The easiest solution is to see him as a son of Akhenaten by a wife other than Nefertiti. He was married to Ankhesenpaaten, the third of the daughters that Nefertiti bore to the heretic king. At the young age of about nine, the couple ascended the throne after the disappearance of Smenkhkare. The exclusivist cult of the Disk (Aten) still reigned at Amarna, but at Thebes, and undoubtedly elsewhere, the long-awaited restoration of the polytheistic order was begun. Soon, Tutankhaten ("Aten is entirely alive") became Tutankhamun, and the name of Ankhesenpaaten ("she lives for the Aten") was changed to Ankhesenamun. Amarna was abandoned by the state bureaucracy, and from then on, the court would frequent Thebes, Heliopolis (where the young king hunted), and especially Memphis.

The strong men were the "divine father" and future pharaoh Aya, a repentent old Atenist; the great majordomo and future pharaoh Haremhab; and the treasurer Maya. The latter two men constructed vast tombs at Saqqara that serve as splendid illustrations of domestic and colonial prosperity, as well as of a new style of bas-reliefs in which Amarna style blends with the classicism of Amenophis III. In his year 4, while resident at Memphis, the king ordered the making of new cult statues and divine barques, and the reconstitution of the priestly personnel and the temporal goods of all the temples. In the belief that impiety had ruined the government and the nation, and that the abandoned gods had turned their backs on humankind, Tutankhamun ordained a restoration of harmony and wellbeing. The former theologico-political discourse was resumed, along with normal relations between the human and the divine realms. After twenty years, Amun regained his preeminence at the summit of Egypt's supernatural edifice and religious institutions. An impressive colonnade was begun at Karnak; beautiful statues were sculpted, giving the king of the gods, as was customary, the visage of the reigning sovereign. A "mansion of millions of years," which has yet to be located, was founded on the west bank of Thebes.

Dead at the age of about eighteen, in year 10 of his reign, Tutankhamun was buried by Aya in a minuscule tomb in the Valley of the Kings that does not seem to have been the one he had prepared for himself. Miraculously preserved, it is the only royal burial of the New Kingdom that has yielded an intact selection of the sacred objects that assured Pharaoh's eternity. It also concealed a prestigious selection of furniture and utensils that bring to life an opulent luxury that was served by the refined arts. These treasures define the image of what it was to be a triumphant king, both in life and in death. An epilogue stresses the distance between this ideal image and the harsh reality of the exercise of power: as widow, Ankhesenamun asked the Hittite king to send her one of his sons so that she might make him her husband and the king of Egypt. The prince was assassinated on route. After his death, the king was not credited with the restoration he had accomplished. On his monuments, Haremhab substituted his own name for Tutankhamun's, and tradition erased his memory, just as it did that of Akhenaten and Aya—all of them, repented or not, tainted by the affair of Amarna.

C. Desroches-Noblecourt, *Tutankhamun: Life and Death of a Pharaoh* (New York, 1963); I. E. S. Edwards, *The Treasures of Tutankhamun* (New York, 1972).
See Amarna; Amenophis IV, alias Akhenaten.

Tuthmosis

Tuthmosis is the Greek form of the Egyptian name Djehutymose, which was borne by four pharaohs of the Eighteenth Dynasty. It means "Thoth is born."

Tuthmosis I 1493–1481 B.C.E., Eighteenth Dynasty

Third pharaoh of the Eighteenth Dynasty, Tuthmosis I was the son of the lady Seniseneb and a father whose name remains unknown. Tuthmosis was thus evidently not a blood relative of his predecessor Amenophis I. He married an Ahmose whose relationship to the royal family is uncertain, and who bore him the future Hatshepsut; the future Tuthmosis II was the product of his marriage to another woman, named Mutnofret. During his eleven years and nine months on the throne, Tuthmosis I established the basics of the policies that would be followed by the other kings of the

Eighteenth Dynasty. In year 2 of his reign, he traveled upstream to Nubia to put down a revolt; he established his southern boundary at the Third Cataract, constructed a fortress, and divided the surrounding territories into five principalities that were entrusted to Nubian vassals. On his return to Egypt, he cleared the canal at Sehel, and he prepared for a new extension of Egyptian influence farther to the south.

During a long tour of Syria-Palestine that took him as far as Carchemish and the Euphrates, the king signaled similar pretensions with regard to the northern regions. For the first time, he clashed with the kingdom of Mitanni, which would later be both the partner and the principal adversary of Egyptian policy in Asia. On his return trip, he hunted elephants in the territory of Niy. From that time on, Asia was the avowed object of Egyptian imperialism, and Tuthmosis I prepared for the future by making Memphis a base for departure: he created Perunefer, a riverine port directed toward the lands of the north, he established a palace, and he stationed an army equipped with chariots, and which was under the command of the heir apparent. The ancient residence of the Old Kingdom was better situated to keep watch over Asia than was Thebes, the dynastic city.

Thebes was not neglected, however. The king began enlarging the temple of Amun at Karnak by constructing a hypostyle hall in front of the bark sanctuary and erecting a pair of obelisks in front of the fourth pylon; he also surrounded the temple with an enclosure wall. All these works were supervised by the architect Ineni.

Ineni was also charged with preparing the king's tomb, which for the first time was located in the Valley of the Kings; it was decorated and inscribed with a new funerary composition, the Amduat. Tuthmosis I's mummy was found in the cachette of Deir el-Bahari.

C. Lalouette, *Textes sacrés et textes profanes de l'ancienne Égypte: Des Pharaons et des hommes* (Paris, 1984), pp. 91–92.

See Ahmose, son of Ebana; Amenophis I; Hatshepsut; Tuthmosis II.

Tuthmosis II 1481–1478 B.C.E., Eighteenth Dynasty

Tuthmosis II was the fourth pharaoh of the Eighteenth Dynasty. He was the third son of Tuthmosis I, and after that king's first two sons, Wadjmose and Amenmose, predeceased him, Tuthmosis became his successor. He married his half sister Hatshepsut, daughter of Tuthmosis I and Ahmose (his own mother was Mutnofret), and they had a daughter named Nefrure. Isis, another of his wives, was the mother of the future Tuthmosis III.

His reign was quite short, probably three years. Like his predecessors, he had to suppress a revolt in Nubia; the expedition he dispatched apparently ended the pretensions of the descendants of the Nubian potentates who had reigned during the Second Intermediate Period. Otherwise, he conducted a police operation against the bedouins of Palestine.

Tuthmosis II was able to make noticeable progress in the enlargement and embellishment of the temple of Karnak; in particular, he erected a pair of obelisks and a pair of colossi. But he did not have time to complete either his tomb or his funerary temple north of Medinet Habu, which was finished by Tuthmosis III. His mummy, which was found in the cachette of Deir el-Bahari, confirms that he died young, at the age of twenty-five to thirty.

See Hatshepsut, Tuthmosis I, Tuthmosis III.

Tuthmosis III 1478–1426 B.C.E., Eighteenth Dynasty

The fifth pharaoh of the Eighteenth Dynasty, Tuthmosis III was the son of Tuthmosis II and a concubine, Isis. He was designated successor to the throne by an oracle of Amun, and he reigned for fifty-three years. But this long reign was anything but bliss. In fact, since Tuthmosis was still a young child when he was crowned, his aunt Hatshepsut, widow of Tuthmosis II, exercised a regency that she soon transformed into a coregency that was made official by her own coronation as pharaoh. Without being entirely ousted—events continued to be dated by his regnal years—Tuthmosis III remained somewhat excluded from the reality of power, especially in domestic policy. As he grew older, Tuthmosis became more and more impatient with this situation. Thus, when Hatshepsut's death in approximately year 22 of his reign left him sole ruler, he had the queen's cartouches mutilated, substituting his own or those of his father and grandfather, Tuthmosis II and Tuthmosis I. At the end of his reign, a new—this time voluntary—coregency was established between him and Amenophis II, his son by one of his wives, Merytre-Hatshepsut.

Tuthmosis III carried Egyptian imperialism to its acme. In Nubia, he extended his power to the area between the Third and the Fourth Cataracts, which was commanded by the city of Napata, while the regions to the south were placed under close surveillance; he even set up a border stela at Kurgus, midway between the Fourth and the Fifth Cataracts. In Asia, at the price of fifteen campaigns, he affirmed and consolidated Egyptian supremacy in Syria-Palestine.

The first of these campaigns was conducted to eliminate the serious threat posed by a coalition of Syrian princes led by the ruler of Qadesh, a city located at the mouth of the Beqaa Valley. In year 23, after making his way via a difficult route that led to Megiddo, Tuthmosis III and his army defeated the enemy coalition, who were awaiting them at the end of the easier route. Megiddo itself fell after a seven-month siege. Scarcely had the ruler of Qadesh been conquered than a new opponent to Egyptian pretensions arose, the ruler of Tunip; after several defeats, his threat was neutralized by the sack of his city. But Egypt's most dangerous rival was Mitanni (Naharin), a state with a Hurrian population that was ruled by an Indo-European aristocracy. Tuthmosis III prevailed over Mitanni, thanks to a clever strategy: ships were conveyed by chariot from the Lebanese coast to the Euphrates, whose banks were ravaged by Tuthmosis. He erected a border stela as testimony to his victory, and then, on his journey home, he gave himself a well-earned diversion by confronting a herd of 120 elephants.

The Egyptian hegemony assured by these brilliant campaigns was solidified by a system of control: though they retained a certain autonomy, the cities of Syria-Palestine had to pay tribute to an Egyptian administration that relied on garrisons placed in strategic locations. Sanctuaries dedicated to Egyptian deities constituted the symbolic pendant to this military presence. Furthermore, the sons of the local potentates were taken as hostages to Egypt, where they were carefully educated in the royal palace, so that if they returned to their native lands to succeed their fathers, they returned entirely Egyptianized. Some of them remained in Egypt, where they made careers, sometimes brilliant ones, for themselves.

This triumphant imperialism brought riches pouring into Egypt in the form of booty and annual tribute. Most of this wealth was dedicated to the domain of Amun, as shown by the Annals of Tuthmosis III, a text that was copied near the holy of holies of the temple of Karnak. As was only to be expected, the temple itself was considerably enlarged and embellished. Wooden columns were replaced by columns of stone, a new bark sanctuary was constructed, the Middle Kingdom court was reworked for the erection of the Akh-menu (a jubilee temple), a new pylon was added, obelisks (one of them now in Istanbul) were erected, and the sacred area was surrounded by a new enclosure wall. Otherwise, Tuthmosis III's building activity was manifest in most of the temples from Nubia, via Upper, Middle, and Lower Egypt, all the way to Byblos; Minmose, "overseer of works in the sanctuaries of the gods of Upper and Lower Egypt," reports that he worked in nineteen temples. In addition to the construction activity, cultic objects were renewed and multiplied. Moreover, besides being a brave warrior, Thuthmosis III was a cultivated man who was enamored of literature; his researches in the sacred archives not only led him to recopy ancient religious texts, beginning with the Pyramid Texts, but also to establish new rituals and ceremonies that were still celebrated in the Greco-Roman era.

Paradoxically, quite unlike that of Hatshepsut, the funerary temple of Tuthmosis III was in no way out of the ordinary. The same is true of his tomb, which was excavated in the Valley of the Kings. His mummy, which was found in the cachette of Deir el-Bahari, indicates that like many great men, he was of short stature.

And he was indeed a great man, undoubtedly the greatest pharaoh of ancient Egypt. His cult still played a part in personal piety under the Ptolemies, and his throne name Menkheperre became a talisman that was reproduced on innumerable scarabs down to the Saite Period and on Egyptianizing objects manufactured elsewhere in the Mediterranean basin.

G. Steindorff and K. C. Seele, *When Egypt Ruled the East,* 2d ed. (Chicago, 1957), chapter 7; J. A. Wilson, in J. B. Pritchard, ed., *Ancient Near Eastern Texts Relating to the Old Testament,* 2d ed. (Princeton, 1955), pp. 234–44, 373–75, and 446–47.

See Amenophis II, Hatshepsut, Rekhmire, Tuthmosis II.

Tuthmosis IV 1401–1391 B.C.E., Eighteenth Dynasty

Tuthmosis IV was the eighth pharaoh of the Eighteenth Dynasty. Son of Amenophis II and Queen Tia, he reigned nine years and eight months; examination of his mummy revealed that he evidently died around the age of thirty. In foreign policy, aside from some police operations against bedouins and Nubians, his principal accomplishment was the peaceful resolution of the Mitannian problem. Amenophis II had obtained only a fragile truce. After a military expedition against Mitanni, Tuthmosis IV concluded a peace treaty with its king, Artatama, and it was sealed with the introduction of a daughter of that king into the pharaoh's harem after lengthy negotiations.

Of his monumental activity, notable accomplishments were his completion an obelisk of Tuthmosis III at Karnak that had been lying uncompleted for forty-two years (it is now in the Lateran) and his clearing of the Great Sphinx of Giza, which he protected with a wall. In fact, while he was sleeping, exhausted from one of his adolescent escapades in the Memphite necropolis, Harmachis, whose hypostasis was the Sphinx, had appeared to him in a dream and promised him the kingship if he would clear the monument from the sands that covered it.

Tuthmosis IV's funerary temple was built southwest of that of his father, Amenophis II. His tomb in the Valley of the Kings needed repair in year 8 of Haremhab, who put the architect Maya in charge of the job. Tuthmosis' mummy was transferred to the tomb of Amenophis II in the Twenty-first Dynasty.

B. M. Bryan, *The Reign of Thutmose IV* (Baltimore, 1991); C. Zivie-Coche, *Sphinx: History of a Monument* (Ithaca, 2002), pp. 47–51.

See Amenophis II, Amenophis III.

Twelfth Dynasty

Founded by Amenemhet I, the former vizier of the last king of the Eleventh Dynasty, the Twelfth Dynasty had to struggle to impose its legitimacy on the partisans of the preceding line. But it succeeded, notwithstanding crises—such as that provoked by the assassination of its founder—thanks to effective propaganda disseminated by talented writers. It maintained power for more than two hundred years, and it lost it only after the reign of Nefrusobk, a queen who became pharaoh under circumstances that escape us; but its policies and its spirit were continued under the dynasty that followed it.

The succession of kings was as follows:

Amenemhet I (1991–1962 B.C.E.)
Senwosret I, his son and coregent (1971–1926 B.C.E.)
Amenemhet II, son and coregent of the preceding (1929–1895 B.C.E.)
Senwosret II, son and coregent of the preceding (1897–1878[?] B.C.E.)
Senwosret III, son of the preceding (1878[?]–1843 B.C.E.)
Amenemhet III (1843–1796 B.C.E.)
Amenemhet IV, nephew (?) and coregent of the preceding (1799–1787 B.C.E.)
Nefrusobk, daughter of Amenemhet III and wife of Amenemhet IV; reigned as pharaoh (1787–1784 B.C.E.) after the death of her husband, assuming the prerogatives and the duties (maintaining the temples) of the royal office.

The history of the Twelfth Dynasty can be divided into two periods. From Amenemhet I to Senwosret II, the pharaohs tried to balance the Theban heritage of the First Intermediate Period (they saw themselves as continuers of the Eleventh Dynasty) with the traditional model of the Old Kingdom. This policy accounts for their choice of Lisht as their administrative capital; it was sufficiently close to Memphis to benefit from its cultural aura (arts and sacred lore), but far enough south to mark its specificity and to signify a search for a happy medium between Upper and Lower Egypt. Even as they forged the concept of "Victorious Thebes," the pharaohs erected pyramids, as had been done in the Old Kingdom.

Though they recruited their ruling elite mostly from their native province, they maintained the overall social organization of olden times; in particular, powerful families of nomarchs still exercised their office in the spirit and with the pomp of the Sixth Dynasty.

After the reign of Senwosret II, a major change occurred in the apparatus of the state. New offices, a new hierarchy, and new titles were created, and there was a redistribution of assignments and responsibilities in the framework of the forces and the administration of production. The system of nomarchs died out, and they were replaced by leaders at the municipal level, not at that of the nome; these leaders were assisted and supervised by "heralds" who were under the immediate jurisdiction of the vizier. All of Egypt was divided into three "departments," which were themselves managed by "heralds."

The supervision of the workforce received great attention because there were never enough workers. A "bureau of the distribution of men" was set up, along with an agency called the "prison," which administered common-law prisoners condemned to forced labor, as well as many Asiatic immigrants or prisoners of war, and statutory laborers who were ever quick to flee the fields or construction sites assigned to them. Order was assured by militias organized into various corps: "followers," "followers of the ruler," "guardians of the table companions of the ruler," "residents of the city," and so forth.

These reforms led to the emergence of a middle class of bureaucrats who worked in the offices of the state and were well enough compensated to be able to provide themselves with inscribed funerary monuments, which had previously been the prerogative of the elite of the high officials. This change in the sociological landscape, which was marked by the multiplication of stelae, statues, and offering tables of middling quality, was one of the most striking traits of the second half of the Twelfth Dynasty.

As a whole, this dynasty extended the geographical range of pharaonic activity. It began the exploitation of the Faiyum, which had previously been covered with marshes, and it forged a veritable foreign policy based on a good knowledge of neighboring lands. This knowledge was demonstrated by the Execration Texts, in which all the names of foreign countries and their rulers are listed in detail on vases or figurines that were used in execration rituals. On a more practical level, the Nile valley of Lower Nubia was integrated into Egypt by means of a complex system of fortresses. In Asia, traditional relations with Byblos were strengthened to the point that its rulers became highly Egyptianized; more generally, trade with Syria-Palestine intensified, and via that area, trade with the Aegean world. Meanwhile, many Asiatics immigrated to Egypt.

The Story of Sinuhe is a good reflection of its times, for most of its action takes place in this Asiatic world to which Egypt had opened itself. It is no accident that this masterpiece of Egyptian literature is set in the reign of Senwosret I. The Twelfth Dynasty's most splendid legacy to Egyptian civilization was its fiction (Story of Sinuhe, Tale of the Shipwrecked Sailor), its prophecy (Prophecies of Neferti), its wisdom texts (Instruction of Amenemhet I, Instruction of Khety, Loyalist Instruction, Instruction of a Man for his Son), and its poems (Hymn to the Nile), which would remain classics until the end of the dynastic period.

G. Posener, *Littérature et politique dans l'Égypte de la XIIe dynastie,* Bibliothèque de l'École Pratique des Hautes Études 307 (Paris, 1956); M. Lichtheim, *Ancient Egyptian Literature: A Book of Readings,* vol. 1: *The Old and Middle Kingdoms* (Berkeley, 1973).

See Amenemhet, Inyotefoqer, Senwosret, Sinuhe.

Twentieth Dynasty

Claiming the patronage of Amun, Sethnakhte (1190–1187 B.C.E.) put an end to the disorders that undid the Nineteenth Dynasty, and he founded the second line of Ramesside kings, which included the nine kings named Ramesses whose reigns followed his own. All these monarchs made their tombs at Thebes, in the Valley of the Kings (that of Ramesses VIII remains undiscovered). The last mention of Pi-Riamsese, the northern capital that Ramesses III often visited, dates to Ramesses VIII; the diminishing flow of water in the easternmost branch of the Nile in the delta led to the abandonment of the city. In any case, the last Ramesside kings seem to have resided permanently in the delta, rather than at Thebes. Ramesses III (1187–1156 B.C.E.), son of Sethnakhte, saved Egypt from attacks by Libyans and Sea Peoples and maintained bases in Canaan. He blatantly copied the style of Ramesses II, while emphasizing the spiritual hold and the revenues of Amun.

Egypt experienced a brief apogee, but it did not outlast the reign of the pious Ramesses IV (1156–1150 B.C.E.); the next three quarters of a century saw a lengthy decline. All the Near East, undoubtedly affected by an adverse climate change, sank into a period of convulsions. Hebrews and Philistines disputed over control of Palestine, Aramaeans poured into Syria, and the empires of Assyria and Babylon declined. Egypt continued to dominate the Sudan, but it withdrew from the coast of Asia: Egyptians did not even set foot in the Sinai after Ramesses VI. In the temples, construction activity was meager: the titularies of these last Ramessides were carved in the blank margins of existing decorations, and only a few statues were sculpted, though they were elegant (Ramesses VI, Ramesses IX).

Toward the end, under Ramesses XI, work was begun anew at the temple of Khonsu at Karnak.

Fortunately, two sources enable us to catch a glimpse of the circumstances of this period when the political will and ritual role of the king expressed themselves more feebly in the south than the decisions and initiatives of the Theban pontiffs. One of these sources is the papyri and ostraca from Deir el-Medina, the village occupied by the workmen charged with excavating and decorating the royal tombs. The other, also from the Theban area, consists of dossiers detailing several judicial inquiries and the inscriptions left by the high priests of Amun at Karnak. Difficulties in subsistence (which led to strikes) and disturbances affecting the public order (conspiracies at the royal court, armed movements) began to occur in the reign of Ramesses III. Descendants of Libyan prisoners of war who had been recruited as soldiers, as well as newcomers driven out of the Sahara by famine, eventually inundated the delta and even began to disturb the south. Over several generations, one family in the Thebais won control over the clergy and the property of Amun, while this priesthood, which had disposal of the worldly goods of the god and steeped itself in spiritual culture, became ever more autonomous and wealthy.

Under Ramesses IX, the high priest Amenhotpe was the actual ruler of Thebes. But during this reign, strikes and shortages of provisions recurred. Tombs were pillaged, even those of the "great gods," the deceased kings. Things worsened under Ramesses XI (1098–1069 B.C.E.), with famine, more tomb violations, the ousting of the high priest Amenhotpe, the appearance of Libyans, military intervention by the viceroy of Nubia, who conducted operations as far north as Middle Egypt, and violence by bands of foreigners. In year 19 of Ramesses XI, a new era was begun; it was called the "renewal of births" (*uhem-mesut*). Its year count ran parallel to the king's, and its purpose was to proclaim a rebirth of the cosmic order, not the substitution of a new family line. Far from this weakling of a Ramesses who lived in the north, Herihor and then Piankh, newcomers who were both high priests of Thebes and military commanders, ruled Upper Egypt like kings under the cloak of the oracle of Amun. They were contemporaries of Smendes, the future founder of the Twenty-first Dynasty, under whom Tanis would supplant Pi-Riamsese as the northern capital. The end of the New Kingdom (which was no longer a single kingdom) bore the seeds of the Third Intermediate Period: the weakening of the moral presence of the pharaoh; the promotion of Amun-Re, the transcendent creator god, into the source of both governance and individual destiny; and the rise of two ambitious powers—the priesthood of that god and the Libyan chiefs who were becoming Egyptianized.

C. Lalouette, *L'Empire des Ramsès* (Paris, 1985), pp. 298–363.

See Herihor, High Priest of Amun, Libyans, Ramesses III, Ramesses IV, Ramessides, Sethnakhte.

Twenty-eighth Dynasty

See Saite (Dynasties).

Twenty-fifth Dynasty

See Kushite (Dynasty).

Twenty-first Dynasty

See Third Intermediate Period.

Twenty-ninth Dynasty

See Mendesian (Dynasty).

Twenty-second Dynasty

See Third Intermediate Period.

Twenty-seventh Dynasty

See Persians.

Twenty-sixth Dynasty

See Saite (Dynasties).

Twenty-third Dynasty

See Third Intermediate Period.

Twosre 1192–1190 B.C.E., Nineteenth Dynasty

Her name—Tahoser, as Champollion transcribed it—was borrowed by Théophile Gautier to baptize the pretty mummy in his novel. However extraordinary her destiny, the Twosre who is the object of historians' attentions had nothing in common with the invented heroine. The chief wife of Sethos II (1204–1198 B.C.E.), Twosre survived her husband. At first, she exercised a sort of regency on behalf of Siptah, the son of a secondary wife, whom the great treasurer Bay "maintained on the throne of his father." Then she succeeded Siptah as pharaoh in her own right. She adopted a throne name and founded a funerary temple of her own at Thebes.

Thus, fifteen years after the death of Ramesses the Great, the monarchy went through a grave crisis. Power was torn between the protagonists of a bizarre triarchy, each of whom had a tomb excavated in the Valley of the

Kings. One member of this triarchy, a canonical pharaoh who was a minor and infirm, changed his name from Ramesses-Siptah to Merneptah-Siptah in the second year of his reign, a sure sign of a change of program. The second was a kingmaker who scholars have every reason to think was of foreign origin, one of those hostages who were raised at the court of Ramesses II and became court officials. The third, Twosre, was a dowager queen, no doubt of royal blood, who in any case exemplified the feminine dimension of royalty in association with the young king and ended up as the fourth female pharaoh in history. Her own reign, which was quite brief, marked the end of the Nineteenth Dynasty. A vase bearing her cartouche has been found at Deir Alla in Jordan. At this time, Egyptian influence was in fact on the wane in Asia, while courtiers of Asiatic descent and the Syrian recruits of the factious power holders dictated the law of the land. As usual, erasures and name replacements were the manifestations, either immediate or deferred, of the settling of scores. Under the Twentieth Dynasty, tradition would ignore the reigns of Siptah and Twosre.

C. Lalouette, *L'Empire de Ramsès* (Paris, 1985), pp. 290–94.

See Erasures, Nineteenth Dynasty, Queens.

Udjahorresnet

One could say that Udjahorresnet was a "pharaoh maker," though in an undoubtedly anachronistic manner, he has often been denounced as a "collaborator." This Saite priest had administered the royal fleet under the last two kings of the Twenty-sixth Dynasty and exercised various administrative offices when, in 525 B.C.E., the Persians occupied Egypt. Taken on as chief physician by Cambyses, he composed the Egyptian titulary of this conqueror and persuaded him to agree that the Persian garrison would cease to pollute the temenos of the goddess Neith with its presence. Later, while resident at Susa, he was commanded by Darius I to return home and to restore the "house of life" (institute of priestly knowledge) at Sais. In his autobiography, Udjahorresnet recounts in simple terms how he introduced the new masters of Egypt to the theology of his native country and initiated them into the ritual duties of a Lord of the Two Lands. His compatriots were less severe than present-day historians in their estimation of this maintainer of sacred order and moral security: one hundred seventy-seven years later, a Memphite priest restored a statue of him in order to perpetuate his memory.

M. Lichtheim, *Ancient Egyptian Literature: A Book of Readings*, vol. 3: *The Late Period* (Berkeley, 1980), pp. 36–41.

See Cambyses, Darius I, Persians.

Unification

The establishment of the pharaonic state and the evidently sudden emergence of its characteristic traits—in other words, the transition from prehistory to history—were for a long time described as a single event: the moment when Upper and Lower Egypt were united, at some time between 3200 and 2900 B.C.E. Menes, the first name in the king lists of the New Kingdom—and, according to Manetho, the first king of the first human dynasty—supposedly unified the land, making Memphis its capital and laying the foundations of its institutions, its economy, and its culture. He was also credited with the organization of a system of irrigation basins, the redistribution of tribes into nomes, and the founding of a central administration that used writing.

This story, which is still sometimes told in discussing the problem of the unification, stems from the conjunction of two sources. One of them is what we read about Menes in the ancient Greek sources; the other consists of the ancient Egyptian concept of the monarchy as a dual one.

According to Herodotus (c. 450 B.C.E.), "Min" reclaimed the land on which he built Memphis from the floodwaters of the Nile, and the subsequent accumulation of silt created the delta. Manetho (c. 290 B.C.E.) characterized Menes as a conqueror of foreign lands. The Greco-Egyptian stories and anecdotes transmitted by Diodorus made him a sovereign who imposed written laws (attributed fictively to Hermes-Thoth), the inventor of material comfort, and the founder of the sacred rites and animal cults.

From the first dynasties on, mythological and iconographic themes presented the kingship as a double one, with different images distinguishing (but also uniting) an Upper Egypt and a Lower Egypt; the former had precedence over the latter. A word for "king of Lower Egypt" was paired with one for "king of Upper Egypt." The gods Seth (the south) and Horus (the north) were united in the person of the sovereign. The goddess Nekhbet of el-Kab had a counterpart in Wadjit of Buto, and they were the mistresses of the white crown and the red crown, respectively; when the former was placed inside the latter, the two crowns together formed the *pshent,* the double crown. The "souls of Hierakonpolis" in the south formed a symmetry with the "souls of Buto" in the north. The order imposed by the state was symbolized by a scene of the "uniting of the Two Lands": under the pharaoh's feet, or on the side of his throne (see figure 8), the stalks of the plants symbolizing the south and the north were tied together around the hieroglyph for the word "unite" (*sema*).

Carved during the Old Kingdom, retrospective annals called the "Palermo Stone" listed kings wearing only the red crown in the place where New Kingdom historiography located the "Followers of Horus" or "demigods." Prior to World War II, Egyptologists who relied on this source, along with certain ritual texts, took it as a given that there was a northern kingdom of Buto whose conquest by kings of the south from Hierakonpolis and el-Kab effected the unification of the Two Lands. In the same vein, in consideration of noted cultural differences between predynastic sites at the apex of the delta and in Upper Egypt, a fashionable theory once claimed (rather arbitrarily) that an "African," pastoral south had annexed an "Asiatic," agricultural north.

Scholars who studied pharaonic thought were soon obliged to challenge these reconstructions: the theme of a united duality was entirely symbolic and could not commemorate a genuinely historical founding event. Supposedly uninhabitable (contrary to paleographic and other evidence), Buto was chosen, according to these scholars, as the counterpart of Hierakonpolis, the two sites ideally marking the two boundaries of the kingdom. More recently, archaeological progress has radically changed our view of the issue, which had relied principally on the interpretation of texts and images expressive of ideological traditions.

Considering the parallelism between the sequence of kings attested by

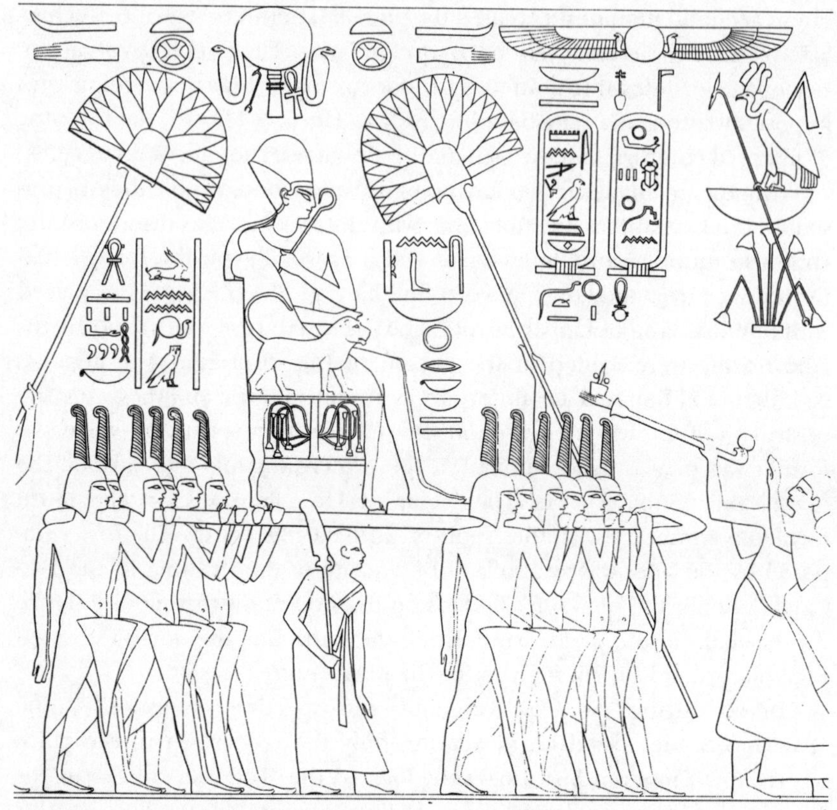

FIGURE 8. *King Haremhab seated on a throne, the side of which is decorated with the symbol for "uniting the Two Lands." From J.-F. Champollion,* Monuments de l'Égypte et de la Nubie, *vol. 2, (Paris, 1845), pl. 111.*

the monuments of the First Dynasty and the king lists of the New Kingdom, Horus Aha seems to correspond to Menes; in both the Abydos region and the Memphite necropolis, Aha's reign is marked by the size of the elite tombs and the richness of their furnishings. But there is no point in seeking to authenticate the accomplishments credited to Menes by a writer like Diodorus; those achievements are those of a fictitious culture hero and legislator. In classical literature, such traits are otherwise assigned to the legendary Sesostris (whose name is also given as Sesoosis and Osiris). Such figures were borrowed from Egypt by Hellenistic historiography at a relatively late point, when traditional mythology held that the basics of Egypt's institutions had been created in the primordial time of the gods: Re had instituted *maat,* the just order of the world; Shu had organized the land; Thoth had been the first vizier and the inventor of writing; Horus and Seth had contended for control over the Two Lands and divided these two parts of Egypt between them; grain had sprung from Osiris; and so forth.

The discovery of protohistorical settlements at Buto and at neighboring sites has lent some substance to the idea that late in the fourth millennium B.C.E., a northern kingdom was conquered by kings of the south. But in both the valley and the delta, excavations have shown that the cultural expansion of the south was a lengthy process, and that the pace that led to the prevalence of a uniform culture and to the pharaonic regime quickened at the time of Dynasty Zero. We must henceforth dissociate the historical birth of the Egyptian state from the ideological structure of the unification of the Two Lands.

See Buto, Crowns, Dualisms, Hierakonpolis and Eileithyiaspolis, Memphis, Menes, Zero (Dynasty).

Uraeus

This word from the earliest Egyptological jargon is the Latinized form of Greek *ouraios,* which according to the *Hieroglyphica* of Horapollo supposedly designated, in Egyptian, the serpent known as the basilisk (from Greek *basilikos,* "royal"). But the snake was not, as this Alexandrian philosopher believed, the large male reptile that symbolized cosmic eternity, but rather a rearing cobra, a female entity called *iarat* that represented the magical power of crowns and the blazing heat of the sun. This divine being was merged with Wadjit, the goddess of the crown of the north, but also, as the "Eye of Re," with many other goddesses, notably the lion-headed Sakhmet. The uraeus, either alone or in a pair (like the royal crowns), was suspended from a sun disc in the iconography. From the Fourth Dynasty on, a single cobra, an exclusive insignia of the royal office in this life, crept along the axis of the pharaoh's headdress and reared its inflated hood in the middle of his brow. Certain princesses shared this insignia, and in the New Kingdom, multiple uraei adorned the crowns of goddesses and queens. In the temples, rearing cobras formed protective friezes at the tops of walls.

See Crowns, Pharaoh.

Valley of the Kings

Buried according to custom in the west of their dynastic home, the Theban kings of the Seventeenth Dynasty had pyramids of middling size built for themselves at Dra Abu el-Naga, at the foot of the mountain across the river from Karnak. The founders of the Eighteenth Dynasty were also buried on the west bank of Thebes; the mummies of Ahmose and Amenophis I were found in the cachette of Deir el-Bahari, though unfortunately, the exact location of their tombs has not been identified. Apparently under Tuthmosis I, the decision was made to excavate rock-cut tombs for the kings in the mountainside. This custom would be followed by all his successors down through Ramesses XI. In contrast to the summit of the pyramid shape dominating the *gebel,* the tombs of nearly all the kings of the three dynasties of the New Kingdom are thus at the bottom of the steep sides of two wadis that run together into a dry valley, the Valley of the Kings (Arabic *Biban el-Moluk,* "the gates of the kings"). Amenophis III and Aya were buried farther away, in the so-called Valley of the Monkeys. (Amenophis IV/Akhenaten, of course, made his tomb in the eastern mountain of Amarna). Certain privileged individuals were admitted into the Valley of the Kings: the prince Maherpra, and then the in-laws of Amenophis III, Yuya and Tuya, in the Eighteenth Dynasty; the upstart treasurer Bay, a contemporary of Siptah and Twosre, in the Nineteenth Dynasty; and the crown prince Mentuherkhopshef, son of Ramesses IX, in the Twentieth Dynasty. Royal wives and mothers, princesses, and other children of the king were normally buried in a wadi to the south that ends behind Medinet Habu, the Valley of the Queens (or *Biban el-Harim*).

Sixty-one tombs are presently known in the Valley of the Kings. A typical rock-cut tomb consisted of a fairly lengthy succession of corridors, some of them flanked by small side rooms, leading to the burial chamber (see figure 9). The walls of the passages, and the pillars as well, were exhaustively decorated, representing the Osiris-king's encounter with the gods of the afterlife, and reproducing compositions that identified the tomb with the depths into which the sun sank at night. These fantastic annotated illustrations symbolized the phases of the regeneration of the heavenly body that rose again in the morning. The earliest of these was the Book of the Hidden Room (or Amduat), which was followed, on the eve of Amarna, by the Book of Gates, and later by the Book of Caverns and other cryptic works. Representing different approaches to the mystery of regeneration, these esoteric rows of illustrations describe the life of the blessed dead and the extermination of the damned. Their chronology and their topography are centered on the nightly navigation of the sun along the river of the netherworld. They recount the defeat of the cosmic enemy

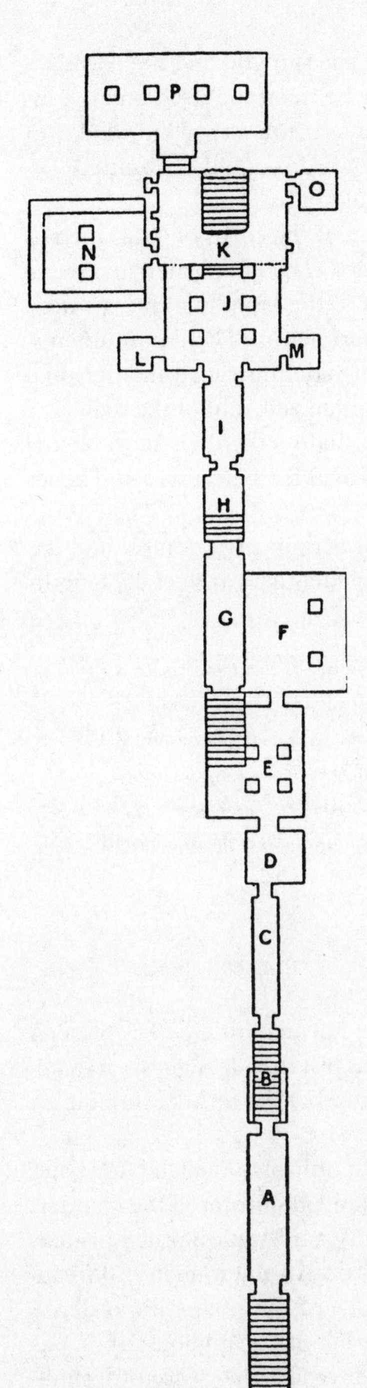

FIGURE 9. *Layout of a typical New Kingdom royal tomb as illustrated by a plan of the tomb of Sethos I. A, first corridor; B, second corridor; C, third corridor; D, shaft; E, first pillared hall; F, side chamber; G–H, lower corridors; I, antechamber; J, sarcophagus chamber; K, "crypt"; L–O, side chambers; P, end room. From E. Hornung and E. Staehelin,* Sethos—ein Pharaonengrab *(Basel, 1991), p. 44.*

Apopis, the transformations of the body of the sun god and the corollary rebirth of Osiris, and the transfer of power between the dead and the living. These recondite treatises were believed to contain total knowledge of the mechanisms of the immanent world. Down through the Twentieth Dynasty, they would be a monopoly of the royal tombs.

The reign of Tuthmosis I saw the creation of the corps of "workmen of the Tomb" and their village of Deir el-Medina. The quarrymen and decorators whose job was to prepare the tombs of the kings and queens were settled there, in the proximity of their workplaces. Their monuments, both tombs and chapels, along with surviving administrative and personal archives, inform us of how their work was organized, and of the daily life, the culture, and the piety of these people. Indirectly, their monuments also reflect the economic and political difficulties that affected Thebes and the kingdom.

The immense size and the perfection of certain royal tombs, and the uncompleted status or the usurpation of certain others, reflect the lengths of reigns and the apogees and crises of power.

J. Černý, *The Valley of the Kings* (Cairo, 1973); D. Valbelle, *"Les Ouvriers de la Tombe": Deir el-Médineh à l'époque ramesside,* Bibliothèque d'Étude 96 (Cairo, 1986); M. Bierbrier, *The Tomb-Builders of the Pharaohs* (New York, 1984); N. Reeves and R.H. Wilkinson, *The Complete Valley of the Kings: Tombs and Treasures of Egypt's Greatest Pharaohs* (London, 1996); L.H. Lesko, ed., *Pharaoh's Workers: The Villagers of Deir el-Medina* (Ithaca, 1994); E. Hornung, *The Ancient Egyptian Books of the Afterlife* (Ithaca, 1999).

See Cachettes.

Vizier

Egyptologists conventionally translate the Egyptian title *tjaty* as "vizier," and this convention should be understood as just that. It suggests an analogy, but evidently not a close resemblance to what the term covered in its original use.

In ancient Egypt, the vizier was the highest official in the land, the chief of the bureaucracy through which the pharaoh administered the country; the vizier was a sort of prime minister. This administration relied primarily on writing; above all, the vizier had to control the immense bureaucratic machine that assured the maintenance of the pharaonic order, a fact that helps us understand how it was that Thoth, the god of scribes, was also the vizier of the gods. In fact, the vizier sealed the decrees promulgated by the pharaoh, and large archives were stored in his office. He kept not only copies of private legal documents, especially those called *imyt-per* (records of property transfers), but also registers of cultivable lands, which were referred to in cases of dispute when it was time to measure the taxable land surfaces. The vizier had the right to access the archives of other institutions, which were obligated to forward the documents he requested of them, according to procedures that were detailed in writing, and which differed according to whether they were classified as "confidential." It was above all because he maintained archives that the vizier played a major role that we would characterize as judicial, though in ancient Egypt there was scarcely any distinction between the judiciary and the executive branch of the government. The vizier searched the written documents to weigh the merits of requests, to resolve disputes according to regulations, and to apply punishments according to the "laws," which were more a matter of the normative substance of decrees and customs than of general and abstract principles.

With these means at his disposal, the vizier controlled production. The natural phenomena that lent rhythm to the agricultural cycle (the heliacal rising of Sothis, the arrival of the annual inundation, episodic rainfalls) were reported to him, and he gave local administrators orders to construct dikes to retain the silt-laden water in the irrigation basins and to prepare the arable soil. He fixed the taxes on the harvests, calculating any arrears, and he supervised the transport and distribution of large cattle. In collaboration with the "overseers of that which is sealed," he saw to the storing of precious commodities, and he assured their procurement by sending expeditions to the mines and quarries, or to distant trade centers.

The vizier controlled the circulation of goods and labor by controlling the round trips made by boats, by moving paramilitary personnel to where they were needed, and by seeing to it that the divine offerings were furnished to the temples. He was able to mobilize these means and forces of production for special tasks, such as the construction or repair of buildings, royal ceremonies, and the preparation of royal funerary monuments. Finally, he had oversight over civil and religious offices.

The scope of the job was so burdensome that in the Eighteenth Dynasty, if not already in the Middle Kingdom, it was divided between a vizier of Upper Egypt, in charge at Thebes, and a vizier of Lower Egypt, in charge in the northern residence (Memphis, Pi-Riamsese, or Lisht). During the first half of the Eighteenth Dynasty, the family line of Amtju, User(amun), and Rekhmire perfected a sort of vizierial tradition that was expressed through a specialized literature that consisted in part of the Duties of the Vizier and the Installation of the Vizier. The former was an enumeration (though more laudatory than systematic) of the vizier's tasks; the latter aimed to define the ethical aspect of the office.

At the beginning of the Old Kingdom, the viziers were members of the royal family, but in the Fifth Dynasty, they began to be recruited from outside it; conversely, the weakening of royal power under the Sixth Dynasty is signaled by the fact that Pepi I was obliged to marry the sisters of the vizier Djau, who was a member of an influential family of Abydos. During the Thirteenth Dynasty, when ephemeral pharaohs rapidly succeeded one another on the throne, the family of the vizier Ankhu imperturbably controlled the conduct of business. Sometimes the importance of the office aroused the ambition of its holder to the point of inciting him to aim higher, as in the case of Amenemhet I, who founded the Twelfth Dynasty, after having been the vizier of Mentuhotpe IV, the last king of the Eleventh Dynasty. In the Third Intermediate Period, the rise of a theocracy that reduced the pharaoh's sovereignty, which was no longer immanent but rather subject to the divine oracle, had repercussions in the weakening of the vizierial office. From that time on, the viziers seem to have been pale figures, compared with the administrators of the domain of Amun.

T. G. H. James, *Pharaoh's People: Scenes from Life in Imperial Egypt* (London, 1984), chapter 2; G. P. F. van den Boorn, *The Duties of the Vizier: Civil Administration in the Early New Kingdom* (London, 1988).

See Ankhu, Herihor, Inyotefoqer, Kagemni, Ptahhotpe, Rekhmire.

War

Protecting his subjects from minor incursions and major invasions was the task of the king, as was the profitable expansion of Egypt's frontiers; theologically, the gods granted these powers to him alone. On the façades of temples, huge scenes of "smiting the enemies" in the presence of a deity lend material expression to this protective action; they do not, however, depict human sacrifice. The presentation of a sword to the king by a god and the presentation of rows of bound prisoners (represented by "fortress cartouches"; see figure 10) to the god by the king express a ritual exchange of victorious force for booty.

Pharaoh's battles and his victorious return from war were archetypal events exemplifying his maintenance of a providential order, and their representations on temple walls actualized their ceremonial meaning. Along with assurances of his divinity and of his pious activities on behalf of temples, epithets describing his success in war and his personal prowess fill the titularies and the panegyrics to be found in the inscriptions carved under every king, even those who were minors or whose armies were inactive. In the New Kingdom, a period well-known for conflicts between great empires, a distinction was made between expeditions led by the sovereign himself at the head of huge contingents, and actions led by officers to pacify tributaries on a local scale. The latter were displays of the "strong arm of Pharaoh." Beyond the sentiment that could always be aroused by representations of the triumph of the incarnation of the creator god, the accounts left behind by kings such as Kamose, Tuthmosis III, Amenophis II, and Ramesses II reveal them to have been inspiring leaders (though not always enlightened strategists). Two gods

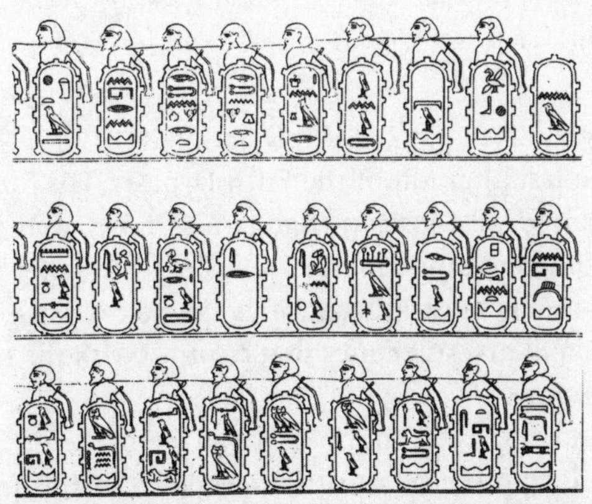

FIGURE 10. *Foreign lands depicted as "fortress cartouches." Temple of Karnak. From J.-F. Champollion,* Monuments de l'Égypte et de la Nubie, *vol. 3 (Paris, 1845), pl. 294.*

were prototypes of the royal warrior: Montu, the original patron of the kings of the Eleventh and Twelfth Dynasties, and Seth, the violent defender of the sun barque.

Weni

A high official of the Sixth Dynasty, Weni is famous because of the autobiography carved in his mastaba at Abydos, which has impressed not only Egyptologists but also the ancient Egyptian themselves, to judge from the number of implicit citations in later works.

Weni's career spanned the reigns of Teti, Pepy I, and Merenre, progressing through the following stages: "overseer of the work house," "inspector of the managers of units of production of the Great House," "companion, prophet of the pyramid city of Pepy I," "judge, mouth of Nekhen," "sole companion, overseer of the managers of units of production of the Great House," "guardian of the Great Mansion, sandal bearer," and finally, "governor, overseer of Upper Egypt." Weni's success was due to the competence with which he handled delicate matters. His assignments included judging the persons implicated in a plot fomented in the harem, conducting several military campaigns in the south of Palestine, and leading expeditions to the quarries of Hatnub, Elephantine, and Ibhat to extract the materials needed for the offering table, the false door, the sarcophagus, and the casing of the pyramid of Merenre. Conversely, one king had items of fine limestone procured for Weni's tomb. With its clarity, its precision, and its literary qualities (it includes a passage in poetic style), Weni's autobiography is one of the most accomplished of its genre from Egyptian civilization.

M. Lichtheim, *Ancient Egyptian Literature: A Book of Readings,* vol. 1: *The Old and Middle Kingdoms* (Berkeley, 1973), pp. 18–23.

Wenis 2350–2321 B.C.E., Fifth Dynasty

Wenis was the last pharaoh of the Fifth Dynasty. His funerary complex behind the pyramid of Djoser at Saqqara is fairly well preserved. The causeway that connected the funerary temple to the valley temple was decorated with bas-reliefs illustrating various themes: a battle with bedouins, artisans at work, and market scenes that contrast with the mournful representation of a famine.

Wenis' pyramid is scarcely more than 130 feet in height; it was restored by Khaemwese during the reign of Ramesses II. In this pyramid, for the first time, the walls of the sarcophagus chamber and the entrance corridor were covered with inscriptions reproducing the collection of funerary spells called the Pyramid Texts.

A. Piankoff, *The Pyramid of Unas,* Egyptian Texts and Representations 5 (Princeton, 1968); E. Hornung, *The Ancient Egyptian Books of the Afterlife* (Ithaca, 1999), pp. 1–6.

See Fifth Dynasty.

Xois

Xois was a city of the northern delta, traces of which remain near the modern village of Sakha; in fact, this Arab name comes from the Egyptian name, with a metathesis. Until the Middle Kingdom, Xois seems to have been a town of little importance, located near the marshes at the border of the delta. It was the capital of a nome whose emblem represented a bull in a pothole, which was later interpreted as a bull in an undulating desert landscape. During the Thirteenth Dynasty Xois became the capital of an independent kingdom of which no monument survives. Xois became important again in the New Kingdom, but the local myths that made it the "place of the monarchies of Re" were perhaps based on its past. Xois was greatly expanded in the Greco-Roman Period.

See Fourteenth Dynasty.

Zero (Dynasty)

This designation is certainly strange, but it appropriately indicates the uncertainties that weigh on the most ancient periods of pharaonic Egypt. When Egyptologists began to reconstruct the history of this land, they adopted the division into dynasties that had been established by Manetho. The First Dynasty thus consisted of the earliest pharaohs who ruled Egypt after it was unified by the first of them, the mysterious Menes, who would have been either Narmer or Aha, or perhaps a fictive pharaoh modeled by tradition on both of them. Still, several indications furnished by royal annals (the Palermo Stone) and by inscribed objects gave reason to think that before Menes, potentates provided with certain attributes that were later assumed by the pharaohs had reigned over regions of Egypt. The archaeologist William Matthew Flinders Petrie proposed making them into a "Dynasty Zero." Colleagues ignored his suggestion, but half a century later, archaeology supplied him with a posthumous revenge. Excavations by the German Institute of Archaeology in the Archaic Period cemetery of Abydos uncovered the burials of kings who antedated the unification: Scorpion I (to be distinguished from Scorpion II, the immediate predecessor of Narmer), Iri-Hor (?), and Ka (or Sekhen).

The rich furnishings of these tombs included royal emblems (scepters), jugs of wine imported from Palestine, and above all, many inscribed objects proving definitively that writing was already in use around 3150 B.C.E., and thus prior to the pharaonic period. The study of these finds has barely begun, and many conclusions remain to be drawn. At the very least, the notion of a Dynasty Zero has been resuscitated as a designation for this group of kings, along with a few others who are known from small objects but whose tombs have yet to be discovered. Even if they ruled over Upper Egypt and even if they were culturally linked to the First Dynasty, however, these kings cannot be considered as full pharaohs, because they did not control the kingdom of Buto in the delta. It was their successors, particularly Menes, who accomplished the unification between 3000 and 2950 B.C.E. The symbol of this unification and thus of the beginning of the properly pharaonic period was the foundation of Memphis, where the earliest pharaohs and/or their high officials built funerary complexes. We thus now know that the First Dynasty emerged not from nothing, but from Zero; there is no stopping progress!

See Archaic (Period), Menes, Narmer, Origins (Prehistory, Predynastic), Scorpion.

BIBLIOGRAPHY

For the most part, the references at the end of entries have been chosen according to the criterion of accessibility, with emphasis on books that are available in affordable editions or in college or public libraries. These will be sufficient for most educated readers in search of more information on a given point.

But those who wish to confront the technical details of a given question will need to consult the basic scholarly publications in the field of Egyptology, which are for the most part written in English, French, and German. For those who can do so, there are certain basic resources.

Egyptology has a basic encyclopedia of its own, in which the entire universe of Egyptian civilization is covered by alphabetically arranged articles that are provided with rich bibliographies: W. Helk and E. Otto, eds., *Lexikon der Ägyptologie,* 6 vols. (Wiesbaden, 1972–1986). All research must begin with this resource, the articles of which are written in the three major languages of the field, and it includes an exhaustive index.

Other valuable scholarship is listed in the yearly volumes of the *Annual Egyptological Bibliography;* it has been published since 1947, and it is currently edited by L. M. J. Zonhoven and published by Aris & Philips, Warminster, England. It is now in the process of being made available on the Internet at http://www.leidenuniv.nl/nino/aeb.html. These volumes have a section entitled "History," but it should not be consulted exclusively, for other sections often include contributions touching on this topic.

Those who wish to delve into the field of Egyptology will also profit from the excellent bibliography published by E. Hornung, *Einführung in die Ägyptologie* (Darmstadt, 1967).

Readers of English also have the benefit of two magisterial encyclopedias. One of these is J. M. Sasson, ed., *Civilizations of the Ancient Near East,* 4 vols. (New York, 1995). It has many chapters devoted to the history and civilization of ancient Egypt. The other is D. B. Redford, ed., *The Oxford Encyclopedia of Ancient Egypt,* 3 vols. (New York, 2001).

The list that follows is a selection of recent works on pharaonic Egypt.

ORIGINS

Hoffman, M. A. *Egypt before the Pharaohs: The Prehistoric Foundations of Egyptian Civilization.* New York, 1979.

Midant-Reynes, B. *The Prehistory of Egypt: From the First Egyptians to the First Pharaohs.* Malden, Mass., 2000.

Spencer, E. *Early Egypt: The Birth of Civilization in the Nile Valley.* London, 1993.

HISTORY OF THE PHARAOHS

The Cambridge Ancient History, 3d ed. Cambridge, 1970–1975.

Clayton, P. A. *Chronicle of the Pharaohs: The Reign-by-Reign Record of the Rulers and Dynasties of Ancient Egypt.* New York, 1994.

Dodson, A. *Monarchs of the Nile,* 2d ed. Cairo, 2000.
Dunand, F., and C. Zivie-Coche. *Dieux et hommes en Égypte.* Paris, 1991.
Grimal, N. *A History of Ancient Egypt.* Oxford, 1992.
Hornung, E. *History of Ancient Egypt: An Introduction.* Ithaca, 1999.
Husson, G., and D. Valbelle. *L'État et les institutions en Égypte des premiers pharaons aux empereurs romains.* Paris, 1992.
Shaw, I., ed. *The Oxford History of Ancient Egypt.* New York, 2000.
Trigger, B. G, B. J. Kemp, D. O'Connor, and A. B. Lloyd. *Ancient Egypt: A Social History.* Cambridge, 1983.
Valbelle, D. *Les Neuf Arcs.* Paris, 1990.
Vandersleyen, C. *L'Égypte et la vallée du Nil.* Vol. 2, *De la fin de l'Ancien Empire à la fin du Nouvel Empire.* Paris, 1995. (Despite some aberrant geographical paradoxes.)
Vercoutter, J. *L'Égypte et la vallée du Nil.* Vol. 1, *Des Origines à la fin de l'Ancien Empire.* Paris, 1992.

KINGS AND PERIODS

Aménophis, le Pharaon-Soleil. Paris, 1993.
Desroches-Noblecourt, C. *Ramsès II, la véritable histoire.* Paris, 1996.
Grandet, P. *Ramsès III: Histoire d'un règne.* Paris, 1993.
Hornung, E. *Akhenaten and the Religion of Light.* Ithaca, 1999.
Kitchen, K. A. *Pharaoh Triumphant: The Life and Times of Ramesses II King of Egypt.* Warminster, 1982.
——. *The Third Intermediate Period in Egypt (1100–650* B.C.). Warminster, 1986.
Kozloff, A. P., and B. M. Bryan. *Egypt's Dazzling Sun: Amenhotep III and His World.* Cleveland, 1992.
Myśliwiec, K. *The Twilight of Ancient Egypt: First Millennium B.C.E.* Ithaca, 2000.
Redford, D. B. *Akhenaten, the Heretic King.* Princeton, 1984.
Schneider, T. *Lexikon der Pharaonen: Die altägyptischen Könige von der Frühzeit bis zur Römerherrschaft.* 2d ed. Düsseldorf, 1997.
Welsby, D. A. *The Kingdom of Kush: The Napatan and Meroitic Empires.* London, 1996.

ASPECTS OF PHARAONIC CULTURE

Baines, J., and J. Malek, *Cultural Atlas of Ancient Egypt.* New York, 2000.
Bonheme, M.-A., and A. Forgeau. *Pharaon: Les Secrets du pouvoir.* Paris, 1988.
Donadoni, S., ed. *L'Homme égyptien.* Paris, 1992.
Grandet, P., ed. *L'Égypte ancienne.* Paris, 1996.
Quirke, S., and J. Spencer. *The British Museum Book of Ancient Egypt.* London, 1992.
Romer, J. *Valley of the Kings.* New York, 1989.

Shaw, I., and P. Nicholson. *British Museum Dictionary of Ancient Egypt.* London, 1995.

Vernus, P. *Affaires et scandales sous les Ramsès: La Crise des valeurs dans l'Égypte du Nouvel Empire.* Paris, 1993.

——. *Essai sur la conscience de l'histoire dans l'Égypte pharaonique.* Paris, 1995.

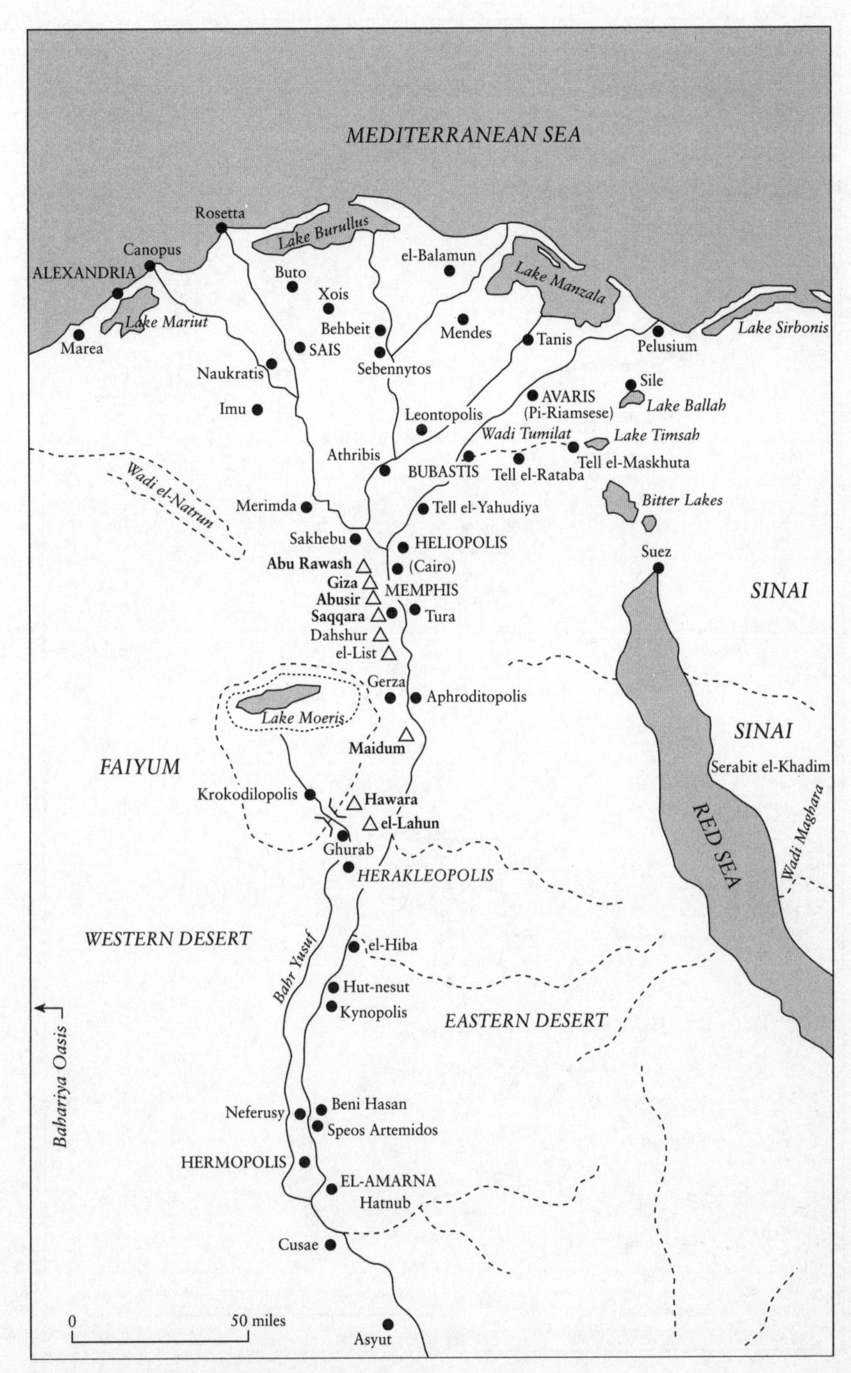

THE DELTA AND MIDDLE EGYPT

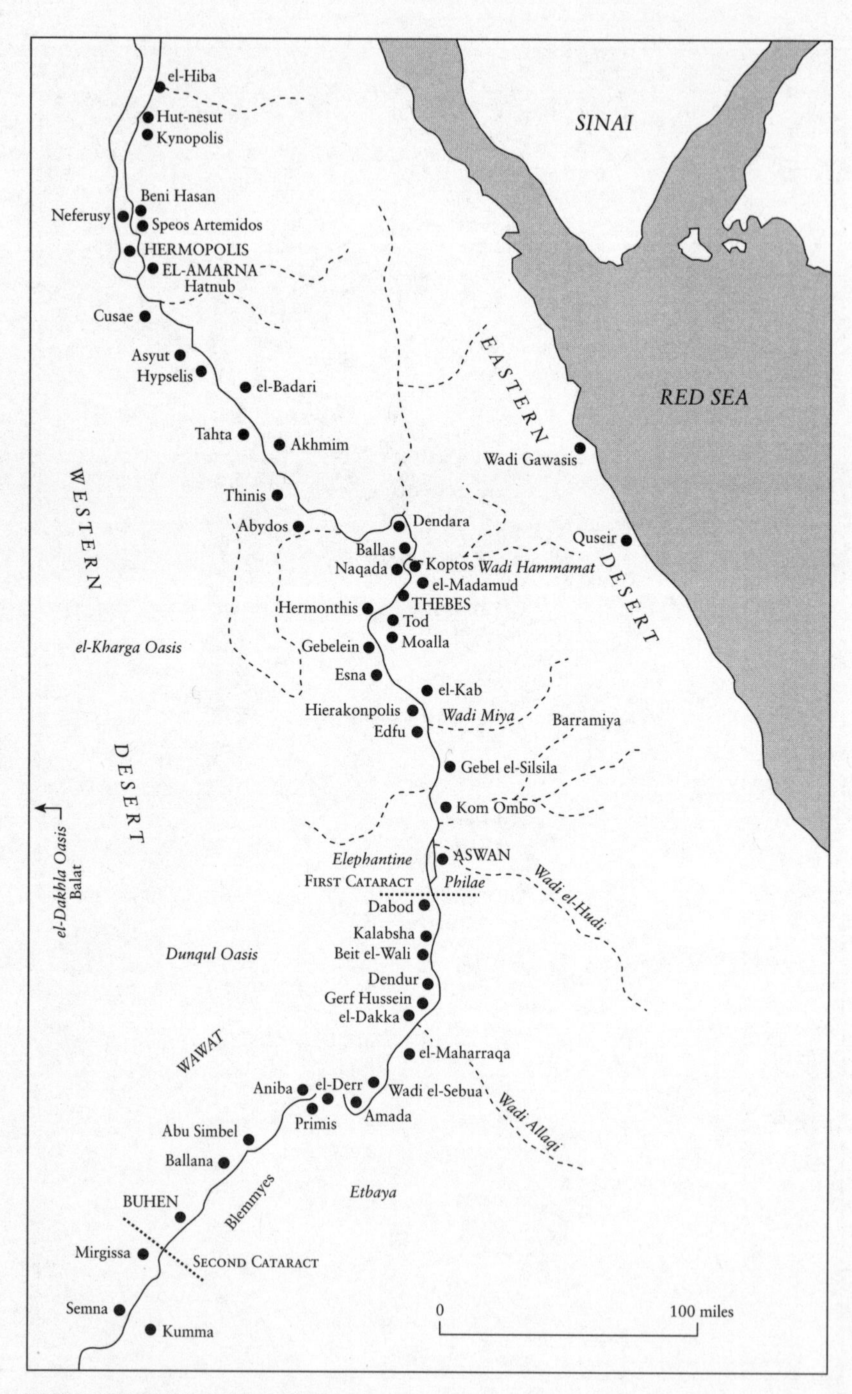

UPPER EGYPT AND LOWER NUBIA

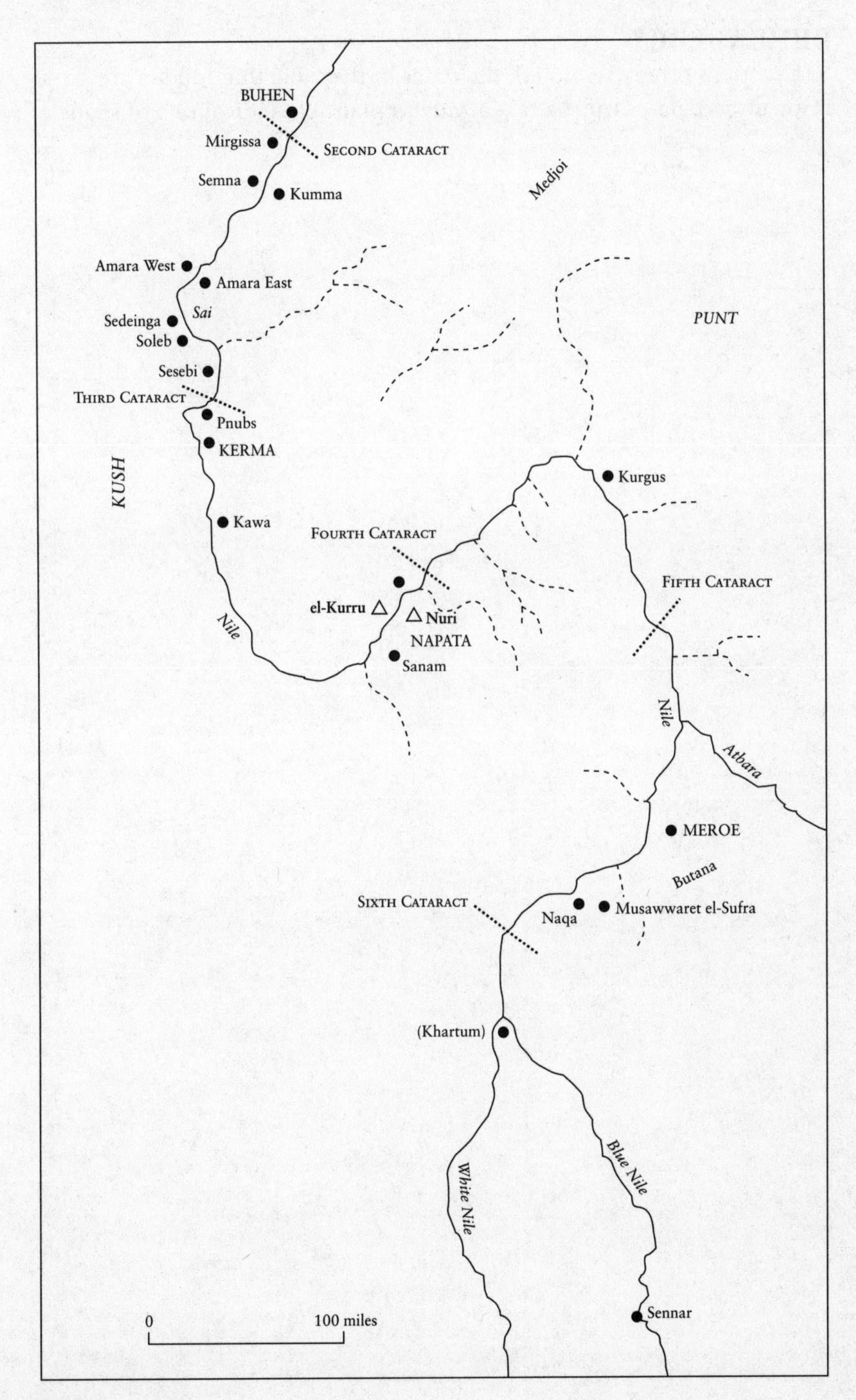
BUHEN
Mirgissa
Second Cataract
Semna
Kumma
Medjoi
Amara West
Amara East
Sai
Sedeinga
Soleb
PUNT
Sesebi
Third Cataract
Pnubs
KERMA
KUSH
Kurgus
Kawa
Fourth Cataract
Fifth Cataract
el-Kurru
Nuri
NAPATA
Nile
Sanam
Nile
Atbara
MEROE
Butana
Sixth Cataract
Naqa
Musawwaret el-Sufra
(Khartum)
White Nile
Blue Nile
Sennar
0
100 miles

UPPER NUBIA

CHRONOLOGY

Except as otherwise noted, the dates in the table that follows are B.C.E. Prior to 700, dates can be taken only as plausible indications of spans of time.

		c. 3500–3000	Dynasty Zero
2950	PREDYNASTIC PERIOD	c. 3000	King Scorpion, Horus Narmer
	ARCHAIC PERIOD First Dynasty	2950–2780	Horus Aha (Menes of tradition), Wadj, Den
	Second Dynasty	2780–2635	Horus Hetepsekhemwy, Horus Ninetjer, Seth Peribsen, Horus-and- Seth Khasekhemwy
	OLD KINGDOM Third Dynasty	2635–2561	Djoser, Sekhemkhet, Huni
	Fourth Dynasty	2561–2450	Snofru, Cheops, Chephren, Mycerinus
	Fifth Dynasty	2450–2321	Sahure, Neferirkare, Neuserre, Wenis
	Sixth Dynasty	2321–2140	Teti, Pepy I, Pepy II, Queen Nitokris
2140	Power crisis; Seventh Dynasty FIRST INTERMEDIATE PERIOD Eighth Dynasty (Memphite)	2140–2130	

2130	Division of the land		
	Lower and Middle Egypt:		
	Ninth Dynasty (Herakleopolitan)	2130–2090	Khety
	Tenth Dynasty (Herakleopolitan)	2090–2022	Merykare
	Upper Egypt:		
	Eleventh Dynasty (Theban)	2130	Kings named Inyotef
2022	Reunification of the land by Mentuhotpe II MIDDLE KINGDOM		
	Eleventh Dynasty (continuation)	2022–1991	Mentuhotpe II–IV
	Twelfth Dynasty	1991–1784	Kings named Amenemhet (I–IV) and Senwosret (I–III), Queen Nefrusobk
	Thirteenth Dynasty	1784	Kings named Sebekhotpe; Khendjer, Neferhotep I
1720	Emergence of regional powers		
	Valley: Thirteenth Dynasty (continuation)		Neferhotep-Iykhernofret
	Delta:		
1650	Fourteenth Dynasty (kings at Xois and Avaris)	1750–1650	Nehesy
	Capture of Memphis by the Hyksos		Salitis

	SECOND INTERMEDIATE PERIOD		
	Hyksos suzerainty over all Egypt		
	Fifteenth Dynasty	1650–1550	Khian, Apophis
	Lower and Middle Egypt:		
	Sixteenth Dynasty: Asiatic chiefdoms and vassal princes	1650–1539	
	Upper Egypt:		
	Thirteenth Dynasty (end)	1650	Dedumose
	Seventeenth Dynasty	1630–1539	Inyotef V, Sebekemzaf II, Seqenenre, Kamose
1539	Expulsion of the Hyksos by Ahmose		
	NEW KINGDOM		
	Eighteenth Dynasty	1539–1293	Ahmose, kings named Amenophis and Tuthmosis, Queen Hatshepsut
1353	Appearance of Amenophis IV; Atenist period	1353–1335	Amenophis IV/Akhenaten, Smenkhkare
1335	Restoration of the traditional religion; post-Amarna period	1335–1293	Tutankhamun, Aya, Haremhab
	Nineteenth Dynasty	1293–1190	Sethos I, Ramesses II, Merneptah, Queen Twosre
	Twentieth Dynasty	1190–1069	Ramesses III–XI

1080	Era of the “Renaissance”		High priest Herihor
	THIRD INTERMEDIATE PERIOD		
	Twenty-first Dynasty (Tanite)	1069–945	Smendes, Psusennes, Siamun
	Twenty-second Dynasty (Bubastite or Shoshenqide)	945	Shoshenq I, Osorkon I, Osorkon II, Takelot II, Shoshenq III
818	Appearance of Pedubaste I		
	Twenty-second Dynasty (continuation)		Shoshenq III
	Division of the land		
	Delta and Memphis:		
	Twenty-second Dynasty (continuation)	773	Pami, Shoshenq V
	Upper Egypt:		
	Twenty-third Dynasty	787–750	Osorkon III, Takelot III
750	Annexation of Upper Egypt by the Kushites		Piye of Napata
	Twenty-second and Twenty-third Dynasties (four local pharaohs)	720	Nimlot, Peftjauawybast, Iuput II, Osorkon IV
	Twenty-fourth Dynasty (Saite)	720–715	Bocchoris
715	Conquest of Lower Egypt by Shabaka, Kushite sovereignty over all Egypt		
	Twenty-fifth Dynasty (Kushite)	715–656	Shabaka, Taharqa

	Lower Egypt		
	Twenty-second Dynasty (final epigones)	660	Gemenefkhonsubak
	Twenty-sixth Dynasty (Saite)	700	The legendary Nechepso
656	Annexation of Upper Egypt by Psammetichus I		
	LATE PERIOD		
	Twenty-sixth Dynasty (continuation and end)	525	Psammetichus I–III, Necho, Apries, Amasis
525	Conquest of Egypt by Cambyses		
	Twenty-seventh Dynasty (first Persian domination)	525–398	Cambyses, Darius I
	In the delta:		
	Twenty-eighth Dynasty (Saite)	404–398	Amyrtaios
398	Total liberation of the land by Nepherites I		
	Twenty-ninth Dynasty (Mendesian)	398–378	Nepherites I–II, Hakoris
	Thirtieth Dynasty (Sebennytic)	378–341	Nectanebo I–II, Teos
341	Reconquest of Egypt by Artaxerxes III		
	Second Persian domination	341–330	Artaxerxes III, Khababash, Darius III
330	Conquest of Egypt by Alexander the Great		
	GREEK PERIOD		
	Macedonian Dynasty	330–323	Alexander the Great

	Ptolemaic (Lagide) Dynasty	323–30	Ptolemy I Soter, Ptolemy II Philadelphos, etc., Cleopatra VII
30	Conquest of Egypt by Octavian		
	ROMAN PERIOD		
	Caesars as pharaohs	30 B.C.E.–313 C.E.	from Augustus to Maximinus Daia
	Christianity becomes the religion of the emperor	c. 320 C.E.	
	Closing of the pagan temples	392 C.E.